WHEN WRITERS WRITE

KATHLEEN MACDONALD

Leeward Community College

Eric P. Hibbison, *Consulting Editor*

PRENTICE-HALL, INC.
Englewood Cliffs, New Jersey   07632

MACDONALD, KATHLEEN
  When writers write.

  Includes index.
  1. English language—Rhetoric. I. Hibbison, Eric.
II. Title.
PE1408.M26 1983   808′.042   82-18098
ISBN 0-13-956490-X

Printed in the United States of America

10   9   8   7   6   5   4   3   2   1

Editorial/production supervision and
interior design: Barbara Alexander
Cover design: Photo Plus Art
Manufacturing buyer: Harry P. Baisley

0-13-956490-X

PRENTICE-HALL INTERNATIONAL, INC., *London*
PRENTICE-HALL OF AUSTRALIA PTY. LIMITED, *Sydney*
EDITORA PRENTICE-HALL DO BRASIL, LTDA., *Rio de Janeiro*
PRENTICE-HALL CANADA INC., *Toronto*
PRENTICE-HALL OF INDIA PRIVATE LIMITED, *New Delhi*
PRENTICE-HALL OF JAPAN, INC., *Tokyo*
PRENTICE-HALL OF SOUTHEAST ASIA PTE. LTD., *Singapore*
WHITEHALL BOOKS LIMITED, *Wellington, New Zealand*

In Loving Memory of my Parents
Kay and Bud Purnell

Contents

part III
WHEN WRITERS WRITE: THEIR PURPOSES AND TECHNIQUES   *123*

Preface

This text draws heavily on recent research into the way writers actually write. It presents the writing process as richly varied and recursive rather than linear. It emphasizes the writer's intended audience and reason for writing to that audience. And, unlike many other texts, it integrates audience and purpose with the writing process.

As we know, when writers write in the real world, their writing process is not divorced from their sense of audience or of why they're writing to that audience. Those three elements—process, audience, and purpose—are intimately connected. For instance, when writers sit down to write with a clear conception of their audience and purpose, that audience and purpose can shape the writing process. When writers sit down to write with no clear audience or purpose in mind, the prewriting and drafting stages of the writing process can help them clarify what they want to say, why they want to say it, and to whom it is to be said.

Unfortunately, students are often unaware of this synergistic relationship between audience, purpose, and the writing process. In fact, they may have little or no conception of the needs and expectations or either general or specific types of readers. They may think that "good" writing is always the same. In addition, they may think that "good" writers always know exactly what they want to say before they begin to write, or that "good" writers write one perfect sentence after another, never blotting a word, much less an entire paragraph.

In short, students often don't know what happens when writers write. They do not know that writing is often a messy, varied process. They do not see that writers write for a reason. Above all, they do not see that when they themselves write something— whether it's a letter of complaint, directions for motorcycle maintenance, a description of last year's backpacking trip, or a history paper on the Spanish American War—they are themselves writers, writing to their readers for a reason.

Thus writing to communicate with others is the main concern of this book. Of course, not all writing has this purpose. Often people need to write in order to sort out their own ideas or simply to get something off their chests in private. Such self-expressive writing is important, both in itself and as a preliminary step to communicating with others. This book therefore encourages students to write to and for themselves whenever doing so will help them. The focus of the book, however, is on helping students to write effectively when they want or need to communicate with others.

STRUCTURE OF THE BOOK

The book is divided into three recursive parts:

I. The Writer's Audience
II. The Writer's Writing Process
III. The Writer's Purposes and Techniques

These parts are interrelated. As an aid to the students, just one aspect of writing is highlighted at a time. However, all three aspects are very much present throughout the text. In fact, many concerns are repeated throughout the book in order to help students view the writing process as a whole.

The order in which the three parts are presented is partly arbitrary, partly based on the students' need for an introduction to "audience" before it is used in the other two parts, and partly a result of the text's narrowing concern from writing in general to techniques that are helpful in specific writing situations.

Part I, "The Writer's Audience," presents the dual concepts of "audience" and of writing as communication with an intended reader. In the first chapter there is an "experiment" that invites the students to become aware of how well they listen to others and of how well others listen to them. By thus drawing on the communication process that students use the most—speaking and listening—students can discover for themselves some of the elements that are important in all communication, including writing. This inductive approach is one I use as often as clarity permits.

Part I also includes two chapters on reading, in order to enable students to see, from the reader's point of view, what happens when writers write. Although our students know how to read, they don't all know how *experienced* readers read. Further, even experienced readers may not be consciously aware of the reading process. Until it is made explicit for us, few of us are. Thus the two chapters on reading make *explicit* what various readers *implicitly* do as they read: what questions they unconsciously ask themselves, what clues they unconsciously look for, and what expectations they may have. This information can help students read their own drafts and final copies as their intended readers would. As the reading process is described in these two chapters, the implications for writers are spelled out.

Part II describes a general writing process that I have arbitrarily divided into seven steps or phases:

Doodling (prewriting)

Drafting

Taking a break

Revising and redrafting

Sharing the draft with others

Polishing

Stopping

These steps are not linear. Some writing may move by spurts through some stages, return to earlier ones, then cycle ahead again. Other writing may fall immediately into place, shortcutting many of the steps. Self-expressive writing may begin and end with the "doodling" stage, if that's all that's needed for the writer's purpose.

Still, it's helpful for students to be aware of the various steps that *can* help them when they write. For instance, many experienced writers try to take a long break after writing a draft. They feel their drafts need time to "cool off" before being revised. Yet students tend to take only the briefest breaks (if any) between a draft and final copy. I've therefore made "Taking a Break" into a separate, short chapter to emphasize the point being made: taking a break can be more beneficial than pushing writing through to completion in a single sitting. To give another example, experienced writers often have someone else read and react to drafts of important letters, reports, and articles. But students are often afraid to do this and therefore keep their drafts to themselves. To help students overcome this problem, Chapter 8, "Share the Draft," offers specific tips on *how* to have others read and react to one's drafts.

Throughout the chapters on the writing process the students are asked to consider both their audience and their purpose in writing to that audience. For instance, in Chapter 4 the devices for finding a subject to write about provide the student with a possible audience as well as a subject. Chapter 7 suggests clarifying the audience and purpose, and, when students are advised to have others read their drafts, they are also advised to ask others to read as the *intended* audience would. Thus, Part II incorporates "audience" into the writing process.

Part II concludes with worksheets that are designed to help students apply the tips in Parts I and II—and also Part III.

Part III (The Writer's Purposes and Techniques) is a compendium of tips and techniques students can use to make particular types of writing more effective. These techniques are meant to be used throughout the writing process, not after it. Why, then, is Part III separate from Part II? It's because the student's audience and purpose in a specific piece of writing should determine what techniques are used. In addition, whether the students use the techniques in an early draft, during later revisions, or during final polishing will vary from student to student and from writing project to writing project. Thus it's more convenient for both students and instructors to have the techniques for effective writing arranged according to purpose and placed in a separate part of the book. Earlier parts of the book do, however, make frequent reference to the techniques in Part III, encouraging students to turn to those chapters that will help them write more effectively in a specific situation. The basic situations covered in Part III are:

Writing to clearly *inform* the reader.

Writing to *interest* the reader in what's being said, or to share a vivid *description*.

Writing to *persuade* the intended reader with tact and logic.

Although some of the techniques suggested in these chapters will be familiar to students, the suggested uses may be new. For instance, the chapter on writing informatively includes information on writing clear comparisons, definitions, and "how to" directions, all techniques that will be familiar to many readers. However, students who have written "comparison" papers in past courses might not have thought of using comparisons to make *other* types of writing clear, or might not have thought of the differences in purpose between explaining "how to do something" and explaining "how something works."

Likewise the chapter on writing interestingly includes "descriptive" writing not just as an end in itself but also as a means of making other writing more interesting to the reader.

Specific writing techniques are means to an end, not ends in themselves. The arrangement of Part III, in which specific techniques may be presented in more than one chapter, emphasizes this. Of course readers may occasionally need to locate information on a given technique or mode of writing. For their convenience, there's a detailed index at the back of the book.

Three other features of the book's structure are worth mentioning here. First, the activities and exercises are an important part of each chapter. Designed to help students learn by doing, the exercises are sometimes integrated into the text and sometimes presented at the end of the chapter. Second, the worksheets at the end of Part II are designed for either the student's own use or to be passed in to the teacher along with each writing project. These worksheets combine audience, purpose, and the writing process in a way that should help students learn by doing. They also refer students to whichever chapters or pages will help them solve a specific problem. Third, the appendices at the end of the book are intended as very brief writers' guides. They make the text self-contained while keeping it as short as possible. Some instructors may want to order additional grammar or documentation handbooks, while others will feel no need to.

BOOK'S STYLE AND CLASSROOM USE

When Writers Write is written in an informal style, addressing the student as a beginning writer, not as a "student." It assumes an audience of college freshman who vary widely in years and experience. The increasing numbers of older or returning students should feel comfortable reading this text, as should the 19-year-old who is working part-time or participating in school or community activities.

A writing class should prepare students to write for a variety of occasions in addition to academic ones. After all, most students will have reason to write to their legislators, friends, co-workers, and bosses, as well as to manufacturers of faulty merchandise and other people who affect their lives, long after they no longer have occasion to write history or psychology papers. Furthermore, many students need practice communicating with a wide variety of people who have values, assumptions, and language patterns different from their own. They need practice adjusting to the needs of their audiences. Quite simply, we can best give students this practice by encouraging them to write for a wide variety of challenging audiences or situations, including nonacademic ones. And we can certainly best demonstrate the principles of such writing by using examples that illustrate personal and business situations as well as academic ones. Thus, the text contains examples in the form of letters and even memos as well as articles and essays. It also provides many student writing samples so that readers can more readily identify with the material.

When Writers Write is designed to be flexible enough for use in a variety of course structures. For instance, some instructors will want to focus on Part II, with each student working on a different type of writing, perhaps prompted by the various suggestions in Chapter 4 for discovering a subject and audience. Other instructors might want to focus on Part III, with all students simultaneously writing, say, a persuasive paper or one that uses comparisons or descriptions. (The Teachers' Guide provides sample course outlines and suggestions for using the book with various sequences.) In addition, *When Writers Write* serves very well as a "resource book" for courses based on the Elbow or Garrison methods of teaching, as well as for courses that use the case study method.

There is still another variable in the way this book can be used. Some teachers may wish to use the nonacademic writing samples solely to illustrate specific writing principles, with the students themselves writing for a variety of academic audiences. Other instructors may encourage their students to write for a wide variety of nonacademic as well as academic audiences. As long as a nonacademic writing situation calls for writing that's especially clear, interesting, or persuasive, it can prove as challenging as academic writing and can provide a realistic, rewarding learning experience.

In summary, *When Writers Write* helps students see that when writers write, it's for a reason. It helps them see that writers write for different audiences and different purposes. It helps them see that the writing process is often one of discovery—and of revision. It helps them see that techniques for effective writing vary with the writer's audience and purpose. Above all, it helps students see themselves as writers . . . by helping them to write.

ACKNOWLEDGMENTS

Many people helped write this book. My colleagues Kay Hayes, Nancy Higa, Steven Hirose, Ruth Lucas, Nancy Mower, and Henry Schaafsma all kindly read manuscript chapters in areas of their own teaching expertise. Mitsue Cook, Liz d'Argy, Mimi Nakano, Pat Ramos, Jim Wilson, and, once again, Kay Hayes, all field-tested the manuscript in their classes. Norman Yoshida, now at Lewis and Clark College, spent long hours reading the manuscript in its earliest, often unintelligible, stages. Dorothy Vella, Director of the Composition Program at the University of Hawaii, Manoa, generously found time to read the finished manuscript with care. My debt to these busy people is great. Their insights and helpful suggestions made the text clearer and more useful than it would otherwise have been. Their generosity and enthusiasm propelled me through difficult stretches. Indeed, without Norman Yoshida's early encouragement and help there would probably be no text at all.

I would like to express my thanks to the following reviewers for their many constructive comments: Professor Douglas R. Butturff (University of Central Arkansas), Professor Tilly Eggers (University of Wyoming), Professor Peggy Buzbee Jolly (University of Alabama), Professor Carol Niederlander (St. Louis Community College), and Professor Jean Wyrick (Colorado State University).

Students also deserve thanks for the many writing samples they contributed and the valuable suggestions they made as the book was being field-tested. My students continue to teach me in many ways; for this, and the marvelous good will they bring each semester, I thank them.

Two Prentice-Hall editors deserve special mention: Eric Hibbison and Barbara Alexander. Eric sweated through the manuscript with me, raising all the right questions and making precisely the right suggestions. Barbara sweated through production, seeing to it that all went smoothly despite my many revisions. Their unfailing tact, good cheer, and efficiency were both needed and appreciated.

Finally, I owe my husband Tom a year or two of our life. Through the chaos of drafts, galleys, and deadlines, he read, edited, provided sound advice, and listened with a sympathetic ear.

To the Student Writer

This book is divided into three parts, all designed to help you improve your writing. The parts are not really separate, however, since they all discuss what happens when writers—including you—write.

Part I discusses an idea that may be new to you: the important role that your audience or intended reader plays in your writing. In the past, you've undoubtedly been aware of the person or people you were writing to. You'll now become more conscious of the differences between various readers and of how those differences can affect your writing. You'll also become more conscious of the way readers read. This too can affect the way you write.

Part II describes seven different steps that can help you when you write. Although you won't necessarily use all the steps each time you write, and you won't always use the steps in the same order, knowing about them can make writing easier for you. As you read about the seven possible steps, you'll find frequent references back to the earlier concept of "audience."

At the end of Part II you'll find a Writing Process Worksheet and a Checklist for Effective Writing. These worksheets and checklists will help you apply the various tips and suggestions found throughout the book. They also refer you to the chapters and pages that will help you most.

Part III presents techniques that will help you write more effectively once you have a clear idea of your audience and reason for writing. Specifically, Part III can help you:

When you want to make your writing clearer or more informative.

When you want to make your writing more interesting or more descriptive.

When you want to make your writing more persuasive.

Sometimes you'll want to use the tips in Part III while you work on a rough draft. Other times you won't be ready to use the tips until you're in the final stages of revision. Either way, you can locate tips that will help you by browsing in the appropriate chapter or by using the *alphabetical index* at the back of the book. That index is designed to help you locate a *specific* tip or technique as quickly as possible.

Learning to write effectively is a bit like learning to drive a car. At first, it seems as though there are at least a hundred different things to keep in mind at the same time. With practice, however, the entire process becomes fairly automatic. Occasionally something unexpected happens and an experienced driver becomes aware of the various decisions that must be made. Generally, however, experienced drivers do what is necessary in a given situation without all the conscious attention that was necessary when they were first learning. So it is with writing.

When writers write, they don't *consciously* do the many things this book will suggest you do. Instead, they often automatically do whatever is appropriate to the writing situation—to the "when" and the "why" of their writing. As you read this book, don't be overwhelmed by the many tips and suggestions. You would never use all of them in the same piece of writing. Further, only at the beginning will you necessarily be conscious of using them at all. Soon they will become automatic.

Finally, use *When Writers Write* as a guidebook, not a rule book. It offers suggestions, tips, and techniques for you to try. But you have to decide for yourself which tips to use in a given situation. And you must decide which tips work for you.

KATHLEEN MACDONALD

Honolulu, Hawaii

part I

WHEN WRITERS WRITE: THEIR AUDIENCE

This book will explore several questions: When and why do writers write? To whom do they write? How do they write effectively? To some extent, the answers will all be the same: "It depends on the situation." This is exactly the point: Knowing *how* writing depends on the situation will help you become a better writer. It will help you write more easily and more effectively whether you're working on a paper for History 151, a letter of complaint, or a description of your recent camping trip. In short, it will help you write in a variety of situations. When do writers write? Sometimes writers write when they want to understand an idea better or want to put something in writing before they forget it. Sometimes they write because they want to get something off their chests, without any one else's seeing it.

Other times writers write because they want to communicate something to someone else. When writers write to communicate with someone else, the "audience" or intended reader is an important part of the writing situation. For instance, when you write a letter to your friend Bill, you probably have a specific reason for writing: Perhaps you're asking Bill to help you get a job, or reminding him that he owes you $20, or inviting him to go camping with you and your friends at the end of the month. As you write, you unconsciously keep Bill's personality, problems, and interests in mind. You may even try to guess what Bill's mood will be as he opens your letter. In short, Bill, who may be too busy to help anyone get a job, who may be nearly broke, or who may prefer a nice warm bed to a sleeping bag, is your audience, and you keep him, and his problems, in mind as you write.

Let's take another example. A student we'll call Elaine may be taking a course in child psychology. She must write a paper on the guilt young children often feel upon learning that their parents are getting a divorce. In her paper, Elaine must communicate an intellectually interesting idea about the subject to her professor. She must also meet her professor's expectations regarding the evidence, documentation, and style appropriate for an academic paper. Because Elaine is familiar with the expectations of an academic audience, she does not make the mistake of writing her paper as she would write to herself or a friend. Instead she writes directly to her real audience: a psychology professor.

Let's say four years pass and Elaine completes her B.A. in developmental psychology. She's still interested in the divorce-guilt experienced by children and wants to write an article on the subject for publication. Who will her audience be now? It won't be Dr. Wolff, her old child psychology professor. As she thinks about it, she realizes that her intended readers won't be college professors at all. She wants to write to two groups of people: parents and elementary school teachers. The best way to do it, she decides, is in two articles, one for *Parents' Magazine* and one for *American Teacher.*

As she writes these two articles, she soon sees that they will have to be quite different. Not only will she use different vocabulary for parents and for teachers, but her main idea and examples will be different too. In the article for parents she will offer tips parents can use to reduce their own children's guilt feelings about a divorce. In the article for teachers, she will describe ways teachers can recognize when a child is suffering from divorce-guilt.

Finally, Elaine may learn that the parents of her favorite young nephew, James, are getting a divorce. The letter Elaine writes to James is totally different from all of her previous papers and articles. This time her purpose is simply to help ten-year-old James feel better about his parents and himself. She therefore uses words and personal examples that James himself can understand and feel good about.

Thus when Elaine writes to others, the people she writes to are her "audience," or intended readers. They are part of the writing situation and help her decide what to say and how to say it. The following three chapters will help you understand the audience in your own writing and will also help you understand how your audience will read the things you write.

chapter 1

Who Is Your Audience?

When you write, you may write for two different types of audiences: yourself and other people. Writing to yourself is a good way to sort out your thoughts and untangle your emotions. It's useful in itself and it's also a fine way to warm up for writing to others. However, this chapter and the next two will focus on what happens when you write to other people. This means focusing on communication. We'll therefore begin not with writing, but with a brief look at the communication process we all use most: conversation.

THE AUDIENCE IN CONVERSATION

What can you as a writer learn from conversation? By paying careful attention to when you "tune out" while others are talking, and when they "tune out" while you are talking, you can learn a great deal. Speaking and writing are very similar in that both speakers and writers want their audiences to pay attention, to understand what's being said, and perhaps to care about it also. There's one very important difference, though: When we speak, we can immediately see when we're losing our audience. We can tell when they begin to tune us out. That's not the case with writing. With writing, our intended audience may be miles away from us. We can't see or hear their reactions as they read what we've written. Fortunately, though, by carefully observing what happens when people speak, we can pick up tips and ideas that may apply to writing as well.

Communication Experiments

1. Make a point of noticing when you "tune out" in the middle of a conversation. (If you can't tell when this occurs, ask your friends to let you know when your eyes glaze over and your mind wanders. They'll probably be happy to help out.) Keep a list until you've noticed at least five or six such occurrences, and then analyze *why* you tuned out:

(1) *The speaker*. Was it something the speaker said? Implied? Did? Didn't say? Didn't do? Was there just something "about" the speaker? What?

(2) *The subject*. Was the subject of no interest to you? Why not?

(3) *Circumstances*. Did external distractions interrupt your concentration? What were they? Was the speaker's timing bad?

(4) *You*. Were you preoccupied? Why? By what?

WHY I SOMETIMES STOP LISTENING

SITUATION	REASON
Friend telling me about his car	Doesn't concern me—I don't care
(example)	(example)

Now think back to occasions when you almost always do listen attentively to what people say. What explains the difference?

This exercise can help you become a better listener by making you more aware of when you listen and when you don't. In addition, it can help you become more aware of when you should pay attention to the literal or strict meaning of the words used and when you should understand that the speaker is using the words for some other purpose. For instance, when a doctor begins a physical examination by asking "How are you?" the doctor means exactly what the words say. He or she wants to know precisely how you feel. But when a casual acquaintance says, "Hello, how are you?" the situation is different. The casual acquaintance isn't asking about your health and doesn't want a litany of aches and pains in response. In this situation, the words are being used as a ritual that means "Let's be civilized to each other." Thus good listening requires attention not only to what is literally being said, but also to who is saying it and *why*.

2. This next exercise is more painful. Make a point of noticing when people stop listening to *you* while *you're* talking. (You'll recognize the signs: their eyes wander, they don't ask you any questions, they change the subject the second you pause for breath.) As with the first exercise, keep a list until you've jotted down five or six occurrences. Try to include the reason the listener wasn't really listening to you. To do this, you might try putting yourself in the listener's place, or, in some cases, you might ask the listener.

WHY OTHERS STOP LISTENING TO ME

SITUATION	REASON
I was telling Mary about my test	She was trying to read
(example)	(example)
_____	_____
_____	_____
_____	_____
_____	_____
_____	_____

Now ask yourself these questions about the situations you've jotted down.

(1) *What was I talking about?* (Were you talking about yourself? Were you rambling?)

(2) *Was I being tactless?* In what way?

(3) *What was my real purpose in speaking?* (Be honest with yourself.)

(4) *Was I monopolizing the conversation?*

(5) *Was my listener preoccupied?* By what? Was my timing wrong?

The more sensitive you are to your listener's feelings, expectations, and interests, the more interesting you'll be when you speak. And, more relevant to this book, the more sensitive you become to your intended reader, the better your writing will be.

3. Compare the reasons you tune out other people with the reasons they tune you out. Are there similarities? Differences? Compare your lists with your classmates' lists. Writers write to different people; the more you explore the differences between yourself and others, the easier it will be for you to write well for a variety of people.

4. People can "tune out" writing just as well as they can tune out things they don't want to hear. Working with your classmates, make a list of the various reasons people tune each other out in conversation. Next, read the list over, checking for problems that might interfere with reading as well as listening. Using your intuition or past experience, decide which of those problems writers could do something about. How?

5. Talking with people who are like ourselves is easy; the more they are like us, the less we need to communicate verbally at all. Talking with people who have different opinions, values, backgrounds, and interests is harder.

Make a brief list of the people you talk with regularly. How many of these people are quite similar to you in outlook, interests, and background? How many have interests or backgrounds very different from yours?

The more you communicate *with* (not talk *at*) people who are different from you, the more you're forced to consider your listener's feelings and assumptions before you speak. If, as a child, you had to communicate with people who were quite different from you and your relatives, you had a head start in communication. If you didn't, what can you do about it now? You can consciously try to talk with a greater variety of people—people who are much older or younger than yourself, who have much more or much less education, or who come from a different geographical area.

You may feel stage fright at first, but remember that you aren't trying to impress them; you're trying to communicate with them. You don't have to lecture them; you do have to try to understand them. An ability to "walk around inside someone else's skin" is crucial to communication, whether it be speech or writing.

SPEAKING AND WRITING

Speaking and writing are basically similar. Both are forms of communication. Both involve not only what's being said, but also when it's being said, by whom, to whom, and why. In short, effective speaking and effective writing both depend on an entire situation. With these similarities in mind, it's time to consider some differences between the two.

When you're talking in person with people, their reaction to what you're saying is immediate. If you're giving a speech, you can note when your audience squirms, when they sleep, and when they eagerly await your next word. If they are about to slip away from you, mentally or physically, you can alter your approach in an attempt to regain their attention.

In writing, you have to imagine your reader's response. You usually can't watch your intended reader while he or she reads your letter or paper, and even if you could, you couldn't alter the words you had already written.

This difference between speaking and writing is crucial. As you learned in the earlier exercises, no one has to listen to you when you talk; your listeners can tune you out. However, at least the signals—the frowns, the questions, the smiles—are there for you to pick up. In writing, you must anticipate your reader's responses in advance. You must ask yourself what information your intended readers will need. What examples will be clear to them? What comments might anger or insult them? Speakers too must ask themselves these questions, but speakers have the advantage of the listeners' questions and body language to help them.

Not only must writers imagine their readers' responses, they must also decide for themselves who their readers will be. This is, of course, also true of public speakers, who can choose to accept an invitation to talk to one group and turn down an invitation to address another group. By and large, though, when we speak to people, our audience is predetermined in a way that's not always true of writing.

The differences between speaking and writing discussed so far make effective writing seem more difficult than effective speaking. In some ways it is. The writer, unlike the speaker, must first decide who the audience or "intended reader" will be and then must write for that audience without being able to watch the reader's face or hear the reader's questions. But at least two differences favor writing.

The first advantage of writing is the time and care you can take. You can't, in the middle of a debate, run to the library to look up a fact. In the middle of writing you often can. When speaking, you can't take five minutes to polish a sentence until it sounds just right. When writing, you often can.

The second advantage of writing is that you can let writing sit. Words spoken in haste or anger can't be taken back. Not so with writing. Wise writers can wait a day or two before mailing an impulsively written letter. Thus writers have some advantages speakers don't have.

YOUR INTENDED READER

When we write, almost anyone may pick up what we've written and start reading it. Someone with no background in astronomy may start reading a technical report on the expanding universe, written for Astronomy 101. Someone with neither a car nor an interest in mechanics might start reading an article explaining how to replace automobile spark plugs. In both cases the readers would soon become frustrated and stop reading, but this is no fault of the writers. The situation would be hopeless if writers tried to write so that everyone could pleasurably and profitably read their writing. Instead, writers must decide for themselves who their intended readers are and then write directly to those readers.

As a student you may be wondering, "How does this apply to me? Won't I be writing to my English teacher?" Not really. Your writing class is designed to help you write for a variety of audiences. Thus as your writing teacher reads your work, he or she will read it as your *intended* reader would. Think of your writing teacher as a coach or editor who reads your writing in order to help you make it effective for your primary audience: the *other* people to whom you are writing.

You may also wonder about the references to letter writing in this, a college composition textbook. There are several reasons for including letters in this book. First, although audience is important in all types of writing, it's easiest to see in letters. Second, much of the writing that people do outside of school and after they graduate takes the form of letters: letters to friends, letters to customers, letters to the editors of papers, letters of complaint, and so forth. The emphasis throughout this book is not on the particular format that writing takes. It's on writing effectively for a particular audience and purpose, regardless of whether that writing assumes the form of a letter, school essay, published article, or formal report.

Your Intended Reader and Your Purpose in Writing

When you write a personal letter, you know who you're writing to. When you write an essay, article or report, you might well think of yourself as writing a letter to a group of people. In either case, there are three questions you should always ask yourself about your intended reader:

1. Is this reader already interested in my subject or idea?

2. Does this reader already know much about the subject or idea?

3. Does this reader probably agree with my idea or attitude, even before reading what I have to say?

It might seem that the more "yes" answers you have, the better. That isn't the case, however. Let's say that you think humpback whales should be protected from extinction. You've decided to explain your thoughts on the subject in a letter to Dale King, president of Save the Whales. Whether you are writing the letter for English class, for your own satisfaction, or both, you should ask yourself three questions: "Is Dale already interested?" Yes. "Is she already knowledgeable about the subject?" Yes, probably more than you. Finally, "Is she predisposed to agree with your position that the humpback whale should be saved?" Obviously. To write to Dale, then, could be a waste of your time and hers. There would be no reason for writing.

What if you still wanted to write to Dale? You could change your subject slightly, perhaps focusing on your appreciation of her organization's hard work on behalf of whales. What if you still wanted to write about your conviction that whales should be saved?

Instead of writing to Dale King, you might change your audience. You could write to the editor of your newspaper persuading people who vaguely agree that "something" should be done that it's important that they themselves help by contributing their time or money to the Save the Whales organization. In this case, your purpose would be to make your readers care enough to actually do something about the problem.

Or you might decide to write to people who don't have much information about the problem, people who don't even know the humpback whale is in danger of extinction. In this case, your purpose would be to provide them with the necessary information so that they could understand. You would probably also want to bring them around to agree with your position, and that also involves giving them information.

Finally, you might decide to write to people who know a bit about the problem but who disagree with your position. These people might feel that the extinction of various animals is inevitable in natural history and that man, in killing whales, is merely functioning as a part of the animal chain. Your purpose in this situation might be to persuade these people to accept your viewpoint.

You may be wondering if, instead of writing three letters or articles, it wouldn't be best to write one to everyone—those people who care but aren't actively involved in saving the whales, those who don't know much about the problem, and those who feel it's necessary to let some species of animals become extinct. It would seem as though one piece of writing should be easier. But it isn't. Alistair Cooke was recently asked if he wouldn't like his British radio show about America to be broadcast in America as well as in England. His response: "No, I always thought that would split the target. I'm talking to the outside world about how things work here [in America] and psychologically it wouldn't be good for me if they were heard here. You can't take a dart and throw it at two bullseyes."[1]

---

[1]"Behind the Best Sellers," *New York Times* Book Review Section, Jan. 27, 1980.

Asking yourself the three basic questions about your intended reader will help you avoid throwing one dart at two bullseyes. The response "Some readers do, some don't" to any of the three questions means you're aiming at more than one bullseye. The response "I don't know" means that you need to give your intended reader more thought. Not knowing if your audience is already interested, knowledgeable in the subject, or in agreement with you is like not knowing exactly where the bullseye is. It's easier to hit it if you know. Of course you can't always know for sure. Sometimes you have to make the best guess or assumption that you can and write as if your readers did have the interest, knowledge, and ideas that you assume they have.

SUMMARY OF CHAPTER

To communicate well with others, you must be able to understand them, to "walk a mile in their shoes." In conversation, your ability to see or hear the responses of others helps you. Sensing when your listeners are confused, bored, or annoyed, you can try to figure out why and what to do about it.

When you write to communicate with others, you must consider your audience with equal care. The following three questions can help you think carefully about your intended reader and why you are writing to that reader:

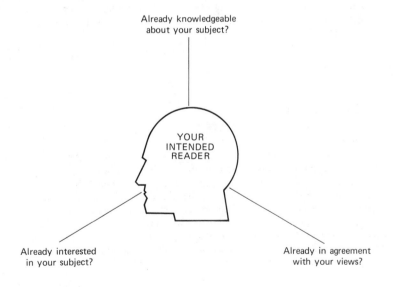

In most cases, the answer to at least one of these questions should be "no." Otherwise, there may be no reason to write.

ACTIVITIES: THE AUDIENCE

I. Below are four written communications. Read each and decide what assumptions the *writer* has probably made about the *intended reader*. Specifically, ask yourself:

1. Does the writer assume the reader already knows about the rat problem?
2. Does the writer assume the reader already knows about Rid-a-Rat and how to use it?
3. Does the writer assume the reader is willing to use Rid-a-Rat or has to be talked into using it?

A.

Hey Bill,

Please put out some more rat poison before you go to work tonight.

Thanks,

Jim

B.

Dear Bill,

Please put out some of the "Rid-a-Rat" poison before you go to work tonight. The Rid-a-Rat is on the top shelf over the washing machine. The directions are on the container.

Since Sue's baby will be here tomorrow, please make sure you put the poison where the baby can't get it.

Thanks,

Jim

C.

Dear Tenant,

As many of you are already aware, we seem to be developing a rat problem. It's not yet a health hazard, but unless we all cooperate, it soon could be.

As part of our rat control program, we're providing each tenant in the building with a free supply of Rid-a-Rat rat poison. We've selected Rid-a-Rat for its safety and effectiveness. It's simple to use—full directions will be given to you with the poison.

If we all put out the poison beginning Monday, May 9, we should have the rat problem under control by the end of the month. Please stop by the office any time between 8:00 A.M. and 4:00 P.M. for your free supply. If you are at work during those hours, please call us at 524-7901 and we'll deliver the poison to you during the evening hours.

Thank you for your cooperation,

Frank Jones
Manager

D. _____

DIRECTIONS FOR USING RID-A-RAT:

Place minimum 4 oz. bait in each location frequented by rats. Use authorized containers only. CAUTION: Baits should be placed in areas inaccessible to children, pets, and wildlife. In cases of ingestion by humans, call a physician.

_____

II. When writers make the *wrong* assumptions about their readers, the readers may "tune out" and not read the writing very carefully. Or they may read it, then either ignore what the writer has said or become angry about it.

    A. Reread the "Directions for Using Rid-a-rat." What assumptions has the writer made regarding the reader's educational level? Do you think the assumption is a good one or not? Explain.

    B. Reread the letter from Frank Jones to the tenants. Assuming that the assumptions Mr. Jones has made about the tenants are *good* assumptions to make, what would be the effect if he wrote the following letter instead? Why?

_____

Dear Tenant,

We just got some rat poison in. Pick yours up in the office any time during business hours: 8:00 A.M. to 4:00 P.M. I expect everyone to use it.

Sincerely,

Frank Jones

_____

III. Select two letters-to-the-editor from your local paper. One should be a letter you feel is well written—clear and persuasive. The other should be a letter that you feel is less clearly or persuasively written. Once you've selected the letters, ask yourself the following questions about them:

    1. How much background information has the writer assumed the reader will have?

    2. To what extent does the writer feel the reader is already interested in the subject or problem?

    3. To what extent does the writer assume the reader agrees with the point being made even before reading the letter?

After you've answered these questions for each letter, ask yourself how well the letters are written for what seems to be the *intended audience*.

Ask yourself to what extent you personally are like the intended audience for each letter. To what extent does your being personally similar to or different from the intended reader affect your reaction to the letter?

IV. Select a magazine article or book that appeals to you and ask yourself the above three questions concerning the writer's assumptions about the intended reader. (*Note:* People sometimes enjoy reading material written for an audience that's really different from themselves. When we read material written for someone who knows less than we do about a given subject, or who has different interests or beliefs, we can temporarily make believe we are like that person ourselves.)

chapter 2

How Do Readers Read?

This chapter does not tell you how *to* read. Rather it describes how most people, especially experienced readers, *do* read. It describes many things that readers do so automatically that they aren't aware of doing them. Just as an experienced driver often slows down or checks the rear view mirror without *consciously* deciding to do so, or just as someone ties a shoelace without *consciously* thinking of each separate movement, so experienced readers may ask questions and make decisions without being aware of doing so.

You may wonder why there's a chapter on reading in a book about writing. The reason is that when you write, you're usually writing someone else's reading. To write effectively, you therefore have to know how people will read what you have written.

TYPES OF READING

Not all types of writing are read—or written—in quite the same way. What are the different types of writing? There is no one correct answer to that question. A similar question might be: What different types of people are there? Since no two people are exactly alike, one answer would be, "There are as many 'types' as there are people." The same is true of writing. Still, readers find it helpful to decide, in general, what "type" of reading they are about to begin. This helps them decide how to read. One classification system readers find especially useful is based on the author's purpose in writing:

Writing for self-expression

Writing to create literature

Writing to communicate with others

As you read the following descriptions of the three types, try to think of examples from your own reading. Of course, you'll find that some writing belongs to more than one "type." In fact, you may find it useful to think of the three purposes as forming a triangle rather than a list: All three may be present in a given piece of writing, but the spotlight or focus is usually on just one or two of the triangle's three points:

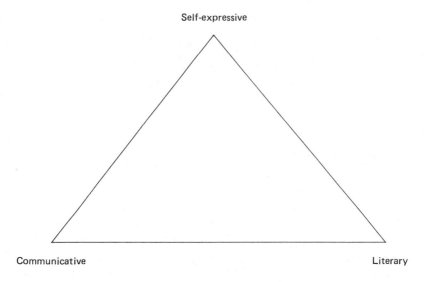

Self-expressive

Communicative   Literary

Self-expressive

The first purpose of writing could be called *self-expressive*. It's the writing people often do in private diaries and journals. It's also the type of writing people do when they are just "thinking out loud" on paper, trying to understand their own thoughts and feelings. There is no reader in mind other than the author himself. Readers can save themselves frustration by recognizing when a piece of writing is primarily self-expression. In general, when readers read such writing, they don't expect the same logic or organization as they would expect in other types of writing. In fact, rather than trying to understand the details, they usually just try to get a general feeling for the author's thoughts or emotions. What self-expressive writing have you read recently? Did you have any difficulties with it?

Literary

The second purpose of writing could be called *literary*. Literary writing typically includes poems, short stories, novels, and some essays. While the self-expressive writer may be concerned primarily with his or her own thoughts and feelings, the literary writer may be primarily concerned with the poem or essay being created, with the writing as a work of art. (It's the purpose, not the quality, that's important for our purpose here. Whether or not a particular piece of literary writing is *well done* is a separate question.) Another chracteristic is that while other types of writing may *tell* readers about something, literary writing often *re-creates* it, letting the readers see or experience it for themselves.

Think of a short story, novel, or poem you've read. How did reading it differ from reading something that's primarily self-expressive writing? How did it differ from reading a newspaper or factual magazine article?

Communicative

The third purpose of writing could be called *communicative:* writing to communicate with others. When experienced readers choose to read primarily self-expressive or literary material, they may be willing to work hard at understanding it. After all, the self-expressive writer's focus may have been on himself or herself, and the literary writer's focus may have been on the work of art itself. But when experienced readers read communicative writing, they expect the burden of responsibility to shift. They expect the writer to focus on communicating clearly and well with the intended readers.

This communicative type of writing includes much of what we read and write: newspapers, magazine articles, love letters, business letters, reports, memos, school papers, self-improvement books, and chemistry textbooks, to give just a few examples. Obviously, not all communicative writing is read, or written, in the same way. Readers therefore divide communicative writing into still smaller categories. Again, these subtypes are based on the writer's reason for writing. We'll consider just three important ones:

Writing to inform the reader

Writing to interest or entertain the reader

Writing to persuade the reader

Just as with the larger categories, one piece of writing may have been written for two or more reasons. Thus these subtypes are often combined. For instance, one paragraph of a letter may be mainly persuasive while another paragraph of the same letter may be mainly informative. Or two different purposes may be intertwined throughout an entire essay. Once again, it can be useful to think of the three types of writing as forming a triangle rather than a list. As before, all three aspects may be present in a given piece of writing, but the spotlight or emphasis is usually on just one or two of the triangle's three points.

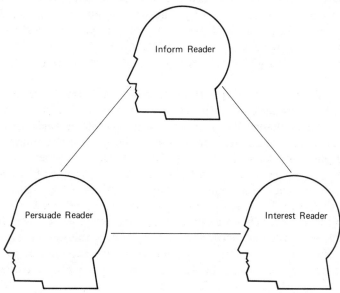

Despite this blending of purposes, readers still find it helpful to subconsciously ask themselves: "What's the writer up to? What's his or her purpose?" How do readers decide what the writer's purpose is? The next time you reach for something to read, observe your own behavior. Before you've read even the first word, you undoubtedly know whether it's a letter, magazine, or newspaper article that you're about to begin. You may also know something about the writing situation: who the writer is, what the writer's relationship to you is, and whether the writing is in response to something you yourself wrote or said. This is so obvious, and so automatic, that most readers don't give it a thought. Yet the "setting" and "situation" help readers decide what type of writing something may be. This helps them know how to read it. As you read the next few pages, keep the "Rid-a-Rat" writing samples from the last chapter in mind.

THE SETTING AND SITUATION

What settings normally cause readers to expect *informative* writing? It varies, of course, but most readers expect to be "informed," to learn something new, when they read newspapers, textbooks, or newsmagazines. They also expect to be informed when they read a report or letter providing information they themselves have requested, when they read directions on the label of a product they've purchased, or when they arrive home and find a short note from their roommate pinned to the door. In all these situations, readers would look for facts and information as they read. They might also look for examples, details, reasons, comparisons, or definitions to help them understand the information being presented. In addition, they would appreciate a writing style and organization that's clear and easy to read.

When do readers expect to find *interesting* writing? When readers pick up general interest magazines, or ones that deal with people or places, they often expect writing that's interesting or entertaining. The same is true of many friendly letters. In both situations, readers may look for vivid descriptions, interesting details, humor, or even suspense. Other situations may cause readers to look for a different kind of interest: they may look to see how the writing applies to them personally or what they can gain from it.

Still other writing settings and situations may cause the reader to expect *persuasive* writing. For instance, when people read newspaper editorials, letters-to-the-editor, and some feature columns, they expect the writer to try to persuade them to a particular point of view. People also expect to find persuasive writing when they read advertisements, sales letters, and letters from friends who write only when they want something. Another situation where persuasive writing is expected is in many college courses. As professors read course papers, they often look to see what idea, what point of view, the student is trying to prove. While reading persuasive writing, experienced readers tend to assume a "prove it" attitude. They look for evidence and hard proof. Further, they expect the writer to have anticipated and answered not only their questions, but also their objections.

As you read earlier, communicative writing need not be just one of these three types. It can be both informative and persuasive. Or both interesting and informative.

Or all three. Think back to the Rid-a-Rat writing samples. Which ones would the intended reader expect to be primarily informative? Which one or ones would the intended reader expect to be persuasive as well as informative?

Setting and the Intended Reader

Another way of thinking about setting is that it lets us, as readers, know who the intended reader is. Then, as we read, we can play that role. For instance, if the cover of a book entitled *City Streets* indicated that the book was an introductory text in sociology, we would expect that the author of the text would be writing for beginning sociology students. While reading the text, we would therefore be prepared to read as beginning sociology students would read. We would look for definitions, explanations, and examples. We might also look for helpful charts, graphics, and subheadings. We'd probably be pleased to find chapter summaries. If, on the other hand, the cover of the book indicated that *City Streets* was a mystery novel, our role as readers would be quite different. Knowing that mystery novels are usually written primarily to entertain people, we would assume the role of someone looking for fun and relaxation. We would then be upset, or puzzled if the book read like a sociology text. And, finally, if we received a letter from the mayor's office concerning the street lights in our city, we would assume a still different role as we read: that of concerned resident or tax-paying citizen. If someone from out of town tried to read the mayor's letter, they'd have to make believe they too were a resident of our city in order to read the letter appropriately.

Implications for Writers

When you write to communicate with someone else, you have to consider the entire writing situation. This includes not only what you want to say, and your intended readers, but also your purpose in writing. Do you primarily want to inform your readers? To excite their interest or curiosity? To persuade them? Do you have a combination of purposes? Part II of this book will help you make these preliminary decisions. Once you've decided on your audience and purpose, the chapters in Part III will help you make your writing more effective.

When you write, the setting or situation is important in another way also. The setting in which your writing appears will determine what your readers expect to find. Thus what you say and how you say it must be appropriate to the setting in which it will appear. For instance, someone reading an article in the school paper would expect a different type of writing than someone reading a friendly letter.

In addition, you can sometimes consciously create special setting to let your readers know how to read. For instance, you might need to let your readers know that they should read your writing humorously. One solution would be to use a comic "pen name" that your readers would see as part of the setting. Another solution might be to play with the physical format of your writing, perhaps borrowing the graphics or format of a well-known humor columnist. By providing a setting that your readers would recognize as humorous, you would be helping your reader know how to read your writing.

Another implication of the setting and situation concerns models of "good writing." What works well in one setting or situation might not work at all in another. For instance, an article on computers written for a computer magazine might be full of technical terminology with few, if any, attempts to make it interesting or clear to non-specialists. Considering the setting and situation, the article could be very effective. The intended readers, people who work with and enjoy computers, might understand the technology and be fascinated by the article. The very same article appearing in *Reader's Digest* or *Time* would attract few readers because the situation and the audience would be different. Thus whenever you look for examples of good writing to use as models, you must take the setting, situation and audience into account.

THE SUBJECT AND LENGTH

Once a reader has observed that the reading in hand is, say, an article in *Time* magazine, and is probably informative, what next? Once again, consider how you yourself read.

First, you might decide whether or not you felt like reading a *Time* article at all. If you decided you did, your next step might be to see what the specific subject of the article was. You would probably, once again, turn to the setting for help. What is the article's title? What do the pictures and the "blurb" near the title indicate about the subject? If the subject interested you, you would probably do one more thing before you actually began reading. You'd check the length.

Length is important to readers. They feel the weight of the book in their hands. They flip the pages of a magazine to see how long a chapter is. They rip open a letter and proceed to count the pages. Why?

First, the length, like the setting and subject, helps readers determine when—and if—they want to read the writing at all. (Writers, take note.)

In addition, the length of the writing can help readers recognize the author's "point" or main idea. This is especially true of material that's written to inform or persuade readers. In general, the longer such writing is, the more the reader expects a main idea that's fairly complex or broad. The shorter the writing, the more the reader looks for a main idea that's simple enough to be fully explained in the short space available. Part of the unspoken pact of informative and persuasive writing is that the writer will fully explain the main idea to the intended reader.

THE MAIN IDEA

How do readers recognize the author's main point, or *thesis*, as it's sometimes called? Keeping the length and the type of writing in mind, the reader generally looks for an idea that "sounds like" the main idea. How readers do this will be explained in more detail later. First, let's look at a piece of writing the way an experienced reader might.

The following article is from a newspaper,[1] but the specific setting indicates that

---

[1]*The Washington Post,* April 20, 1972, See A, p. 20, col. 3. © 1972, The Washington Post Company, reprinted with permission.

it is probably persuasive as well as informative. Look first at the title and length, then read the first paragraph. Underline what seems to be the thesis, then continue reading to see if that is, indeed, the author's main idea.

WILL WE LET POLLUTION NIBBLE US TO DEATH?

Ecologists warn that unless a firm brake is applied soon to our feverish abuse of earth's resources, man himself may become an endangered species. But first things first. Instead of worrying about deadlines for man's extinction, we should give immediate thought to a closer danger: adaptation. The horror is not only that we are killing the land and possibly ourselves, but that we calmly *adapt* to it, often without even a fight.

For example, a city park is taken over for a new highway, so the neighborhood people adapt and use another park a mile away. Then a stream through that park is contaminated by the town's power plant, and the people are told to fish 30 miles upstream. But there a chemical factory's black smoke makes breathing bad. In desperation they go across the state line 100 miles away, to where there are tough clean-air laws. But there a new airport for jumbo jets has gone up, and the noise prevents sleep at night.

Because adaptation to pollution is made in small fits, we see each giving-in as only a minor loss. Why sweat the penny-ante stuff? But in the end we find our fortune—our environment—taken away.

The statistics of pollution show that we have been adapting very well; much of America lives comfortably with the following:

> Fifty percent of the nation's drinking water has been discharged only a few hours before by some industrial or municipal sewer.
>
> Water pollution killed 23 million fish in America in 1970.
>
> Strip mining may soon claim 71,000 square miles of land, an area the size of Pennsylvania and West Virginia combined.
>
> In one Washington inner-city neighborhood, 25 percent of the children under six who were tested showed dangerously high levels of lead in their blood. The source: not only peeling, lead-based house paint (which the children eat) but lead-laden car-exhaust fumes.
>
> Forty million pounds of dung a year are deposited by dogs on New York City streets.

That most people become good sheep and adapt to these outrages may be a tribute to human flexibility; but isn't something subtracted from the sum of the person's individuality and emotions? A clear equation is created; adapt to the subhuman and you may become subhuman too. As bacteriologist Rene Dubos says, "It is not man the ecological crisis threatens to destroy but the quality of human life."

Jerome Kretchmer, head of New York City's Environmental Protection Administration, tells of a ghetto mother who was seen "air mailing" her garbage: putting it into bags and hurling them from her tenement window into a vacant lot four floors below. When asked why she air mailed, she said she used to carry it down but grew afraid of running the gauntlet of addicts roaming the hallways of her building and afraid of a rat attacking her child while she was out. In other words, as offensive as air mailing is, it had a sound internal logic according to the conditions under which she was forced to live. She had adapted.

Is there anyone who isn't adapting to pollution? Surprisingly, large numbers of lone citizens, groups, even whole communities, are part of a new environmental resistance. City officials in Oberlin, Ohio, for example, passed a stiff law . . . making it illegal to sell, offer for sale, or even possess nonreturnable cans or bottles. As a result, the city officials say, "a significant dent" has been made in their solid-waste problem. In eastern Kentucky and Tennessee, two citizens' groups are campaigning to stop strip mining, the first time the voice of impoverished mountain people has been heard on this outrage.

If groups like these multiply, and the philosophy of non-adaptation spreads, then it is possible that the swelling tide of pollution may be halted or even reversed. Hopefully, while there is still time, Americans will see the danger of adapting, and fight instead.

Colman McCarthy

The first sentence in McCarthy's article *could* be the main idea of persuasive writing. It sounds like a possible thesis: "Man himself may become an endangered species." However, because the statement is so broad, because it's not exactly a "new" idea, and because it is the very first sentence of the article, most readers would suspect that it's probably just an introduction. This suspicion is confirmed by the next sentence: "But first things first." This brief sentence clearly indicates that the author's real point is still to come. The next sentence introduces McCarthy's real concern: " . . . we should give immediate thought to a closer danger: adaptation." The idea that adaptation is a closer danger than extinction is then repeated in the following sentence. Clearly this more limited, and original, idea seems to be McCarthy's real thesis or main idea.

The difference between a subject and a main idea is important to readers. Someone reading about pollution, for instance, needs to know what the author's idea is concerning pollution. For instance, is it that society cannot financially afford stringent pollution controls? Is it that pollution of the Chesapeake Bay must stop? Is it, as in McCarthy's article, that man seems to be adapting to pollution?

Of course the reader's final test of an author's main idea comes at the end of the writing. In rough drafts and self-expressive writing the author may begin with one idea, explore it, change it, and finally end with an entirely different idea. In such writing, written primarily for the writers themselves, this would be no problem. However, in communicative writing it would present a problem for the reader. There the reader would expect the writer to have thought his or her ideas through before presenting them for others to read. In short, experienced readers expect the main idea of communicative writing to be consistent throughout the writing. Further, they expect the conclusion to confirm that main idea. When this doesn't happen, they are likely to feel confused and annoyed.

What about the end of McCarthy's article? Does it confirm the main idea developed up to that point? Yes and no. Yes, McCarthy confirms his concern with the dangers of adaptation. But he goes a bit beyond that idea. It's as though McCarthy can imagine his reader asking: "Are all people adapting to pollution? Is no one fighting it?" In answering that imagined question, McCarthy admits that some people are fighting pollution instead of adapting to it. And this leads him to modify—not change—his main idea. At the very end, the reader sees that McCarthy believes that although adaptation to pollution is very dangerous, there is still time to fight it. Thus the thesis isn't changed so much as the reader is motivated to want to do something about it. In short, McCarthy has offered the reader a conclusion that's easy to follow and more interesting than a flat summary of what has already been said.

Recognizing Different Types of Main Ideas

In *persuasive* writing such as McCarthy's, the main idea is usually an opinion, judgment, or proposal. One way readers recognize a persuasive main idea is to see if the words "I'm writing to persuade you that . . ." would make sense in front of the idea. Consider the following examples:

> The best way to close your home when on vacation is to follow a set procedure.
>
> The college cafeteria should serve food that's more wholesome and less costly.

In *informative* writing, the main idea or thesis may be a fact that the writer wants to communicate or explain to the reader. One way readers recognize the main idea in informative writing is to see if the words "I'm writing to say (or explain) that . . ." could easily be imagined in front of it. Another clue is that the main idea or thesis of informative writing sometimes indicates the number of points the writer will make. For instance, most readers would agree that the following sentences sound as though they could be the thesis or main point of a brief (1 to 3-page) piece of informative writing.

> This is to inform you that, effective Friday, January 14, I must resign from my job with D & J Supermarket.
>
> In yesterday's elections in Canada, the voters replaced most of the major incumbents.
>
> There are three important procedures to remember in case of hotel fire.
>
> There are four basic reasons most people don't listen to others as carefully as they should.

You may wonder if the last example couldn't be considered persuasive as well as informative. The answer is yes. The author might simply want to explain the four reasons people don't listen. But there's also a chance the author might be writing to persuade the readers that they should become better listeners. The experienced reader would be alert to both possibilities, as well as to the possibility that the writer wants to do both: inform and persuade.

How do readers recognize the main idea in writing that's primarily *interesting?* We've already said that most writing is a combination of types. The thesis of most interesting writing is often either informative or persuasive. The difference is not the thesis so much as the author's purpose: to present the main idea as interestingly and vividly as possible.

You may wonder if knowing the type of writing helps the reader recognize the main idea, or if the main idea helps the reader decide what type of writing something is. It works both ways. A reader who expects informative writing will recognize the above main ideas more quickly than would a reader who expected some other type of writing. However, readers who had no idea what type of writing they were reading might still recognize the author's main idea. (For instance, they might imagine the general words *"My main point is that . . ."* in front of appropriate sentences.) They could then use the main idea to decide whether the writing would most likely be informative, interesting, persuasive, or some combination of these.

Location of the Main Idea

Where do readers expect to find the author's main idea? To some extent that depends on the type of writing. For instance, with much humorous and descriptive writing, readers don't expect the main idea to be spelled out at all; instead, they expect the author to plant enough hints so that they can figure the idea out for themselves. With other types of writing they may expect the author to wait until the end of the writing to actually state the thesis. They know this technique is sometimes used to stimulate their interest or curiosity. However, with most informative and persuasive writing, readers expect the main idea to be clearly stated within the first paragraph or two, just as it was in Colman McCarthy's article. If readers don't find the main idea as early as they expect it or need it, they may give up and stop reading. Just as listeners often tune out a conversation or lecture they find confusing, so readers often tune out confusing writing.

This is not to say that readers expect to find the main idea in the very first sentence. They know that in almost all writing, the first sentence, or even the first paragraph, may be introductory. In addition, they know that they can't be sure of the author's thesis until they've finished reading the entire piece of writing.

Implications for Writers

When you, the writer, want to inform or persuade your reader, it's important to make your main idea clear. Often readers will expect to find the thesis stated within the first two paragraphs. If they don't find the thesis there, they may become confused as to what your point is, and they'll soon stop reading. As a rule of thumb, remember that the greater the chance your intended reader may misunderstand you, the earlier you should state your thesis or main idea.

Another implication of the way readers read communicative writing is that you should do all your preliminary "thinking-out-loud-on-paper" in your rough drafts. That way you can write a final copy that presents a consistent main idea from beginning to end. Writing that doesn't stick to the point confuses readers just as much as does writing that seems to have no point at all.

FULL DEVELOPMENT

You read earlier that one reason readers are so aware of length is that it helps them recognize the author's main idea. Since the thesis is a kind of unspoken pact between the writer and reader, the reader expects that, once a thesis is clearly stated, the writer will fully explain or develop that idea for the intended audience.

Another way of thinking about development is to say that readers expect the author to anticipate answers to their questions. For instance, while reading the first paragraph of McCarthy's article, readers might wonder "Exactly what does McCarthy mean by 'adaptation to pollution'?" The second paragraph, which gives examples, answers that question. While reading that second paragraph, readers might think of a new question, such as: "So what? Aren't these just a few isolated examples?" And so it goes: The reader forms questions and then looks for answers to those questions:

WILL WE LET POLLUTION NIBBLE US TO DEATH?

Ecologists warn that unless a firm brake is applied soon to our feverish abuse of earth's resources, man himself may become an endangered species. But first things first. Instead of worrying about deadlines for man's extinction, we should give immediate thought to a closer danger: adaptation. The horror is not only that we are killing the land and possibly ourselves, but that we calmly *adapt* to it, often without even a fight.

Reader's question: For example?
McCarthy's Answer:

For example, a city park is taken over for a new highway, so the neighborhood people adapt and use another park a mile away. Then a stream through the park is contaminated by the town's power plant, and the people are told to fish 30 miles upstream. But there a chemical factory's black smoke makes breathing bad. In desperation they go across the state line 100 miles away, to where there are tough clean-air laws. But there a new airport for jumbo jets has gone up, and the noise prevents sleep at night.

Reader's question: So what?
McCarthy's answer:

Because adaptation to pollution is made in small fits, we see each giving-in as only a minor loss. Why sweat the penny-ante stuff? But in the end we find our fortune—our environment—taken away.

The statistics of pollution show that we have been adapting very well; much of America lives comfortably with the following:

> Fifty percent of the nation's drinking water has been discharged only a few hours before by some industrial or municipal sewer.
> Water pollution killed 23 million fish in America in 1970.

Strip mining may soon claim 71,000 square miles of land, an area the size of Pennsylvania and West Virginia combined.

In one Washington inner-city neighborhood, 25 percent of the children under six who were tested showed dangerously high levels of lead in their blood. The source: not only peeling, lead-based house paint (which the children eat) but lead-laden car-exhaust fumes.

Forty million pounds of dung a year are deposited by dogs on New York City streets.

Reader's question: Doesn't that just show we're flexible? What's wrong with that?
McCarthy's answer:

That most people become good sheep and adapt to these outrages may be a tribute to human flexibility; but isn't something subtracted from the sum of the person's individuality and emotions? A clear equation is created; adapt to the subhuman and you may become subhuman too. As bacteriologist Rene Dubos says, "It is not man the ecological crisis threatens to destroy but the quality of human life."

Reader's question: For instance?
McCarthy's answer:

Jerome Kretchmer, head of New York City's Environmental Protection Administration, tells of a ghetto mother who was seen "air mailing" her garbage: putting it into bags and hurling them from her tenement window into a vacant lot four floors below. When asked why she air mailed, she said she used to carry it down but grew afraid of running the gauntlet of addicts roaming the hallways of her building and afraid of a rat attacking her child while she was out. In other words, as offensive as air mailing is, it had a sound internal logic according to the conditions under which she was forced to live. She had adapted.

Reader's question: But is everyone adapting like this?
McCarthy's answer:

Is there anyone who isn't adapting to pollution? Surprisingly, large numbers of lone citizens, groups, even whole communities, are part of a new environmental resistance. City officials in Oberlin, Ohio, for example, passed a stiff law . . . making it illegal to sell, offer for sale or even possess nonreturnable cans or bottles. As a result, the city officials say, "a significant dent" has been made in their solid-waste problem. In eastern Kentucky and Tennessee, two citizens's groups are campaigning to stop strip mining, the first time the voice of impoverished mountain people has been heard on the outrage.

If groups like these multiply, and the philosophy of non-adaptation spreads, then it is possible that the swelling tide of pollution may be halted or even reversed. Hopefully, while there is still time, Americans will see the danger of adapting, and fight instead.

Thus while reading McCarthy's article, his intended readers find answers to their questions. Further, their questions are answered as they arise.

Implications for Writers

When readers read informative writing, they naturally look for answers to their questions. When they read persuasive writing, they look for answers to their objections as well as to their questions. In order to fully develop their main ideas, most writers therefore try to imagine the questions and objections that might occur to their intended readers. You've seen that McCarthy explained his thesis by anticipating and answering his readers' questions and objections. When you write, you can use this same technique yourself. (Part II of the book will show you how.)

READERS' FEELINGS

When readers read, they do not become mere reading machines. They do not process words and ideas as a computer would. Indeed, people read with their emotions, and their interests, as well as with their intelligence and reading skills. If they feel they are being lectured, readers will usually stop reading, just as listeners in a similar situation would stop listening. The same is true if they feel insulted or attacked. For instance, how many of McCarthy's intended readers would have kept reading if his first paragraph had read as follows:

People like you don't know what you're doing. Not only do you poison the air with your aerosol spray cans, your automobiles, and your cigarette smoke, but you calmly adapt to all this pollution. You're like sheep. In fact, you've probably never even thought about this before.

Compare the above paragraph with the one McCarthy actually wrote. What differences do you notice?

Implications for Writers

The implication for writing is obvious: When you write, always keep in mind that you're writing to people with feelings. Whether your intended reader is your boss, your teacher, the governor, or people who read a particular newspaper, keep in mind that your reader is a person, not a machine. In rough drafts it can feel good simply to sound off and get things off one's chest. However, if the writing is to accomplish anything else, the draft must be revised with the reader's feelings in mind.

READERS' REASONS FOR READING

In addition to tuning out if they feel insulted, readers may also tune out if they simply have no reason to read. In fact, "What's this got to do with me?" or "Why should I read this?" may be the most important question in the reader's mind. Sometimes the answer to this question is obvious: The reader may need the information or be very interested in the subject. Other times, however, the answer is not so obvious. That's when the reader expects to find an answer within the writing itself.

In "Will We Let Pollution Nibble Us to Death?" McCarthy's title gives the reader one reason to read: to learn the answer to the question asked in the title. The first paragraph gives the reader another reason for reading: adaptation to pollution, it would seem, affects us all, including the reader.

Sometimes, however, there is no practical reason for a reader to read. Consider the following paragraphs, taken from a student's description of her boss.

I had always been afraid of my boss. He was not tall, but his extremely large girth made him seem so. His wide, meaty shoulders supported a large head that sprouted thick, dark hair in constant disarray. His face was partially hidden by a wiry mustache that curved downward at the ends, giving him an appearance of a constant scowl. Underneath his shoulders a massive paunch bulged over his bathing suit—his only attire in the two years we worked together in his palatial home.

He was a very nervous, aggressive man, constantly moving in circles, always puffing on an endless chain of cigarettes. Great clouds of smoke billowed from underneath his mustache, punctuated by an incessant smoker's cough. The more nervous and excited he became, the faster he would twirl in circles, his elbow working like a motorized hinge pumping cigarettes to his mouth while keeping pace with his feet.

My desk was in the library, his was around the corner in the living room. Unfortunately, he chose to share my desk. Every day he sat across from me on one of the kitchen stools that he dragged across his freshly vacuumed Chinese rugs, leaving tracks like skis over newly fallen snow. Smothering the stool with his large frame, he would bend over his work, hunched shoulders supported by elbows resting on my desk. He looked like a great vulture hovering above his prey. Day after day we sat there, the vulture and I, working at breakneck speed, shuffling our respective piles of paper to and fro. . . .

Linda Hee, student

Most of Linda's intended readers would find this description very interesting, even though they would have no practical reason for wanting to know about Linda's boss. Their reason for reading this description would be curiosity—a curiosity developed by Linda's vivid descriptions.

Implications for Writers

Readers read for a purpose, and they won't read without one. Sometimes the purpose is fairly obvious. Other times, however, the subject holds no natural interest or importance for the intended readers. In such cases, it's up to you, the writer, to give the reader a reason to read. You can do this in many ways. For instance, you can appeal to your reader's self-interest, as McCarthy does. You can use vivid descriptions to arouse your reader's interest and curiosity, as Linda Hee does. Or you can use a variety of other techniques described in Chapter 13. What's important is answering, as quickly as possible, the reader's unspoken question: "Why should I read this?"

SUMMARY OF CHAPTER

Readers don't read all types of writing in the same way. They don't even read all communicative writing in the same way. How they read and what they look for are determined in large part by the situation, the setting, and what the writer's purpose seems to be.

Readers do, however, look for certain things in nearly all communicative writing. They look for a clear main idea. They look for the writer's purpose. They look for answers to their own questions or objections. And they look for a reason to read. If there seems to be no reason for them to read, they probably won't. Just as listeners don't have to really listen when someone is talking to them, so readers don't have to read, not even when they are the intended audience. Writers have to give them a reason to read.

ACTIVITIES: READING

I. Two articles on dining out follow. Assume that both articles appeared in a special "leisure activities" column of the school newspaper. Assume further that this column is frequently written in the first person ("I") and usually carries articles that offer either helpful advice or interesting information. As you read the two articles, ask yourself:

1. What questions and reactions do I have as I read *each* article?
2. Which article has a clearer thesis or point to make?
3. Which article seems more appropriate for the column?

Article 1

EATING OUT

I ate out last night and had the prime rib. My companion had the scampi. Scampi is one of her favorite dishes, especially when it's prepared with plenty of garlic. I like garlic too, but since I don't care for shrimp, I never have scampi when we're out. Of course I like fish, so I order that sometimes.

Anyway, my prime rib was served well done even though I had asked for it "rare." I don't like well-done meat. It doesn't have much taste. My brother likes his meat well done. I've never been able to understand that. Maybe he's just too unsophisticated to appreciate good food. Anyway, when my prime rib came, I raised my voice and said I wanted it done the way I'd asked for. The waiter took it back.

We like a nice view of the city lights when we eat out. That's one reason we go to this place. There are lovely night views in all the big cities, but perhaps the views in San Francisco and Hong Kong are best. I hope to get to Hong Kong some day. Anyway, we sat in the bar while we waited for a better table. I had scotch, and Sue, my companion, had white wine. We didn't talk about much while we waited for the table. The first table they offered us didn't have any view.

When we were finally seated, we started with soup, then had a salad, and finally the scampi and prime rib. The salad was nice but could have been a little fresher. The soup was good. We had wine with our dinner. The waiter almost forgot to bring it, but I reminded him.

There are over 30 fine restaurants in this city. Six of them have won national awards. How many of them have you dined at? Isn't it about time?

Article 2

HOW TO HAVE IT YOUR WAY

You have probably been out to dinner at one time or another. Dining out is fun. But sometimes little problems with the service, if not handled correctly, can ruin an evening.

These problems often seem to involve the waiters or waitresses. Even if the problem is with ill-prepared food, your waiter or waitress is your main line of communication to the kitchen. Therefore these people hold an important position. They will be a key factor in your having a pleasant or unpleasant evening out.

Let's say you're dining out in a restaurant that has waiters. I believe the waiter should be at your table to help you feel welcome. A smile or a hello can make your day brighter. If he is too busy, at the moment, to take your order, he should at least be there to acknowledge your presence. Even then, he should take your order in a reasonable amount of time. It's up to you to judge how long is reasonable. I waited half an hour once. I was so angry when the waiter arrived, I couldn't enjoy my meal.

Has your steak come to your table rare when you asked for it well-done? Or have you received only the lobster of a steak and lobster dinner? If you have, you have probably been through what I feel is an all too frequent occurrence. It's not funny when you receive something completely different from your order. I used to think it was rude to return the dinner, but I've recently grown tired of eating restaurant's mistakes. I now politely refuse to eat what they give me and request my original order. Sometimes, all it takes is a customer (you) to complain to the waiter or waitress that there's been a mistake. "I ordered a rare steak and I received it well-done. Please exchange this." Or you might inquire, "Has the restaurant run out of steak for the steak and lobster dinner?" Since such comments need not be offensive, they work well. The main thing to remember is that you, as a customer, should enjoy the meal you are paying for.

You may on occasion be seated in a cute little booth in a dark corner next to the busboys' cart, where you can dine to the music of clattering dishes. If this annoys you, then by all means ask to be seated elsewhere. I had dinner in a classy English restaurant, seated in a cramped booth next to the kitchen. The prices on my menu weren't any different than the prices on the menu of the people sitting in the large spacious booth next to the piano bar, but I paid a high price by having a miserable evening when I didn't ask the head waiter for another table. The restaurant has a wonderful English comic who sits at the piano bar. Unfortunately, I was unable to see or hear him.

Tipping can be another problem. The general rule on tipping is to tip approximately 15 percent of your bill. However, in my experience, the quality of the service and the price of the meal haven't always been directly related. A 15 percent tip may be a good guideline, but it's just that: a guideline. You may go to a very expensive restaurant and receive the worst service you've ever had—or have very good service at a coffee shop. In my opinion, you should base your tip on the quality of service received.

All in all, restaurants can be a source of many pleasurable experiences, but only if you make it that way. So, have it your way and enjoy.

Frances Katano, student

II. Below is part of an article that appeared in a newspaper, *The Honolulu Star-Bulletin,* on January 19, 1981. The article appeared on the paper's second page, a regular news page. As you read the article, ask yourself:

1. Is it primarily informative, entertaining, or persuasive? (Or some combination?)

2. What is the article's main idea?

3. What questions and reactions do I have as I read the article?

4. What type of person seems to be the intended reader?

5. In what ways is this article similar to or different from McCarthy's article?

A-2 Honolulu Star-Bulletin Monday, January 19, 1981

The Future Is Visible from Mauna Loa Peak

By Helen Altonn
Star-Bulletin Writer

MAUNA LOA, Hawaii — Within a matter of decades, carbon dioxide in the atmosphere may cause an increase of global temperatures with potential catastrophic effects on the earth.

This alarming possibility comes from Kinsell Coulson, director of the Mauna Loa Observatory, which has the best records of CO-2 in the world.

"In 22 years, carbon dioxide has built up about 7 percent, which is very rapid...a virtual explosion of CO-2 coming into the atmosphere," Coulson said in a recent interview.

"We expect it to double in the next 50 years," he said, stressing: "It's a very serious problem worldwide, not only for the science community but for everybody.

"When—not if—the CO-2 doubles," Coulson explained, "there is a potential for warming the worldwide temperature by five degrees Fahrenheit. Certain areas will be affected more than others.

"You may say, 'what's five degrees? It will be 95 degrees here instead of 90.' But this is very important because it could start melting

Hawaii's mountain peaks offer perhaps the Earth's clearest views into space for defense purposes and for understanding the wonders of the universe. Star-Bulletin writer Helen Altonn and chief photographer Terry Luke went to the Big Island, Maui and Kauai recently to take a close look at summit activities—an illustrious new state industry. This article is the first of four reports from them.

the ice in Greenland and the Antarctic continent. A great deal of ice will turn to water," he said.

"The level of oceans would be increased something like 400 feet if all the ice melted. No one expects all of it to melt, but if it was only 10 percent, the ocean level would rise 40 feet.

"It would be a catastrophe," he said, pointing out that vast coastal areas and farm lands would be inundated by the rising seas.

"Chances are that our grandchildren will see the beginning of this, and our great-grandchildren will be affected. It's a matter of a few decades," Coulson said.

THE carbon dioxide content of the atmosphere is the most serious problem under study at the 11,150-foot high Mauna Loa Observatory, which has broad responsibilities for "geophysical monitoring for climatic change."

Under the observatory's scrutiny are the sizes, numbers and composition of particles (dust haze) polluting the atmosphere, the ozone, carbon monoxide, solar radiation and rainfall acidity, in addition to wind, rain and other meteorology measurements.

Carbon dioxide occurs mostly from burning of fossil fuels, and Coulson said scientists don't know how to decrease it significantly in the atmosphere.

The United States and other governments are concerned and a big effort has been mounted to assess and understand the carbon dioxide buildup and carbon cycle.

The Mauna Loa Observatory's records are a vital component of this study—attracting a stream of international scientific visitors, Coulson said.

Helen Altonn, "The Future is Visible from Mauna Loa Peak," HONOLULU STAR-BULLETIN, January 19, 1981, p. A-2.

III. Below are two versions of a letter in which Mike Jones gives the required written notice that he's resigning from his job. Assume that Mike's boss has been good to him. If you were Mike's boss, how would you react as you read letter 1? Letter 2? If Mike were later to ask for a letter of recommendation, or perhaps for a summer job, which letter would make you want to help him out?

LETTER 1

112 Rocky Hill St.
Seattle, Oregon 98103
January 2, 1982

Mr. Joe Bossman
Bossman's Service Station
1204 Main Street
Seattle, Oregon 98101

Dear Mr. Bossman:

I'm going to quit my job with Bossman Service Station. January 16 will be my last day. That gives you the two weeks' written notice you want.

I'm quitting to attend school full-time. I sure don't want to spend the rest of my life being nothing but a "grease monkey" in a gas station. It's good enough for some people, but not for me.

Sincerely,

Mike Jones

Mike Jones

LETTER 2

112 Rocky Hill St.
Seattle, Oregon 98103
January 2, 1982

Mr. Joe Bossman
Bossman's Service Station
1204 Main Street
Seattle, Oregon 98101

Dear Mr. Bossman:

This letter is to say that March 16 will be my last day of employment with Bossman Service Station. Although you've always arranged my work schedule to fit my school hours, I feel I should become a full-time student now. As you can imagine, it's been a hard decision to make.

My experience working at Bossman's has been a good one. During my three years with the station, I've appreciated the increasing responsibilities you've given me. For instance, training the new employees probably taught me more about psychology than my college course could have.

Thanks again for a good three years. I wish you and the station continued success.

Sincerely,

Mike Jones

Mike Jones

IV. In a book, magazine, or newspaper, locate an example of writing that you find especially interesting, informative or persuasive. Ask yourself the following questions about it:

1. What seems to be the author's purpose? (What type of writing is it?)
2. Who is the intended reader? How much am I myself like the intended reader?
3. Whats the writer's main idea or thesis? (If possible, underline a sentence that states the thesis.)
4. What questions does the writer seem to anticipate and answer?
5. Why do I find the writing interesting, informative, or persuasive?

Bring the writing, and your answers to the above questions, to class. Exchange the writing with a classmate. Does your classmate react to the writing the same way you do? Why or why not?

chapter 3

What Else Helps Readers Read?

In the last chapter you read that experienced readers unconsciously ask themselves, "Why should I read this?" Then, while reading, they look for the author's purpose and main idea as well as answers to their own questions.

That's not all that readers look for. As they read, they also look for helpful paragraph divisions, logical organization, clear transitions, and readable sentences. Once again, an experienced reader does not *consciously* look for these things. In fact, when they're present, most readers take them for granted, not noticing them at all. But when they're missing—when the paragraphing or organization is confusing or the sentence style is hard to read—the reader notices immediately. Let's explore why.

PARAGRAPH DIVISIONS

Paragraph divisions help readers in three ways. First, they provide a visual break. Second, they provide a place where readers can "digest" the paragraph they've just read, to be sure of its meaning, before moving on to the new material in the next paragraph. Third, they can signal a new idea.

Readers are helped by paragraphs in the same way that they're helped by chapters in a book. Each chapter is part of the book as a whole, yet each is also a unit that the reader can understand, or absorb, before going on. So it is with paragraphs.

Long Paragraphs

In general, a long letter or article without paragraph divisions looks less inviting to read than one with such divisions. The reason, of course, is that it looks harder to read. And, indeed, it usually is. The same is true of writing that has very long paragraphs.

In the last chapter you read an article by Frances Katano entitled "How to Have It Your Way." The same article is typed without the paragraph indentations on page 33. Does this version look easier or harder to read than the paragraphed version in chapter 2? As you read this version, mark the spot where you first become tired or confused.

HOW TO HAVE IT YOUR WAY

You have probably been out to dinner at one time or another. Dining out is fun. But sometimes little problems with the service, if not handled correctly, can ruin an evening. These problems often seem to involve the waiters or waitresses. Even if the problem is with ill-prepared food, your waiter or waitress is your main line of communication to the kitchen. Therefore these people hold an important position. They will be a key factor in your having a pleasant or unpleasant evening out. Let's say you're dining out in a restaurant that has waiters. I believe the waiter should be at your table to help you feel welcome. A smile or a hello can make your day brighter. If he is too busy, at the moment, to take your order, he should at least be there to acknowledge your presence. Even then, he should take your order in a reasonable amount of time. It's up to you to judge how long is reasonable. I waited half an hour once. I was so angry when the waiter arrived, I couldn't enjoy my meal. Has your steak come to your table rare when you asked for it well-done? Or have you received only the lobster of a steak and lobster dinner? If you have, you have probably been through what I feel is an all too frequent occurrence. It's not funny when you receive something completely different from your order. I used to think it was rude to return the dinner, but I've recently grown tired of eating restaurants' mistakes. I now politely refuse to eat what they give me and request my original order. Sometimes, all it takes is a customer (you) to complain to the waiter or waitress that there's been a mistake. "I ordered a rare steak and I received it well-done. Please exchange this." Or you might inquire, "Has the restaurant run out of steak for the steak and lobster dinner?" Since such comments need not be offensive, they work well. . . .

How far did you get in reading this version of Frances' article? Most readers would become muddled by the fourteenth line or so—and with good reason. Although the subject is an easy one to understand, paragraph divisions are necessary to help the reader organize and digest the material.

Short Paragraphs

If overly long paragraphs are hard on the reader, are short paragraphs easy to read? Not always. Imagine trying to read something in which each sentence begins a new paragraph:

HOW TO HAVE IT YOUR WAY

You have probably been out to dinner at one time or another.

Dining out is fun.

But sometimes little problems with the service, if not handled correctly, can ruin an evening.

These problems often seem to involve the waiters or waitresses.

Even if the problem is with ill-prepared food, your waiter or waitress is your main line of communication to the kitchen.

Therefore these people hold an important position.

They will be a key factor in your having a pleasant or unpleasant evening out.

Let's say you're dining out in a restaurant that has waiters.

I believe the waiter should be at your table to help you feel welcome.

A smile or a hello can make your day brighter.

If he is too busy, at the moment, to take your order, he should at least be there to acknowledge your presence.

Even then, he should take your order in a reasonable amount of time.

It's up to you to judge how long is reasonable.

I waited half an hour once.

I was so angry when the waiter arrived, I couldn't enjoy my meal.

Has your steak come to your table rare when you asked for it well-done?

Or have you received only the lobster of a steak and lobster dinner?

If you have, you have probably been through what I feel is an all too frequent occurrence.

It's not funny when you receive something completely different from your order.

I used to think it was rude to return the dinner, but I've recently grown tired of eating restaurants' mistakes.

The difficulty here is that each sentence is presented as a separate unit of thought. Thus readers have no guidance as to how they should organize the various ideas presented. In fact, a series of very short paragraphs can be just as hard to read as overly long paragraphs.

There's another problem with writing that has too many very short paragraphs. Such writing can look superficial or immature. In effect, some readers wonder, "How can such short paragraphs include enough details and information to answer all my questions and objections?"

Paragraph Variety

That's not to say that readers don't enjoy any short paragraphs. Consider your own reaction to various paragraph lengths. The chances are you appreciate writing that has relatively short first and last paragraphs. Most readers do. A short introductory paragraph looks especially inviting since it looks "easy" and requires little commitment from the reader. A short concluding paragraph looks like a welcome "farewell." In addition, most readers are happy to see very short paragraphs—even as short as one line—sandwiched between longer ones within the body of something they're reading. The short paragraphs provide a welcome break. Thus the most appealing writing often has a variety of paragraph lengths.

Paragraph Logic

Do readers expect to find a new subject in each paragraph? No, not always. Readers know that writers sometimes divide what would otherwise be a very long paragraph into two or more shorter paragraphs, just to keep the length reasonable. Still, readers *do* expect a certain logic from paragraphs. Earlier you read that in some ways paragraphs are similar to chapters in a book. One of the similarities is that readers expect both paragraphs and chapters to stick to the subject. They expect each paragraph to be a unit, to make sense as a paragraph. If it doesn't, they may become confused.

To help yourself develop a feel for the "logic" of paragraphs, reread the original "How to Have It Your Way" as Frances wrote it (see page 28). As you read, mark the subject of each paragraph in the margin. Can you see how Frances' paragraph divisions help you organize her ideas? Did any of Frances' paragraph divisions confuse you as a reader? Which ones? Why?

Paragraphs in Newspapers and Business Letters

You may wonder about newspaper paragraphs and the nonindented paragraphs in business letters. Newspaper paragraphs are generally short to make them seem easier to read and to compensate for the small print and narrow columns. In many news articles you'll notice a double space between some of the paragraphs in a long article. That double space sometimes marks what would be the regular paragraph divisions if the news article were typed on a regular typewriter.

In modern business letters, double spacing is used between all paragraphs, with single spacing used otherwise. Thus the double spacing sets off the paragraphs so clearly that the reader does not need paragraph indentations to know where each paragraph begins. (See the format guide in Appendix D for a sample business letter.)

Implications for Writers

You don't have to be an artist to be concerned with the appearance of your writing. The way you divide your writing into paragraphs can have a significant visual impact on your reader. You can use paragraph divisions to make your writing look more inviting. You can also use them to help your readers organize and digest one unit of material before they move on to the next.

Chapter 7 offers suggestions for dividing rough drafts into paragraphs that will appeal to your readers and help them read.

CLEAR ORGANIZATION

In the last chapter you read that people don't read all types of writing in the same way. For instance, when reading writing that's basically informative, readers may look primarily for the author's main idea and for clear explanations and details. In writing that's primarily persuasive, they may look for proof and evidence as well as the main ideas. In writing that's primarily entertaining or descriptive, they may look for something to arouse and sustain their curiosity or interest.

Despite these differences, there are some similarities in the way readers expect almost all writing to be organized. For instance, they almost always expect to find a clear beginning, middle, and end.

Beginnings and Endings

In some types of writing the introduction is important because it helps develop the reader's interest or sets the stage in some way. In other types of writing it's important because it clearly states the author's thesis or main idea. Many times the introduction serves both purposes. In all cases, it's important to the reader.

The ending is also important to readers. It lets them know they have indeed come to the end. Writing that simply "stops," instead of "ending," leaves the reader feeling vaguely uneasy. It's as though someone has lifted the needle off a phonograph record before the end of the song, or as though someone has unexpectedly ended a phone conversation by hanging up without saying "Good-bye."

How do readers recognize endings? In general, they expect endings to be short, although there are definitely some long ones. They also expect the ending to refer in some way to the writer's main idea or purpose in writing. In informative writing, especially when the subject is difficult, readers may expect the ending to include a brief summary. In other types of writing, readers recognize that a brief, often clever, reference to the overall subject or purpose indicates the end. And, of course, readers recognize endings that begin, "To conclude. . . ."

Here are the beginning and ending paragraphs from Frances Katano's article, which you read earlier. Can you see how her beginning and ending help the reader?

HOW TO HAVE IT YOUR WAY

Beginning:

You have probably been out to dinner at one time or another. Dining out is fun. But sometimes little problems with the service, if not handled correctly, can ruin an evening.

These problems often seem to involve the waiters or waitresses. Even if the problem is with ill-prepared food, your waiter or waitress is your main line of communication to the kitchen. Therefore these people hold an important position. They will be a key factor in your having a pleasant or unpleasant evening out.

Ending:

All in all, restaurants can be a source of many pleasurable experiences, but only if you make it that way. So, have it your way and enjoy.

Frances Katano

In the last chapter you read an article by Colman McCarthy. Here's the beginning and ending of that article. Can you see how his beginning helps his reader and how the ending sounds like an ending?

WILL WE LET POLLUTION NIBBLE US TO DEATH?

Beginning:

Ecologists warn that unless a firm brake is applied soon to our feverish abuse of earth's resources, man himself may become an endangered species. But first things first. Instead of worrying about deadlines for man's extinction, we should give immediate thought to a closer danger: adaptation. The horror is not only that we are killing the land and possibly ourselves, but that we calmly *adapt* to it, often without even a fight.

Ending:

If groups like these multiply, and the philosophy of non-adaptation spreads, then it is possible that the swelling tide of pollution may be halted or even reversed. Hopefully, while there is still time, Americans will see the danger of adapting, and fight instead.

Colman McCarthy

Middles

How do readers expect the material between the beginning and end to be organized? There is no one set pattern they expect. However, if the author has announced a plan or pattern in the introduction, readers expect the writing to follow that plan. Or, if the writing begins to assume a particular pattern, readers often expect that pattern to continue throughout the writing.

For instance, the first paragraph of an article comparing the pleasures of eating at home with the pleasures of eating out might announce that three points of comparison will be explored: the food, the atmosphere, and the convenience. Most readers would then expect the author to discuss the three points in that order: first the food, then the atmosphere, and finally the convenience. Further, if in exploring the first point, food, the author discussed first home cooking, then restaurant food, many readers would expect that pattern to continue throughout the writing. They would thus expect the atmosphere of eating at home to be discussed before the atmosphere of eating out. And finally they would expect the convenience of eating at home to be discussed before the convenience of eating out.

When no set pattern is announced or established, most readers simply expect that the writer will discuss one subject or idea at a time and will provide information, details, and explanation when, and as, the readers need them.

So far you've read examples of effective writing by at least three writers: Colman McCarthy, Frances Katano, and Linda Hee. How did these writers organize their material? In the last chapter you saw that McCarthy organized his material by anticipating and answering his readers' questions. Frances Katano's article is organized in a different way. After announcing that she will discuss some of the "problems" of dining out, she then discusses four specific problems, devoting an entire paragraph to each one.

Linda Hee's writing, which you read in the last chapter, is organized in still another way to help her readers: Not only does each paragraph describe a different aspect of her boss, there is a clear progression or movement within each paragraph as well.

Implications for Writers

When writers write rough drafts, their ideas frequently fall onto the page in a jumbled order. That's natural. After all, most writers aren't sure precisely what they want to say until after they see what they've written.

However, when writers present their writing for others to read, it should be organized as the reader expects: with a clear beginning, middle, and end. Further, the writing should stick to the point, follow patterns once they are established, and answer the reader's questions as they arise.

How do writers turn their disorganized rough drafts into writing that's clearly organized? Part II of this book, especially Chapter 7, offers tips for doing that.

TRANSITIONS

If there were a set pattern that all writing followed, readers (and writers) would have it easy. For instance, readers could know that the third paragraph would always contain an example and the fifth paragraph would always contain a description. But that's not the case. The second and fifth paragraphs, as well as all the others, are likely to contain anything: examples, comparisons, descriptions, explanations, evidence, or humorous anecdotes, to name just a few possibilities.

Thus, as readers read, they subconsciously look for signals or clues to help them keep track of what they've already read and what they can expect to find next. These clues are often called *transitions*. Basically, transitional clues are words or phrases that help readers see the connections between the sentence or paragraph they've just finished reading and the sentence or paragraph they are about to begin. Some transitions, such as the words *for example, to summarize,* or *however,* are very obvious to the reader. They clearly spell out the connection between the old and the new material. They are almost like billboards or traffic signals. Other transitions are less obvious. For instance, the repetition of an important word may alert the reader that the subject under discussion has not changed, and a question may indicate a new subject or concern.

Sometimes the connection between the old sentence or paragraph and the new sentence or paragraph is so clear, at least to the intended reader, that no explicit transitional clues or signals are necessary. In this case, the reader is reading between the lines, seeing the connection between the old and the new without any specific clues to help.

To see how transitional clues help the reader—and how readers are sometimes able to read between the lines and provide their own transitions—let's look again at Colman McCarthy's article:

WILL WE LET POLLUTION NIBBLE US TO DEATH?

> Ecologists warn that unless a firm brake is applied soon to our feverish abuse of earth's resources, man himself may become an endangered species. But first things first. Instead of worrying about deadlines for man's extinction, we should give immediate thought to a closer danger: adaptation. The horror is not only that we are killing the land and possibly ourselves, but that we calmly <u>adapt</u> to it, often without even a fight.
>
> *transitional clue: "for example."* — (For example,) a city park is taken over for a new highway, so the neighborhood people adapt and use another park a mile away. Then a stream through that

park is contaminated by the town's power plant, and the people are told to fish 30 miles upstream. But there a chemical factory's black smoke makes breathing bad. In desperation they go across the state line 100 miles away, to where there are tough clean-air laws. But there a new airport for jumbo jets has gone up, and the noise prevents sleep at night.

Because adaptation to pollution is made in small fits, we see each giving-in as only a minor loss. Why sweat the penny-ante stuff? But in the end we find our fortune--our environment--taken away.

The statistics of pollution show that we have been adapting very well; much of America lives comfortably with the following:

Fifty percent of the nation's drinking water has been discharged only a few hours before by some industrial or municipal sewer.

Water pollution killed 23 million fish in America in 1970.

Strip mining may soon claim 71,000 square miles of land, an area the size of Pennsylvania and West Virginia combined.

In one Washington inner-city neighborhood, 25 percent of the children under six who were tested showed dangerously high levels of lead in their blood. The source: not only peeling, lead-based house paint (which the children eat) but lead-laden car-exhaust fumes.

Forty million pounds of dung a year are depositied by dogs on New York City Streets.

That most people become good sheep and adapt to these outrages may be a tribute to human flexibility; but isn't something subtracted from the sum of the person's individuality and emotions? A clear equation is created; adapt to the subhuman and you may become subhuman too. As bacteriologist Rene Dubos says, "It is not man the ecological crisis threatens to destroy but the quality of human life."

transitional clue: Summary of last ¶

transitional clue: "But."

transitional clues: - Repetition of "adapting." - Use of "with the following:"

Reader must read between the lines and recognize that the items on the list are "outrages." The word "these" is a clue.

transitional clue: "But."

Jerome Kretchmer, head of New York City's
Environmental Protection Administration, tells of a
ghetto mother who was seen "air mailing" her garbage:
putting it into bags and hurling them from her tenement
window into a vacant lot four floors below. When asked
why she air mailed, she said she used to carry it down
but grew afraid of running the gauntlet of addicts
roaming the hallways of her building and afraid of a rat
attacking her child while she was out. In other words,
as offensive as air mailing is, it had a sound internal
logic according to the conditions under which she was
forced to live. She had adapted.

Reader must read between the lines and understand that this is an example.

Spelled out at the end.

Is there anyone who isn't adapting to pollution?
Surprisingly, large numbers of lone citizens, groups,
even whole communities, are part of a new environmental
resistance. City officials in Oberlin, Ohio, for
example, passed a stiff law ... making it illegal to
sell, offer for sale or even possess nonreturnable cans
or bottles. As a result, the city officials say, "a
significant dent" has been made in their solid-waste
problem. In eastern Kentucky and Tennessee, two
citizens' groups are campaigning to stop strip mining,
the first time the voice of impoverished mountain people
has been heard on this outrage.
If groups like these multiply, and the philosophy of
non-adaptation spreads, then it is possible that the
swelling tide of pollution may be halted or even
reversed. Hopefully, while there is still time,
Americans will see the danger of adapting, and fight
instead.

transitional clues: question and repetition of "adapting."

transitional clues: "If" and "groups like these."

To check your own ability to recognize transitional clues, read the following writing, marking the words and phrases that would help readers see the connections between one paragraph and the next and also between the various paragraphs and the author's main idea. The author, student Zabrina Giron, wrote "A Noontime Proposal" for publication in the campus newspaper.

A NOONTIME PROPOSAL

Today for lunch I had a Pepsi, a package of nuts layered in salt, and a burrito supreme. I'll have something similar tomorrow. Am I becoming a junk food addict? Yes, it appears that way, at least for as long as I attend Shelton College. Certainly, among Shelton's four dining options I should find something nutritionally wholesome. Let's visit each of the four and see if I can.

First, we have the lunch wagons to tempt us with a variety of plate lunches, Mexican food, and hamburgers. But it doesn't take a discerning eye to spot the grease in which these are prepared. Along with the lunches, the wagons offer us chips, candy, sodas . . . everything to whet the appetite of a junk food junky.

Let's try the cafeteria next. It has a wide range of food, you can't beat the price, and, if you're in the mood for a hot lunch, they've got it. But that hot lunch comes with greasy meat, two servings of starch, and, at best, a small scoop of canned vegetables. And what about the sandwiches? White bread, stained caramel colored, imitates whole wheat, the meats are smothered in nitrates, and there's only one slice of tomato, with a sliver of wilted lettuce.

Our third option is the vending machine—hunger's salvation. Perhaps we'll find what we're looking for in one of the 10 machines on campus? No, it would seem not. Most of the machines are empty, and the few that still have food offer only soggy sandwiches, heavy in mayonnaise and nitrates but light in nutritional value. For dessert, we're offered candy or an ice milk bar covered with imitation chocolate.

Admittedly, there's one more option: an innovative idea called the Gourmet Dining Room. Certainly it is an adventure in epicurean dining and the food is nutritious. But the Gourmet Room has three drawbacks: The dining room holds a total of only sixteen people, the hours of operation are very limited, and, above all, it's so expensive that most of us can afford it only as a special splurge.

Of course I can bring my lunch, but there are no refrigerators or lockers in which to store it. I could leave it in the car, but can you imagine how appetizing that lunch is going to be after it has sat in a closed car in the boiling heat for four hours? So, I'd have to lug my lunch to all my classes, thus increasing the chances of losing it or having it squashed.

Driving off campus to eat is another alternative, but in the interest of conserving energy, not a viable one. Besides, for those of us who must return for afternoon classes, the only places where food can be prepared quickly enough are at the "fast food restaurants." Surely their food is as high in empty calories as is the food at the lunch wagon.

Let's face it. There's a problem. Well, what can we do about it? I suggest that the cafeteria offer certain meals of lean, broiled meat, accompanied by two servings of fresh vegetables. There should be *real* whole wheat sandwiches containing meat not laced with nitrates. The vending machines should have some nutritional foods such as fruit juices without sugar or artificial colorings or flavorings, and whole wheat sandwiches containing liberal quantities of lettuce and tomatoes (we need the roughage). Also, the health food stores should be encouraged to send a lunch truck. . . .

Granted, most students are at school for only one meal a day. And many of us don't want to eat nutritiously—at least not every day. But nutritionists stress that every meal counts. So when good judgment prevails, shouldn't we be able to find wholesome foods with relative ease? I'm suggesting that S.C. help us by giving us a choice at lunch time—a real choice.

Zabrina Giron

You might now reread "How to Have It Your Way" on page 28. You'll notice that the author, Frances Katano, counts on her reader's ability to read between the lines and recognize that the information introduced in the third, fourth, and fifth paragraphs are all "problems" with eating out. Do you think her assumption that the reader needs no specific transitional clue is a good assumption to make? (Did you have trouble understanding her article?)

Implications for Writers

Readers need transitional signals to help them see the connection between "old" information they've already read and "new" information they're about to begin. These clues can be as obvious as words like *for example,* or as subtle as the use of a pronoun such as *this* or *these*.

Sometimes, of course, readers don't need specific clues at all. For instance, in Colman McCarthy's article, the intended readers are counted on to recognize that "airmailing" is an example of adaptation. And in Frances Katano's article, the intended readers are expected to recognize that a restaurant table near the kitchen is a "problem" when one is dining out.

By and large, however, readers do need transitional clues, and writers must provide them. Chapter 7, "Use Transitions to Link Your Paragraphs," describes six different types of transitional clues you can use in your own writing.

READABLE SENTENCE STYLE

Have you ever had trouble reading something, even though you understood what all the words meant? If so, you're not alone. Sometimes this difficulty arises because you are not the intended reader. You therefore find it difficult to read between the lines as the author intended.

Even simple words and short sentences don't guarantee easy reading. For instance, a joke can go right over someone's head even though the words and sentences are short. The difficulty may be that the listener lacks the personal experience or background information necessary to understand the joke. The same is true for much reading: anyone can have trouble reading something that's written for another type of person—someone with different experiences or more background information.

Other times, however, you may be exactly the type of reader the writer had in mind, but still you may find the writing difficult. Assuming that the paragraphing and organization are easy to follow, the difficulty may be that the sentence style isn't as readable as it could be.

Vocabulary

Obviously, if a reader doesn't understand the meaning of the words in a sentence, the sentence will be difficult to read. But even when a reader knows what all the words mean, the sentence can still be difficult to read if it contains too *many* long or uncommon words. The reason is that long or unusual words require extra effort, even for readers who know what they mean.

As you read the following sentences, notice which ones you can understand with no difficulty at all and which ones you have to think about for a few seconds:

1. We request that all participants finalize their arrangements for the forthcoming autumnal journey.
2. We ask that everyone make final plans for the autumn trip.
3. Dissemination of information by affixing printed material to the sides of structures is prohibited.
4. Don't put posters on the buildings.

Imagine if traffic signs read: "Deaccelerate vehicle to point of inertia" instead of the more familiar "Stop." Or "Circumvention of normal route" instead of "Detour." Two words readers often use to curse such unnecessarily difficult writing are *foggy* and *gobbledygook*.

Sentence Length

In general, short sentences are easier to read than long ones. For instance, compare the ease with which you can read the following sets of sentences:

Version 1

I had always been afraid of my boss, who was not tall, but whose extremely large girth made him seem so, and whose wide, meaty shoulders supported a large head that sprouted thick, dark hair in constant disarray above a face that was partially hidden by a wiry mustache that curved downward at the ends, giving him an appearance of a constant scowl, and underneath whose shoulders a massive paunch bulged over his bathing suit—his only attire in the two years we worked together in his palatial home.

Version 2

I had always been afraid of my boss. He was not tall, but his extremely large girth made him seem so. His wide, meaty shoulders supported a large head that sprouted thick, dark hair in constant disarray. His face was partially hidden by a wiry mustache that curved downward at the ends, giving him an appearance of a constant scowl. Underneath his shoulders a massive paunch bulged over his bathing suit—his only attire in the two years we worked together in his palatial home.

Like short paragraphs, short sentences can be easier to digest than long ones. Of course sentences that are *too* short can sometimes be as annoying as ones that are too long. Consider the following versions of the same passage. Which is easier to read? Why?

Version A

A man walked down the street. He wore a sweater. It was blue. He was walking slowly.

Version B

A man wearing a blue sweater walked slowly down the street.

Although each separate sentence in version *A* is easy to read, many readers will find the overall effect less pleasant than version *B*.

Coherence

There's still another factor that can make it hard to read sentences. Sometimes the reader, even the intended reader, has to be a mind reader to figure out the connection between the writer's various ideas. Sometimes the word order is confusing. Sometimes the use of pronouns such as *it* or *he* isn't clear. Sometimes there just aren't enough transitional clues to show the connection between two sentences or between two parts of the same sentence. Just for fun, read the following passages.

Version A

Our age is one of space age technology. Scientists do not know if the atmosphere is about on earth to warm up or cool down. If it does just 5°F, the rise in the oceans could be 350–400 feet. Many of the cities along coasts being destroyed, they would affect the patterns of weather on the globe. If it cools down just 3°F to 8°F the ocean levels may drop. An ice age may be, the water being frozen into the glaciers, in store for us. Man may be accelerating the warming due to his pollutants. The same is true of the cooling.

Version B

Despite our space age technology, scientists do not yet know whether the earth's atmosphere is about to begin warming up or cooling down. If it warms up just 5°F the ice caps could start melting and the level of the oceans could rise 350–400 feet. This would destroy many coastal cities and would affect weather patterns across the globe. On the other hand, if the atmosphere is cooling down just 3°F to 8°F, another ice age may eventually be in store for us. If that's the case, water will be frozen into the ice of glaciers, causing the ocean level to drop. Ironically, both the warming and the cooling could be accelerated by man's pollutants in the air.

Study the differences between the two versions to see *why* one is so much clearer than the other.

Implications for Writers

Lively, clear sentences can keep your readers reading. Foggy, unreadable sentences can defeat even the most devoted readers.

In rough drafts, sentences are often long and the vocabulary more suited to the writer than to the intended reader. In addition, sentences might have words, especially transitional clues, missing and the word order might be confusing to anyone other than the writer. Since rough drafts are often written to clarify the writer's own thinking, this is no problem.

However, before writing is presented for others to read, the sentences must be cleaned up. At that point, it's helpful for writers to keep in mind that their readers aren't mind readers. If a sentence is too long or a word too hard, the writer must rewrite it—with the intended reader in mind. If the word order or the pronouns are potentially confusing, they too should be reworked—with the intended reader in mind. Finally, wherever the writer has assumed the reader can read between the lines and fill in missing information or transitional clues, the writer should stop and ask him or herself: "Am I assuming too much?"

Chapter 9 offers tips for polishing the sentences in your rough drafts. Chapters 12 and 13 offer additional tips for writing sentences that readers will find clear and vivid.

SUMMARY OF CHAPTER

As readers read, they expect to find material organized into a beginning, middle, and end. Further, they expect the material to be divided into paragraphs that will help them digest one idea before going on to the next.

In general, writing is easy to read when the relationship between the *last* sentence or paragraph and the *new* one is clear. Readers therefore look for transitional clues and logical word order to help them see this relationship.

Because readers bring background information and personal experience to their reading, they can often be counted on to "read between the lines." However, writers must remember that their readers are not mind readers.

ACTIVITIES

(There are several activities within this chapter itself. If you didn't do them as you read the chapter, you might do them now, before beginning the following exercises.)

I. Select a magazine or newspaper article that you find easy and pleasant to read.

A. Notice the paragraphs. How long or short are they? Are they the same length or varied? What is the subject of *each* paragraph?

B. Notice the transitional clues. Circle the transitional clues between paragraphs and also the important transitional clues within paragraphs.

C. Notice if there are places where you've had to read between the lines because there were no transitional clues. Mark those places. What information did you have to recognize or supply on your own? Is it reasonable for the writer to assume the *intended reader* could supply that information?

D. Exchange the article with someone else in class. Do you agree on the transitions?

II. Select a magazine or other article that you find *difficult* to read and for which someone like you is the intended reader. As you answer the following questions, try to figure out what made the reading difficult.

A. Are the paragraphs too long? Too short?

B. Are too many transitional clues missing? Are the clues given confusing instead of helpful? Why?

C. Does the sentence style have a high "fog" factor? (Are the words difficult? Are the sentences long?) Is the word order within the sentences confusing? Is it hard to see the connection between sentences or between parts of the same sentences?

D. Is the article really written for someone who is different from you? (Does the article assume you have background information you don't have? Personal experiences? Perhaps certain feelings or values?)

E. Ask someone else in class to read the article you found difficult. Do they find it difficult too? If not, why not?

III. What is the difference between asking an intended reader to "read between the lines" and asking him or her to be a "mind reader"? (You may want to use the above articles to explain the difference.)

part II

WHEN WRITERS WRITE: THEIR WRITING PROCESS

How do writers go about writing? What do they do? In what order? The next seven chapters will answer these questions and describe steps that you yourself can use when you write. Before you read what the book has to say, it might be interesting to jot down some notes on your present writing process. Think of the last important writing you did for school or work. What steps did you follow? In what order? Think of the last informal letter or note you wrote. What steps did you follow? In what order? Jot your steps down so you can compare them with what you read in these chapters. As you read, you may find some surprises.

Many people believe successful writers take pen in hand, contemplate the ceiling for a few seconds, receive inspiration, and then begin writing—one perfect sentence after another. Not so. Most experienced writers write in a very circular, messy fashion. They start not with perfect sentences, but with lists and rough ideas. They find out what they want to say only after they've said it.

Furthermore, writers know this will often be the case. From the very beginning, they often plan to change, revise, snip, scotch tape, splice, and revise some more, until they have prodded their writing into shape. How do writers know when all this revising and polishing is finished? That's easy: it's finished when they've done enough to satisfy their audience and purpose. Or when they run out of time. Or when they suspect that any further snipping and changing will make it worse instead of better.

This section of *When Writers Write* walks you through seven different steps you can use when you write:

Doodling
Drafting
Taking a Break
Revising
Sharing
Polishing
Editing and Finishing

Of course these steps are merely guidelines. When you write a friendly letter, you'll probably skip many of them. When you write just for yourself, to understand your own feelings and ideas, you'll probably skip most of them. Even when you write something like a history paper or an important letter of application, you might find that some of the steps aren't necessary. You might also find that you have to double back to the same step over and over again. Such circularity is natural: it's the way most writers write. Playwright Neil Simon once said, "In baseball, you only get three swings and you're out. In rewriting, you get almost as many swings as you want and you know, sooner or later, you'll hit the ball."[1]

---

[1] Quoted by Donald Murray, "Internal Revision: A Process of Discovery," *Research on Composing,* NCTE, 1978.)

chapter 4

How to Begin with a Doodle

What's the hardest part of writing? Getting started! For many of us, putting the first words on paper is like summoning the courage to jump into the water in very early summer. The more we think about it, the harder it gets.

One thing that holds us back is a myth we carry in our heads: the one-perfect-sentence-after-another myth. When you write, don't think of your first words as the beginning of your paper. They're not. You'll undoubtedly change them later. Since the first words don't count, think of them as doodling—as a warm-up to get the juices flowing and ink running. This chapter describes two popular ways to doodle or warm up: brainstorming and freewriting. It also gives techniques for finding subjects and audiences, for organizing lists of material, and for arriving at possible main ideas or theses.

BRAINSTORM

Brainstorming is an easy, nonthreatening way to begin writing. The rules are simple: On a given subject, you jot down, in a *list,* all the ideas that come to your mind. The trick is to resist being critical of yourself. In brainstorming, nothing counts but the length of your list. Grammar, spelling, and being "right" or "wrong" don't count. In fact, if you think about spelling or grammar, you'll find that the "storm of ideas" in your head slows down . . . often to a stop.

If you're tense before you begin brainstorming, try the relaxation technique of shaking out your hands. Hold your fingers in an open, relaxed position and rapidly shake your hands from side to side from the wrist. Usually seven or eight quick shakes will do the job. If you still feel nervous about making mistakes, don't write your brainstorm in a list at all. Instead write your ideas on the page in random fashion, with some words sideways, some off in a corner, and so forth. Finally, if you find yourself stumped in the middle of brainstorming, simply repeat the last word you wrote. The physical act of writing will often help break your writing block.

Example of Brainstorming

The following brainstorm was written by Frances Katano, the student who wrote "How to Have It Your Way," which you read in Chapter 2. It's complete with misspellings and repetitions, as are most writers' brainstorms.

> *Things That Annoy Me*
>
> *Slow drivers on freeway*
> *People who keep me waiting*
> *People who don't do what they say there'll do*
> *Eating out in expensive places*
> *Motor boats*
> *Noise*
> *Barking dogs*
> *Barking dogs*
> *Barking dogs*
> *Politicians*

Frances' brainstorm list helped her in two ways: First, it got her started writing, and second, it provided her eventual subject: eating out in expensive places.

ACTIVITY: BRAINSTORMING

Let yourself go and simply list as many things as occur to you on the following topic:

TOPIC: THINGS THAT ANNOY ME

Your Brainstorm:

USE STRATEGIES TO FIND A SUBJECT AND AUDIENCE

Even professional writers sometimes have trouble selecting a subject to write on. For example, a public relations writer working for Security Bank has to keep the bank in the news but may not be able to think of anything interesting or newsworthy to write about. People who write free-lance articles for magazines such as *Psychology Today* or *Motor Trend* are always on the lookout for story ideas. If you're a writing student who draws a complete blank when your instructor says "Choose your own subject for the paper next Monday," don't worry: you have lots of company. You also have, on the next few pages, five techniques to use when you're in need of a subject or reason to write:

1. The "Dear People" Log
2. The "I'm Not Going to Take It Anymore" Catalogue
3. The Smile Roster
4. The Wish List
5. The Idea File

The ability to generate good subjects for writing is not dependent on instinct or luck. It's a skill you can learn.

1. The "Dear People" Log

This technique involves brainstorming a list of all the *People* you can think of. Start yourself off with the word *my,* as in: "My . . . boss, wife, teacher, neighbor." Next, prompt yourself with the word *the,* as in: "The . . . people in my class, people in my carpool, union officials, state legislators." Finally, brainstorm a list of the people you know, or know of, using their names. Example: "Joe, Kim, Mr. Wilson, Jerry Brown." This brainstorm records those people who, for one reason or another, are on at least the backroads of your mind. Many of them are people you have something to say to. The next step is to discover what it is you might say—or write—to them. To find out, mentally substitute each person (or group of people) from your brainstorm list in the "person" blank of the following sentence:

> *One thing I'd really like to explain to* _____ *is* ____.
> (person)   (idea)

After inserting the person's name, stop for a moment to see what ideas come to you to complete the sentence. When an idea occurs, write it in the "idea" blank.

Example

> *One thing I'd really like to explain to* my boss *is* that the store could make more
> (person)   (idea)

money by hiring extra help during the rush hours.

ACTIVITY: THE "DEAR PEOPLE" LOG

A. In the space below, brainstorm lists of people:

MY: _boss_   THE: _people in my class_ NAMES: _Joe_

_____   _____   _____

_____   _____   _____

_____   _____   _____

_____   _____   _____

_____   _____   _____

_____   _____   _____

_____   _____   _____

B. Substitute each of the people above in the model sentence:

One thing I'd really like to explain to _____ *is* _____.

If a particular name doesn't generate any ideas for you, just go on to the next name. Copy below the ideas that seem most worth writing about.

One thing I'd really like to explain to . . .

PERSON		IDEA
the athletic director	is	_that weightlifting is a legitimate sport_
_____	is	_____
_____	is	_____
_____	is	_____
_____	is	_____

You can try the following variations on the above model sentence:

One thing I'd really like to *describe* to _____ is _____
                                           (person)   (idea)

One thing I wish I could *persuade* _____
is that_____.   (person)
   (idea)

2. The "I'm Not Going to Take It Anymore" Catalogue

This technique should be familiar since it's one you began earlier when you brainstormed a list of "things that annoy me." You have now only to ask yourself, "Who could do something about this?" to have an audience and reason for writing. Here are examples of how one item on that brainstorm list could lead to at least three different types of writing.

Example

One thing that annoys me is <u>noise from loud televisions and stereos.</u>

Who could do something about it? <u>my neighbors themselves, contractors who build apartments, the apartment manager, the city council.</u>

Possible Writing Situations

1. A letter to the editor or city council, proposing a noise code for your city.
2. A letter to the editor or zoning board, proposing that noise abatement measures be made part of the building code for apartments.
3. If it's not possible just to talk with them, a letter to your noisy neighbors, asking their cooperation.

Of course the letters suggested in 1 and 2 above wouldn't solve your immediate problem, but they could be part of a long-range solution.

ACTIVITY: THE "I'M NOT GOING TO TAKE IT ANYMORE" CATALOGUE.

A. Review your "Things That Annoy Me" brainstorm earlier in this chapter, or brainstorm such a list now. Review your list, putting a check mark by those items that someone could do something about. Copy the most interesting one below, listing all the people who could do something about it.

ITEM	WHO COULD DO SOMETHING ABOUT IT? WHAT?
_____	_____
	_____
_____	_____
	_____
_____	_____
	_____

B. Now decide who you should write to—and why.

Possible Writing Situations

1. _____

_____

2. _____

_____

3. The Smile Roster

This is similar to the "I'm Not Going to Take It Anymore" Catalogue, but you begin by brainstorming things that *please* you. After you've brainstormed such a list, you ask yourself, "Who should be told about this . . . and why?"

Example

One thing that pleases me is <u>the way Jane Mintz (night school secretary) was so patient and helpful during registration last week.</u>

Who should be told and why: <u>Jane herself (to reward her and say "thank you").</u>
<u>School paper (they're always griping about reg).</u>
<u>Secretaries in general (so they'll be more helpful).</u>

Possible Writing Situations

1. A thank you letter to Jane herself, describing what a difference she made to your first night at school. A copy should go to Jane's boss.
2. A letter to the school paper, registering a word of praise for registration.
3. A report to secretarial students, describing the important public relations function secretaries play in an organization.

ACTIVITY: THE SMILE ROSTER

A. Brainstorm of a list of things that please you:

_____   _____

_____   _____

_____   _____

_____   _____

_____   _____

_____   _____

_____   _____

_____   _____

B. Review your list above, checking the items that someone should be told about. Copy the most interesting items below, indicating who should be told, and why.

ITEM   WHO SHOULD BE TOLD AND WHY

_____   _____

_____   _____

C. Now decide who you should write to and why.

Possible Writing Situations

A. _____

_____

B. _____

_____

4. The Wish List

This technique helps you discover questions and problems that are important to you as well as to others. Repeat a given sentence until you think of ways to complete it. Don't force yourself; if no idea comes to you, so be it. Useful sentences to use in this technique are:

I wish I could understand why . . .

I wish I could decide if . . .

I wish I could figure out how . . .

Examples

I wish I could understand why . . .

Why I'm so often late for meetings, dates, class . . . everything.

Why child abuse is on the rise.

Why birds all have different songs.

I wish I could decide if . . .

If <u>I should go into business for myself or work for someone else.</u>

If <u>nuclear power is potentially more damaging or beneficial to society.</u>

I wish I could figure out how . . .

How <u>we can have both recession and inflation at the same time.</u>

How <u>I should explain grandma's death to my five-year-old.</u>

Some of the topics you arrive at using this technique might seem to be of great interest to you but of minimal interest to others. An example might be the question, "Why am I so often late?" Yet even this question, once it's answered, could lead to interesting writing for others: an article offering insight and advice for others who are habitually late, a paper for psychology class, or even a letter to a friend you always keep waiting. Of course, before you can write to anyone else, you first have to solve the problem, or answer the question, for yourself. This is true of all writing, but it's especially important with the subjects you generate using this technique. Keep in mind that the Wish List will help you find subjects to research, think through, and answer to your own satisfaction. Only after you know what you think will you be ready to share your thoughts in writing with others.

ACTIVITY: THE WISH LIST

Following the examples above, jot down your own thoughts:

A. I wish I could understand why . . .

Why   *I'm so often late*   .

Why _____ .

Why _____ .

B. I wish I could decide if . . .

If _____ .

If _____ .

C. I wish I could figure out how . . .

How _____ .

How _____ .

5. The Idea File

Finally, here's a technique that doesn't involve brainstorming. When professional writers notice newspaper and magazine articles on subjects that interest them, they clip the articles out and put them in a special "idea file." You can do the same. Whether you're interested in photography, alternate energy sources, health diets, rebuilding automobile engines, or the newest developments in socio-biology, you can start clipping articles and making notes to yourself. (If you're interested in more than one subject, keep a separate file for each one.) When a writing assignment comes due—or you just feel an urge to write— you'll have not only a subject but a ready source of ideas and up-to-date facts.

ACTIVITY: THE IDEA FILE

A. If you have a special interest, begin an "idea file" on it. Narrow the subjects to specific areas— for example, "Baseball salaries" instead of just "Baseball," or "Alternatives to Nursing Homes" instead of just "Care of the Aged."

B. Set up your files and start looking for information to clip. Be sure to make a note of where the information came from, including the date and page.

MAKE LISTS OF INFORMATION

Let's say that you already have a subject to write on. The next step is to gather relevant information, details, and ideas. Why? The answer might seem obvious: so you'll have examples and proof to include in your writing. That's not the only reason, however. When writers first begin to write on a given subject, they often don't know exactly what it is they want to say. They don't know what they think—what their main idea is—until *after* they've gathered information and doodled with it a bit. Thus one reason to gather information is that it helps you decide what you think.

There are many ways of researching new information. In Chapter 1 you were asked to keep a list of why you sometimes don't listen while others are talking, and another list of why others sometimes stop listening while you're doing the talking. While making those lists, you were researching information. Careful observation, combined with precise record keeping and analysis, is an excellent research technique. A second research technique involves seeing what the "experts" have to say. This entails both library research and interviewing people who have experience or expertise in the subject you're writing about. (Appendix B offers tips on this type of research.)

In addition to gathering new information, writers also need to remind themselves of information they already know. In general, there are two different strategies writers use to accomplish this. One of these may be new to you. It's called *free-writing* and is discussed later in this chapter. The other strategy is one you are already familiar with: brainstorming. You have seen how brainstorming can help you decide who to write to and what to write about. Brainstorming can also help you once you have a subject, by providing you with a quick list of facts and ideas about that subject.

For instance, when Frances Katano reviewed her list of "Things That Annoy Me," she decided that she was most annoyed by "eating out in expensive places." (If you look back at her list in the section on brainstorming, you'll notice that the item "barking dogs" appears several times. However, that doesn't mean that she was most annoyed by barking dogs. Perhaps she was just repeating the phrase "barking dogs" while waiting for new ideas to come to her.)

Once Frances chose "eating out" as her subject, she asked herself who could do something to improve the situation. She suspected that other restaurant customers might, but she wasn't sure. She first had to discover what really annoyed her about eating out. So she brainstormed a new list of ideas and details about "eating out." Here's her new list, complete with the repetitions and misspellings that are a normal part of brainstorming.

EATING OUT

food
fish
fancy restrants
Mc Gees
dark
Churchills
beer
hard to see
no waitress
disappointment
bad table / bad time
had to wait
noisy
noisy
noisy
screaming kid
tip expensive
loud
mad
waste of money
meat overcooked
cold food
sefy hostess
Tom
car
good talk
pizza
unpredctable
louzy service
expensive

ORGANIZE LISTS INTO SMALLER GROUPS

What do writers do with lists? First, they cross out repetitions and obviously irrelevant items. At the same time, they usually circle or asterisk items that seem especially important or interesting. For example, Frances worked on her "eating out" brainstorm in this way:

fish

fancy restrants

Mc Gees

~~dark~~

Churchills

beer

hard to see

no waitress

* disappointment

bad table / bad time

had to wait

noisy

~~noisy~~

~~noisy~~

screaming kid

tip expensive

loud

~~mad~~

waste of money

meat overcooked

Cold food

~~sety~~ ~~hostess~~

~~Tom~~

~~ear~~

good talk

~~pizza~~

unpredctable

lousy service

* expensive

The writer's next step is to look over the items left on the list to see which items seem logically to go together. At this stage writers usually think of new items to add and also may decide to omit unimportant items that don't fit into any groupings. Frances' preliminary groupings eventually looked like this:

PRELIMINARY GROUPINGS

fish
cold meat
hot iced tea

fancy restaurants
Churchills
Mc Gees
Pizza place
beer

no waitress
disappointment
bad table   *screaming kid*
had to wait   *noisy*
lousy service

                       tip
                       expensive
                       waste of money
                       can't count on a good time

Frances' next step was to decide what the items in each group had in common so she could give each group a heading. For example, the group "fish, cold meat, and hot iced tea" all involve "food," so she labeled that group "food." With the other four groups she was able to move a word from the list itself up to become the general heading.

REVISED PRELIMINARY GROUPS

Food   *Fancy Restaurants*
fish   *Churchills*
cold meat   *Mc Gees*
hot iced tea   *Pizza place*
                                beer

Lousy Service   *noisy*
no waitress   *screaming kid*
disappointment   ~~*noisy*~~
bad table
had to wait   *Waste of money*
~~*lousy service*~~   *tip*
                                expensive
                                ~~*waste of money*~~
                                can't count on good time

Once Frances had headings for the groups, she could think about them more clearly, making changes as necessary. For instance, she decided that "pizza place" and "beer" didn't really fit with "fancy restaurants" and decided to cross out "fish," relabeling that group "poor food."

FINAL GROUPS

Poor Food   *Fancy Restaurants*
~~*fish*~~   *Churchills*
cold meat   *Mc Gees*
hot iced tea   ~~*Pizza* place~~
                                ~~*beer*~~

60

Lousy Service
  no waitress
  disappointment
  bad table
  had to wait
  ~~*lousy service*~~

Noisy
  screaming kid
  ~~*noisy*~~

Waste of money
  tip
  expensive
  ~~*waste of money*~~
can't count on good time

You may have noticed that when Frances began organizing her brainstorm list into smaller groups, she did not begin with the headings for the various groups. She began instead by organizing preliminary groups and *then* selecting headings or labels that seemed appropriate to the groups. Is this the only way to do it? No, of course not. But letting the groups determine the headings rather than the other way around is a good way to discover new ideas or insights. Of course, once you have formed the preliminary groups, you usually have to revise them, adding some items and deleting others.

ACTIVITIES: BRAINSTORMING, AND DIRECT OBSERVATIONS

I. A. Think of someone you live with now or lived with in the past. Write that person's name on the Person line below, then quickly brainstorm all the ideas that come to you *about* that person. Don't worry about spelling, grammar, or being "right."

Person _____

Brainstorm:

B. If the person you chose above is someone you still see regularly, carefully observe the person for one day, copying below your observations of what the person does, says, and looks like.

Person _____

Observations:

C. As a point of interest, compare the lists in A and B above. Then combine them into one list, eliminating duplicates and items that aren't true.

II. A. Select one idea from your "Dear People" Log, "Not Going to Take It Anymore" catalogue, or Smile Roster. Write that idea on the Subject line below, then brainstorm on that subject.

Subject _____

Your Brainstorm:

(continue at top of next page.)

B. If the topic you chose above is one that would lend itself to direct observation, observe the situation carefully, copying your observations below:

Subject _____

Observations:

C. Compare your lists in A and B above. Then combine them into one list eliminating duplicates and items that aren't true.

I. A. Below is a brainstorm of reasons people are late to parties. Decide what items have something in common and arrange those items in groups. Next decide on an appropriate heading for each group, revising the groups as you need to. You don't have to use all of the items on the list, but you should try to use most of them.

WHY PEOPLE ARE LATE TO PARTIES

> afraid of feeling out of place
>
> can't decide what to wear
>
> traffic jam
>
> nervous about not having anything to say
>
> think it's "correct" to be late
>
> have a fight with someone while getting dressed
>
> think the party will be boring—don't want to go
>
> feel important rushing in after everyone's there
>
> hate to be the first to arrive
>
> afraid of not knowing anybody there
>
> got lost
>
> didn't start getting dressed on time
>
> had to go someplace else first
>
> wrote down the wrong time
>
> better choice of people to talk to when late

B. Share your groupings with others who have done this exercise. Although your groups should be logical and consistent, there is no one correct way of arranging these items.

II. A. A few pages back you brainstormed about someone you know. Organize that list into logical groups with appropriate headings. (Remember, you can add, delete, and change items as you go.) When you're satisfied with the groups and headings, copy them below.

B. A few pages back you also made lists of information on a subject selected from your "Dear People" Log, "Not Going to Take It Anymore" catalogue, or "Smile" Roster. Organize that list into appropriate groups with headings, copying them below.

ARRIVE AT A TENTATIVE THESIS

When readers read, they want to know what the writer is getting at. They want to know what the thesis or "point" is. But how does the writer know what his or her point will be? The question isn't as silly as it seems. Sometimes writers can simply sit down, know what they want to say, and say it. More often, they sit down knowing only roughly what they want to say. They have to discover their own ideas and feelings—their tentative theses. We call these *tentative theses* (or *working theses*) because they often change as the writer begins to write rough drafts. Still, it's useful for writers at least to have a *starting* place.

How do they go about discovering a working thesis? One strategy they use is to talk their ideas over with someone else. As they listen to themselves, they can better understand what makes sense and what does not. Another strategy is to freewrite as described at the end of this chapter. Still another technique is to study the preliminary groupings of their brainstormed ideas. As they do this, they may silently say to themselves something like "I think (or feel) that_____." Let's see how this strategy worked with Frances Katano.

Saying to herself, "I think that . . . ," Frances studied her preliminary groups, looking for possible connections between them. She soon said to herself, "I believe that— poor service is inexcusable in good restaurants." Then she asked herself, "So what?" Looking at her groups again, she saw what she needed: Poor service was not only inexcusable, it was an expensive waste of her money. She then decided that what she really wanted to say was that people should not pay good money for poor service.

The main idea or thesis helped her decide on her audience: She would write to people who eat out and dutifully leave a large tip despite the poor service they receive. She felt that if everyone left tips that corresponded with the service, the service might soon improve.

With her thesis and audience in mind, Frances could decide which of her preliminary groups to include in her paper and what order to include them in. She could also revise the groups, combining some items and eliminating others. This is what her final plan looked like:

MAIN IDEA: DON'T LET RESTAURANTS WASTE YOUR MONEY

1. *Fancy Restaurants*
   Churchill's McGee's
   Costumes & extras

2. *Poor Service*
   Tips (15%)
   Expensive
   Having to wait
   Being rushed
   Waste of money/bad time

3. *Poor Food*
   Cold meat
   Hot iced tea

Now let's look at the rough draft Frances eventually wrote, using the above groups as her guide. As you read, remember that this is a rough draft. It contains the spelling and other errors that are a normal part of rough drafts. Even with the changes you see here, Frances later changed her paper much more before she regarded it as finished.

ROUGH DRAFT

> In our busy and affluent society, eating out has become Americans' favorite pastimes. Many of us enjoy eating out as a form of recreation, a stopping point in our busy lives, or just a necessary part of human existence.
>
> There are many fine place to dine in Town. To name only a few-- Churchills, The Olde Colony and Mrs. McGees. I've enjoyed myself at these establishments, but I don't feel I received what I paid for. We pay are too loose with our money when it comes to restaurant dining.

Each of these restaurants has their specialty. Whatever it may be. Prime rib, the costume, The English fare are all fine. But is it all really worth the $40.00 you paid for the dinner and wine not to mention the tip, and which is 15% of $40.00 or $6.00? Would you pay that much tip in a cheaper establishment and feel justified? No! I feel we should pay for the service we receive not 15% of the bill. I have received had waiters that couldn't bring the food soon enough, so you've we've rushed through our meal to accomodate our pushy waiter--and paid him for his service. Never shoed until you I decided not to wait any longer and showe up just in the knick of time. Or waitresses that can't say excuse me, but push my arm so they can grab something a plate off the table. And being a good customer I used to pay 15% of the bill because that's the rule. But I'll not follow a silly rule that puts me the person customer being served the person paying just in jeopardy of becoming loosing control of the situation. You must stay in control--you are paying. You are the customer, therefore the waiter is there to serve you not vice versa. And you should only pay for what you believe.

The Quality of the food is another problem. If food is cold, like the cold prime rib I got received once then sent it back. Or warm like my iced tea was many times then politely ask for an <u>iced</u> tea. Don't The rule is not to accept anything and that is not cooked prepared as specified. And if they don't accomodate you, then I can only suggest one thing--refuse to pay for it.

In our day of the dwindling dollar we cannot afford to throw our money away. If restaurant dining is a pleasure do it, but be selective in what and how much you'll pay.

Now that you've read the rough draft, look back at Frances' revised brainstorm groupings. You'll notice that not only do her three revised groups show up in her rough draft, they each form the basis of a separate paragraph. In each case, the heading of the group became the subject of the paragraph, and the items in the group became the specific details with which Frances developed that paragraph. Frances' rough draft really "wrote itself" from her brainstorm groupings. All Frances had to do was add details and write an introduction and conclusion. Of course Frances was lucky. Quite often drafting goes less smoothly than Frances'. In fact, as the next chapter indicates, many times several drafts are necessary before a writer begins to see exactly what he or she wants to say— and why. Indeed, Frances changed her own draft considerably before it became "How to Have It Your Way," reproduced at the end of Chapter 2.

ACTIVITIES: DISCOVERING A TENTATIVE THESIS

I. A few pages back, you organized into logical groups a brainstorm list on someone you know. Turn back to those groups now and try to see a possible thesis resulting from one or more of the groups. (Remember: The words "I believe that . . ." can help you get started, although those words probably wouldn't appear in your writing itself.) When you see a tentative thesis, jot it down below, indicating which groups you would probably use to develop it. At this point don't worry about who your intended readers might be. Sometimes that decision is made later in the writing process.

Subject: _____

Tentative thesis: _____

_____

Groups used to support it:

II. A few pages back you also organized a brainstorm list on a subject from your "Dear People" Log, "Not Going to Take It Anymore" Catalogue, or "Smile Roster." Follow the directions in the above exercise, but decide on a tentative audience as well as thesis.

Subject: _____

Tentative audience: _____

Tentative thesis: _____

_____

Groups used to support thesis:

III. In Chapter 1 you were invited to make lists of when you stopped listening to others and when they stopped listening to you. Refer back to those lists if you like, and write a quick brainstorm on "Why people don't listen to me" or "Why I don't listen to others." Organize your list and arrive at a tentative thesis and audience.

Is Your Tentative Thesis an Idea?

As you already know, a thesis is an idea, not just a subject. "Eating Out" is a subject or title. "Eating out can still be fun" is an idea. The difference is that "eating out" is just part of an idea; it doesn't say what the writer *thinks* about "eating out" or why the writer is writing about it. For instance, does the writer think that eating out is a big bore? Too expensive? Good for the economy? On the other hand, "Eating out can still be fun" is a complete idea; it tells what the writer thinks about "eating out." It could thus be the tentative or working thesis of a draft.

There's another way of looking at the difference between a subject and a thesis. Whereas a subject is usually not a complete sentence, a thesis usually is. The reason is simply that sentences have two parts: a subject and a verb that tells us something *about* the subject. This is why a simple test such as saying to yourself *"I think that . . ."* can help you recognize a thesis—and a sentence. "I think that . . . eating out" doesn't make any sense, but "I think that . . . eating out can still be fun" does.

Let's take another example: "How to eat out." Could "How to eat out" be a thesis? Give it the *"I think that . . ."* test. "I think that . . . how to eat out" does not make sense because it's not a complete idea. "How to eat out" is just a subject. It doesn't tell us what the writer thinks about it.

A question can't be a thesis either. "Why eat out?" can't be a thesis for the same reason that "How to eat out" can't be. The *answer* to a question, however, can be. For example, "Eating out provides a change of food, scenery, and even conversation," could be a thesis. It passes the "I think that . . ." test.

It's true that a subject, title, or question helps a writer organize and limit material, but none of them help as much as a tentative thesis does.

Arriving at a tentative thesis need not be difficult. For instance, looking at Frances' preliminary groupings on page 60 and saying to yourself "I think that . . . ," you might arrive at the following tentative theses:

Restaurants should provide better training for their staffs.

Parents shouldn't take very young children to fancy restaurants.

Despite the prices, eating out is still fun.

Each of the above possible theses would draw on different groups from Frances' preliminary groupings. Each thesis would also be written for a different set of readers. For example, Frances' own paper is written to people who dine out and tip even when the service is poor. But the first thesis above might belong in a letter or report to restaurant owners. The second thesis might be appropriate in a letter to the editor of the local paper.

The last one might be the thesis of a vivid description of a fine meal out written for people who haven't eaten out lately.

There's almost always more than one possible thesis. Your brainstorming, research, preliminary organization, and reason for writing will help you discover ideas and formulate a tentative thesis. The thesis, in turn, will help you decide which of your preliminary groups to include in your rough draft and which to save for another paper.

Here's a final tip: remember that the thesis is just tentative at this point. If it seems vague, uncertain, or dull, don't worry about it now. As you write the rought draft, your thesis may very well change. In fact, tips on sharpening the thesis are included in the next chapter.

IS THE THESIS A THESIS?

I. The list below contains some subjects, some titles, and two statements that could serve as the tentative thesis of a draft. Identify which is which. Tip: Use the *"I think that . . . "* test.

_____Going back to school at age 32.

_____Tips for better listening.

_____Fast-food chains are taking business from traditional restaurants.

_____How to conserve energy without sacrificing convenience.

_____Three simple tricks can make you a better listener.

_____Deciding on your future career as a biologist.

II. Review the theses you arrived at in the last set of activities. Do they pass the *"I think that . . ."* test? Are they complete ideas or just subjects?

TRY FREEWRITING

In addition to the brainstorming technique, there's another technique to discover what you want to say. To use this technique, which is called *freewriting,* you simply start writing on a subject, almost as though you were writing a messy, disorganized, chaotic letter to yourself. The point is not to communicate with others, but rather to find out what you have to say. For instance, if Frances had begun by freewriting instead of by brainstorming, she might have begun with a preliminary doodle like this:

We're going out to eat again this weekend. I sure hope it works out better than the last couple of times, they were such a waste of money and spoiled our evening. Damn service just makes me mad these days, lousy tables and having to wait, wait, wait. Then we have to leave a tip too. That's a waste of time. Course people would think we were cheap if we didn't tip, but why should we. We shouldn't even bother to eat out at all anymore. How come everyone leaves a tip. Are they that intimidated by the system? Eating out's supposed to be a treat, not a treatment. Somebody should do something about it.

In this doodle, notice that Frances would discover what she really wanted to say (that something should be done about poor service) *as a result of the writing.* She might not have noticed that idea while she was writing, but on rereading what she had written, she might notice it immediately. She could then brainstorm on that idea, use it as the beginning of a new freewriting, or use it to write an early draft.

ACTIVITIES: FREEWRITING

I. Select any idea from your ''I'm Not Going To Take It Anymore'' Catalogue or your ''Dear People'' Log. Freewrite on the topic, writing not to your intended audience so much as to yourself, just to get your own thoughts straight. Write as long as you like, and don't worry about grammar, spelling, logic, organization, or anything else. When you run out of steam, read what you've written, asking yourself, ''What do I really want to say here?'' (You'll often find that what you really want to say is near the end, not the beginning, of what you've written.) Take that idea and use it either to brainstorm or to do another freewriting. Either way, you'll probably find that your thesis changes or becomes more specific each time you repeat the freewriting.

II. In Chapter 1 you were asked to conduct an experiment to see why you tune out while others are talking and why they sometimes tune out while you are talking. Imagine that you want to write an article summarizing what you learned. (Your eventual audience could be other college students or some other audience of your own choice.) Freewrite on the subject for one half hour. Rest, then reread what you've written. What thesis seems to emerge from your writing? Take that thesis and either brainstorm or do another freewriting. Do you see still a new thesis? Repeat the procedure until you feel that you have discovered what you really want to say.

GET STARTED NOW

Do you owe anyone a letter? Are any of your reports for school overdue? Is there a problem you could resolve by writing to someone and have you put off doing so? If so, you may be an expert in *avoidance behavior,* at least when it comes to writing.

Avoidance behavior is the psychological catchword for substituting one activity— such as cleaning a room, walking the dog, or sharpening a month's supply of pencils— for another activity that really needs doing. Writers can carry avoidance behavior to extremes.

One strategy to combat avoidance in writing is to have a special place where you do your writing and where you keep your paper, pens, pencils, paperback dictionary, and so forth. When you sit down there, you'll know it's time to write—not to wash the car or make phone calls.

Another strategy is always to have at hand a small notepad on which to make personal notes. That way when you suddenly remember, right in the middle of writing, that the car needs gas or a library book needs to be returned, you can make a note to yourself. You can then put the errand out of your mind and continue writing, knowing that the note will remind you of what needs doing when you are through writing.

A third technique is to divide a writing project into manageable parts. Don't try to produce the finished product in one sitting. Instead, set yourself limited, realistic goals for each session. Your goal for the first session might be to do no more than doodle, whether it's brainstorming, freewriting, or a combination. For the second session, your goal might be a very rough draft and a clear sense of your audience, purpose, and thesis. If all is going well, your goal for the third session might be to revise and polish the draft, after you've had someone else read it and react to it. By thus dividing the writing task into more manageable pieces, you won't feel so overwhelmed, and you won't be trying to do the impossible.

Ideas and writing take time to incubate. Still, incubation time shouldn't be confused with out-and-out procrastination. You know your own temptations. You know what you should be writing—and when. Get started today.

ACTIVITY: GETTING STARTED

A. Make a list of everything you've written during the past two or three months. (Include letters, reports, poetry—everything.) Read the list over and mark those things you wrote later than you should have. Now brainstorm *another list* of those things you *should* have written during the past few months but didn't.

B. Compare the two lists. Is there a particular type of writing you put off? Why? Do you put *all* writing off?

C. Plan a strategy for combating your avoidance behavior. Would a set place to write help? Would you do better if you worked in more isolation? Less isolation? Would dividing the writing task into smaller sessions with specific goals help?

D. Is there something you should be writing right now? Get started on it!

chapter 5

How to Write a Messy First Draft

© 1972 United Feature Syndicate, Inc.

A rough draft is exactly that: rough. Like the rough sketch of an architect or a cabinet-maker, the writer's rough draft merely sketches some possibilities. The draft is a way of discovering what you, the writer, want to do and say. Because drafts don't represent the finished writing product, their roughness is no reflection on the writer's grammar or logic. In fact, a professional journalist once wrote, "When I finish a first draft, it's so bad it wouldn't get 'D' in a high school English course. Then I rewrite, usually about six times."

SEE WHAT YOU HAVE TO SAY

How do you go about writing a rough draft? It depends on the situation. Sometimes you know exactly what you want to say, why you want to say it, and to whom. Let's say, though, that despite your preliminary doodling, you're still not at all sure of your thesis. In that case, you might try writing a preliminary draft that's similar to freewriting. You might write such a draft as a letter to yourself, focusing on the idea you are trying to understand. You might also begin such a preliminary draft by stating your tentative thesis. If you don't have a tentative thesis, you could begin with a question rather than a statement. For instance, if you were writing about the problems of public transportation, you might ask yourself, in writing, "Is the inconvenience of riding the bus worth the savings?" Or,

"How could the city improve the bus system?" As you write your draft, ideas will emerge and you'll eventually see what you now think or want to say. You are then ready to move on to a second type of draft, written with a reader in mind. Frances' rough draft, reproduced in Chapter 4, is this reader-oriented type of draft.

Your reader-oriented draft can also be written as though it were a letter, but, in this case a letter to your intended audience. (If your audience is a group of people, you can focus on one person who is typical of that group.) Some writers find this strategy especially helpful, as it encourages them to actually picture their reader. They try to visualize the reader—to see the yawns, frowns, and smiles on their reader's face as he or she moves from sentence to sentence. This reader-oriented draft is also a way of discovering what you want to say to a particular audience. As you draft, you may therefore find that your ideas change. This is normal; it's why writers usually write more than one draft.

Some ideas seem to offer an almost built-in audience. (This is often the case with ideas springing from the "Dear People" Log, "I'm Not Going to Take It Anymore" Catalogue, and the Smile Roster.) Other ideas may not immediately suggest any audience at all. (This may happen with ideas arising from the Wish List or Idea File.)

What can writers like yourself do when your subject or idea doesn't suggest any particular type of audience? You can ask yourself three questions: "Who needs to know this?" "Who would benefit from knowing it?" and "Who would be interested in it?" The answer to *one* of the questions—not all three—should provide you with an appropriate, specific audience. For example, if your idea were that riding the bus is worth the effort, you might decide to try to persuade people who don't ride the bus that they should. Or you might write to the bus company's public relations department, suggesting ways they could persuade folks to switch from cars to buses.

Whether you're writing a preliminary letter to yourself or a draft with your reader in mind, concentrate on drafting ideas and content, not style. The time for polishing and revising your style will come later. For now, draft the raw materials: ideas.

TIPS FOR WRITING ROUGH DRAFTS

1. Some practical points: Use colored or obviously scrap paper to remind yourself that you're just drafting. (This will help you overcome the temptation to write as though the draft is a final copy.) Also, write on the front of the paper only. (That way you can later use scissors and tape to rearrange your paragraphs.)

2. Don't worry about your first paragraph. When you revise, you'll probably omit it or change it anyway. For now, just plunge on with the rest of the draft.

3. If you've worked out preliminary groupings of information as recommended in the last chapter, use the groupings as a guide. Each group can become one or more paragraphs.

4. Place your tentative thesis early in the draft; it will help focus your attention.

5. If you find that your thesis is changing, let it. Remember—drafting is an exploration of possibilities. If you discard a good idea just because it would change the direction of your draft, you're cheating yourself.

6. As a rule, don't use a dictionary or thesaurus (book of synonyms) while you draft. Since you may later discard entire pages of the draft, it's faster to just circle or otherwise mark places where you're not sure of spelling, grammar, or word choice.

7. If you feel blocked and unable to start writing, try dictating the draft into a tape recorder. Listen to the tape later, taking notes of what you want to include in your writing. You can later use these notes to begin a written draft.

8. If you're still blocked, the problem may be that you, like many of us, are a bit afraid to "see what you think," or to find out that you don't yet know enough about the subject. When this happens, just recognizing the cause and knowing you have company can help. If it doesn't, ask yourself "What's the worst thing I can find out from this draft?" Once you've verbalized "the worst" to yourself, it may not seem so bad.

9. If you type fairly fast, experiment with drafting on the typewriter. It can help you get ideas down on paper almost as rapidly as they occur to you.

10. Above all, remember that these tips are only tips, not rules.

Examples of Drafts

The following few drafts were retrieved from my own trash can. The first one shows what happens when I get stuck while drafting. I simply keep going, using all the paper I need to become "unstuck":

SAMPLE DRAFT

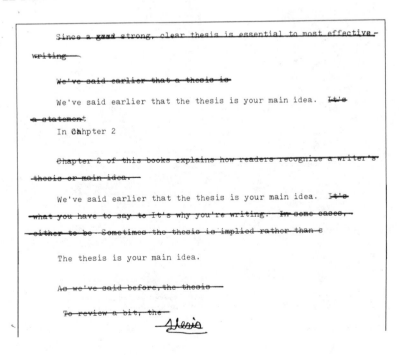

```
        Sometimes the most important

    The following tips may help you improve your thesis before,
xauxdxxftx during, or after your first draft.

1. Thesis too broad.

    1. THESIS TOO BROAD.
```

The next sample shows what can happen when I draft something as seemingly straight-forward as the Tips for Writing Rough Drafts. I stop, read what I've already written, change things, write some more, circle back to the beginning to reread and change some more, push on, and then repeat the process, cutting and taping as I go. It's anything but straightforward. You'll note, by the way, that before I typed the final copy of the drafting tips, I made still more revisions. Don't try to read this draft—it's too messy. Just observe what it *looks* like.

SAMPLE DRAFT WITH REVISIONS

5 —Don't use a dictionary or Thesauras(book of synonyms) while you
write your draft. The early drafts are usually attempts to get
your ideas,not your style, in order. If you slow down over spelling
or to find the "precise" word, you may find that
the entire sentence you've labored over

6 —

7 —If you feel blocked and unable to start writing your draft,
try dictating it into a tape-recorder. Some people are more
comfortable talking than writing, and you may be one of
them. If you use a tape-recorder for your draft, you can later
listen to the tape making notes to yourself
what you want to say in your writing. Then
you can write a draft, using your notes

FIND YOUR THESIS

One thing above all should be evident from the drafting tips: drafting is a discovery
process. When writers draft, they typically write a bit, stop, reread parts of what they've
written, scratch things out—sometimes whole pages—and then continue drafting. As they
reread the draft, they sometimes find that it doesn't really have a thesis. When this

happens, writers can discover their thesis by asking themselves "What's my point?" or "What do I believe about this subject?" A student, Allison C. Clough, III, wanted to write about his recent fire-fighting training for readers who were not familiar with a firefighter's job. Below are two drafts: one is an early draft that's similar to freewriting, the other is a later draft, written with both an audience and thesis in mind. Which is which? (Neither draft was originally as neat or straightforward as appears here.)

DRAFT A

I'm almost through with my training program to become a fireman. I've wanted to be a fireman for a long time. How do I feel about it now?

The training program included lots of things. We studied books on things like construction techniques, water systems, first aid, community relations, and chemistry. We learned fire-fighting techniques too.

The reason I wanted to be a fireman when I was a kid is because they always looked so important. Firemen helped rescue kitty cats from treetops. They rushed around in the big red fire truck with the lights flashing and bells ringing. I used to enjoy the parades, too. The firemen always looked very proud, marching in front of their red truck.

Our trucks are yellow now, because yellow is more easily visible. We're getting very scientific and use face masks with airpacks on our backs. This helps combat the dangerous gases from new materials like foam rubber and plastic. The trucks take a lot of polishing to make them shine. We also give building inspections to make sure the buildings conform to regulations and are safe.

DRAFT B

I remember being asked as a child, "What is it you want to be when you grow up?" Like most children at that time, my immediate answer was, "I'd like to be a fireman." Now that I'm close to being one, firemen seem to be changing.

When I was a child, firemen always seemed gloriously noble. I'd see them climbing up a tree to free a crying kitty, or rushing down the street on a big bright red fire truck with lights flashing and sirens screaming. Other times I'd see the firemen marching in a parade, sharply dressed with their shiny fire truck following behind. But no matter where or when I saw the firemen, they were always doing something highly dramatic and very respectable.

Now, after seven months of training, I see some changes. Today if a cat is stuck in a tree, firemen are instructed not to go up and get it. Our response to the poor owner must be, "Don't worry, the cat will come down." And some add, "You've never seen a cat's skeleton in a tree before, have you?" We spend many hours on necessary—but nondramatic—building inspections. We also spend hours simply sitting at a desk and reading: books on construction principles, books on water systems, books on electrical systems, and books on first aid procedures. In short, we must become apprentice contractors, civil engineers, medical technicians, and even chemists.

Even when we do go to fires, we don't look or act like the fireman of old. In the early days of fire fighting, firemen used to grow long beards so they could wet them down and hold the beards over their mouths as filters against the smoke. Today we are not allowed to wear beards because they might interfere with the face mask of our breathing backpacks. We have to wear these backpacks because of the highly dangerous gases produced by new materials such as foam rubber and some plastics.

Of course we still ride on fire trucks, light and sirens pulsing, but the fire trucks I remember from childhood were exquisitely large and shiny and red. Today the fire trucks are still large and, with an extreme amount of hard work, they do shine. But they're no longer red. Now they are "high-visibility" yellow. True, yellow is more readily seen. But yellow is yellow, not glorious red.

Now when I see a fire truck rolling home toward the station, I no longer picture a group of firemen later sitting leisurely around the station, talking over the weather and playing cards, a pet Dalmation at their feet. No, I now see a group of firefighters, as we're currently called, routinely inspecting buildings, studying regulations, and, alas, putting the shine on that bright yellow truck.

A. C. Clough, III

Sometimes writers know exactly what their thesis is when they begin writing. (Frances Katano did, for instance, when she wrote her rough draft on eating out.) But how do writers discover their real thesis after they have finished a first draft? Usually they simply reread what they've written, asking themselves, "What's my point? What do I want to say?" Sometimes it helps to take a break between writing the draft and rereading it. Can you see what sentences, or even individual words, might have seemed to be Allison's point as he reread his early draft? What *is* the thesis of the later draft?

SHARPEN YOUR THESIS

From Allison's two drafts, we can see why a thesis is so important to the *reader*. (Which draft is easier to read? Which is more interesting?) We can also see how a thesis can help the *writer*. While Allison's second draft has been revised for many things other than just the thesis, it's the thesis that made the other changes possible.

A helpful thesis has four main characteristics. First, it's a complete idea that can be (and usually is) stated in just one or two sentences. Second, it's limited or narrow enough so that the writer can fully explore it in the number of pages to be written. Third, it's appropriate to the writer's purpose and intended readers. Finally, it's reasonable and true. Often the thesis of a draft is too broad, too dull, or too false to satisfy the writer. The suggestions that follow will help you sharpen such a thesis before, during, or after your first draft.

What If Your Thesis Is Too Broad?

You'll know that the thesis is too broad if you find that you'll need volumes—or at least more than you're willing to write—to fully explain or prove the idea. One approach is to review your preliminary groupings of ideas and select just the one most interesting group to write about. For example, instead of writing a paper that tries to explain that

"Managers have a tougher job than workers do," you might decide to concentrate on just the psychological burdens that make the manager's job tougher. Or you might focus on just your own problems as a gas station manager.

A common tactic, especially in school writing, is to select a specific number of ideas to cover. Such a thesis might read: "Railroads affected the development of America in three important ways." Another approach is to focus on the causes of something. The simple trick of including the word *because* or *reason* in a thesis can help narrow it. For instance, rather than writing "Promotions to management are often frustrating," you could write "Promotions to management are often frustrating because there's no pay for the overtime or for the loss of one's former friends."

A third way of narrowing a thesis is by narrowing the intended audience. For instance, if you were writing about creative use of leisure time for an audience that included people of all ages and interests, your thesis might be very broad. However, if you narrowed your audience to, say, retired people, your thesis could become more focused. Can you see why?

What If Your Thesis Seems Dull?

Overhauling a dull thesis can be fairly easy. If you chose the thesis in the first place, something about it must have interested you. The job now is to find out what. The direct approach may be best. Reread your thesis, and then say to yourself, *"This is interesting because . . ."* For example, you may have written, "I enjoy vacations at my uncle's house." Your draft may contain numerous examples of times you've had fun at your uncle's. However, when you say "This is interesting because" to yourself, you realize that you don't do anything at your uncle's house that you don't also do at home. This might lead you to decide that what's interesting is that at your uncle's house someone else decides what to do and when to do it. Your new thesis might be, "The most enjoyable thing about a vacation at my uncle's house is not having to make decisions."

Another way to add interest to a dull thesis is to reconsider your audience. A draft that carefully describes how to tune an acoustic guitar may seem dull if you're writing for experienced guitar players. However, beginning guitarists might find the paper fascinating; it would tell them just what they need to know. Sometimes a change of audience is all that's necessary to make the thesis work. (Incidentally, there really is no such thing as an "interesting thesis": one needs to know, "Interesting to whom?")

What If Your Thesis Oversimplifies the Issue?

You'll know that your thesis is an oversimplification if you have trouble making your facts and examples fit what you're saying. In addition, if your thesis contains words such as *all, none, always,* or *never,* beware. It's quite common to see only one side of an issue as you begin writing. The truth of the other side emerges as you write. When this happens, you should modify your thesis. For instance, you can add words (called *qualifiers* or *qualifications*) that limit your meaning. Suppose you've written, "Jogging is good for people," a statement that is not universally true. You could modify it to "Jogging is good for healthy people," or "Jogging is good—in moderation." Other useful qualifications are: *some, perhaps, seems,* and *usually*. Although you don't want to qualify your ideas out of existence, you do need to make your thesis accurate. When you say something "is," you're saying it's a fact. When you say it "appears" or "seems," you're simply saying the evidence points in that direction. The latter is usually easier for writers to prove and for readers to accept.

A second way to avoid oversimplification is to make an *although, however,* or *but* part of your thesis. If your draft reveals there are major exceptions to your ideas, don't ignore them. For example, suppose you started drafting a letter with the idea that your town should provide more bus service. As you wrote, you might become aware of the increased noise and pollution the buses would cause. You could then modify your original position from "Our town should provide expanded bus service" to "Although ways will have to be found to deal with potential noise and pollution, our town should expand the bus service." With a thesis such as this, you would discuss the noise and pollution problems as well as your basic contention that the bus service should be expanded. (To avoid confusion, make sure you do *not* put your main idea in the clause that begins with *although*. The *although* introduces the less important, or subordinate, idea. The opposite is true with *however* and *but*; these two words introduce the more important idea. For example: "Increased bus service will create noise and pollution; however, it's still necessary that we expand the bus service.")

What If Your Thesis Turns Out to Be False?

When your original thesis turns out to be not just an oversimplification, but actually false, there's little to do but return to the drafting board. This may be painful, but it's much better to find out before you mail the letter or submit the report than after that you don't "think what you thought you thought." It's always a good idea to double-check your thesis to see if it is really sound. Ask yourself if the most important details, examples, and arguments in your draft prove your thesis or run counter to it. Even if all the evidence in the draft *is* in harmony with the thesis, you may still be fooling yourself. Try making a list of all the exceptions to your thesis. Make another list of all the reasons your reader could disagree with the thesis. Study these lists with an open mind before accepting your thesis as sound.

What If the Thesis Is Best Left Unstated?

There are, indeed, times when you shouldn't beat your reader about the head and shoulders with the thesis. For instance, when Allison wrote his second draft about firemen, he spelled out half his thesis, namely that firemen had changed since his childhood. However, he didn't spell out the other half of his thesis: that he doesn't like the changes. Instead, he clearly lets the reader know how he feels about the changes through his choice of examples and language. (This technique is discussed more fully in "Build Curiosity or Suspense" in Chapter 13.)

When might it be best to just imply part, or even all, of your thesis? If you are writing a description, you might want to imply your ideas and attitudes rather than state them outright. The same is true when you are writing a letter of complaint or an argumentative paper requiring great tact. Too, when you use humor, a light touch with the thesis is often best. However, these are very special writing situations. Implying a thesis— or even holding it until the end of the paper—can be tricky. Because readers look for a statement of the thesis to guide their reading, writers must take great care to ensure that readers won't misunderstand or be confused if the thesis is just implied. Thus it's best for the writer at least to have in mind a clear statement of the thesis, as Allison did in Draft B.

ACTIVITIES: THESIS AND DRAFT

I. The following ideas are probably too broad and/or oversimplified to be useful as theses. In addition, few readers would find them of compelling interest.

   Brainstorm, freewrite, or discuss each idea, then sharpen it into a thesis statement that could be fully explained or explored in $2\frac{1}{2}$ to 3 pages of writing. Be sure to specify an appropriate audience.

A. People should listen to each other more carefully.

   *Improved thesis:*_____

   _____

   *Appropriate audience:*_____

   _____

B. Getting a college degree will mean getting a better job.

   *Improved thesis:*_____

   _____

   *Appropriate audience:*_____

   _____

C. To be happy, one must be free.

   *Improved thesis:*_____

   _____

   *Appropriate audience:*_____

   _____

D. Television is ruining our children.

   *Improved thesis:*_____

   _____

*Appropriate audience:*_____

_____

E. We have to stop pollution.

*Improved thesis:*_____

_____

*Appropriate audience:*_____

_____

F. Women are equal to men.

*Improved thesis:*_____

_____

*Appropriate audience:*_____

_____

G. Our public schools need some improvements.

*Improved thesis:*_____

_____

*Appropriate audience:*_____

_____

H. Our college needs some improvements.

*Improved thesis:*_____

_____

*Appropriate audience:*_____

_____

II. A. Ask a classmate or friend to look over the theses you've revised above, telling you which of your revisions seems best, and why. Do you agree?

B. If any of your revised theses contain an *although* or *however*, have a classmate or friend read them and underline what seems to be the *main* idea. Was your emphasis where you wanted it?

III. Now it's time to try writing a rough draft of your own. You may want to continue with one of the ideas you were working on in Chapter 4, or you may want to write on an entirely new idea. Either way, follow the Tips for Writing Rough Drafts given in this chapter. Remember: Drafting is a discovery process, not a finished product. (Keep your draft. In Chapter 7 you'll find tips for revising it.)

chapter 6

How Taking a Break Can Help

BREAK AWAY

Perhaps the most closely guarded secret about writing involves the easiest part: breaking away from it. Why is a break so important? Mainly, because it gives us a fresh perspective. An experienced writer recently said, "My cardinal rule in revising is never to fall in love with what I have written in a first or second draft. An idea, sentence, or even a phrase that looks catchy, I don't trust. Part of this idea is to wait a while. I am much more in love with something right after I have written it than I am a day or two later. It is much easier to change anything with time."[1]

Besides loving them, we're so close to our own thoughts while drafting, that we subconsciously fill in missing words and ideas. After a break, we can reread the draft with fresh eyes and see what's really there—or isn't there. Then, too, drafting takes creative energy. It's exhausting. When we're mentally tired, we can't trust our judgment. (Have you noticed that a piece of writing sometimes becomes worse the longer you work at it?)

Taking a break is especially important when we draft letters and such to "get something off our chests." We feel good getting it all down on paper. Then that particular purpose is satisfied. The irate letter or impassioned report is really for ourselves—and shouldn't be mailed or given to anyone else. A cooling-off period helps us see this.

How long a break to take—and when to take it—depends on the writing itself. Sometimes things just seem to fall into place. In that case, a brief break will do, and it can come near the end of the writing process. At other times the draft seems a mire in which we—and our ideas—are stuck. At such times a longer break or two is called for. Even though writers can't be sure exactly when they'll need the break, or for how long,

---

[1]Anonymous writer quoted by Nancy Sommers, "Revision Strategies," *College Composition and Communication*, 31 (December 1980), 384.

they must plan for it if they are to take it at all. The safest assumption is that at least a 24-hour break will be helpful right after the preliminary draft.

SCHEDULE YOUR WRITING

A simple technique familiar to business executives and anyone who has had to plan a wedding or banquet can help you schedule your writing to include the necessary break as well as the other steps in the writing process. The technique is called *backward planning* because it involves working backwards from a given deadline. If, for example, you need to have a short report written by the 10th of the month, and you already have the necessary information, you might plan to have it finished the day before, on the 9th. You would then plan backwards, allotting the day of the 8th for typing, the 7th and 6th for final revisions and sharing your drafts with others, the 5th for the all-important break, and the 4th for doodling and writing the preliminary rough draft. You would therefore mark the 4th, as well as the other days, on your calendar.

CALENDAR

Sunday	Monday	Tuesday	Wednesday	Thursday	Friday	Saturday
		1	2	3	4 *Begin draft of report*	5 *Take break from report*
6 *Reread + revise draft*	7 *10:00 A.M. meet John. Have DRAFT for him to read*	8 *Type report*	9 *Is report finished?*	10 *Report due!*	11	12
13	14	15	16	17	18	19

If you marked just the deadline of the 10th on your calendar, the chances are that you would end up writing the report at the last minute, probably the night of the 9th. Needless to say, there would then be no possibility of taking a break. This is a problem familiar to professional writers as well as beginning ones. The trick is to give yourself a lot of little deadlines instead of one big one. Thus you can have the advantage of deadline pressure without the disadvantage of having to leave out important steps like taking a break.

ACTIVITY: THE BREAK

I. A. When was the last time a deadline pressured you into doing a less than ideal job of planning? (It need not have been writing. It might have been putting together a trip, organizing an event for your business or club, or preparing a special meal.) Think about it, then work out a backward plan that would have helped you.

B. Use backward planning to organize your time for a deadline (not necessarily writing) that is coming due. (Allow leeway just in case things don't go according to plan.)

II. A. Locate something you wrote at the last minute. Read it over to see what you would now change. Do you see how taking a break can help?

chapter 7

How to Revise Your Drafts

After taking a break, writers reread their drafts. Sometimes they find the drafts are effectively written and need just a bit of light polishing. More often, however, they find that their drafts need a major overhaul.

CLARIFY YOUR AUDIENCE AND PURPOSE

In early drafts, a writer's purpose may be to discover and clarify his or her own ideas or feelings about a subject. Writers may tell themselves they're writing the draft to beginning tennis players, newspaper readers, or the boss. But often they're really not: they're really writing to and for themselves. When they reread their rough drafts, they can see this and clarify their purpose.

When we reread our own rough drafts, we too have to ask ourselves what we really want to accomplish. Do we want to write to ourselves or others? If we want to work our ideas or emotions out on paper, that's fine. Frequently it's all that's necessary. However, if we want eventually to communicate in writing with someone else, our purpose is different. Then we must be very specific about what we want to accomplish. Do we want to write an article on how to improve the backhand shot in tennis, or do we want beginning players to use our suggestions? Do we want people to read about the school play, or do we want the tickets to sell out? Do we want the boss to think about our request to attend a seminar at company expense, or do we want the boss to approve it?

Purpose and audience usually go hand in hand. Clarifying one helps to clarify the other. If you can't decide who your audience is—or should be—ask yourself, "Who (what type of person) would be interested in this idea?" "Who would benefit from it?" "Who could do something about it?" The answer to one of these questions should help you decide on both audience and purpose. You can then revise your draft as necessary.

Once you have drafted with a specific audience in mind, your next task is to read that draft the way your audience would read it. Try to imagine the questions and reactions they would have. For instance, where might they ask for an example? A definition?

Where might they ask, "Why are you telling me this?" Or "What's your point?" Would they continue reading or stop? Understand you or not? Come to agree with you or not? (Chapter 2 offers some insights into the way readers read.)

In order to read the draft as your intended audience would, you have to put yourself in your reader's shoes. One way of doing this is to ask yourself questions about the reader. You won't always know the answers, but you can at least decide what your assumptions are. For example, you can ask yourself: "Does this reader know me? If so, how well?" If the audience doesn't know you, you can't assume they will understand your sense of humor, background, or values. To help them understand you, you must take less for granted when you write. You might also ask yourself, "Is this reader like me or rather different from me?"

Finally, you can ask yourself three basic questions regarding your reader and your subject. These questions were mentioned in Chapter 1 but are important enough to mention again. These questions also form a major part of the Writing Process Worksheet provided in Chapter 11. Each time you have something to write, make a copy of that worksheet and use it to guide yourself through the writing process.

1. Is Your Audience Already Knowledgeable About Your Idea or Subject?

No?

If your audience is not already knowledgeable in the subject, your purpose will include informing them. You must therefore take great care to explain yourself in terms that the uninformed reader will understand. Think of the insurance representative trying to explain a policy to clients, the experienced sales clerk writing a "how to" handbook for the benefit of new employees, and scientists writing popularizations—books that explain scientific or technical concepts in terms nonscientists can understand. This type of writing can be seen whenever we have to give directions or explain something that's new to our reader. William Thackeray, the British novelist, believed that one of the most "engaging powers of an author" is the ability to "make new things familiar." Chapter 12 offers tips to help you make new information seem familiar—or at least clear—to your readers.

Yes?

If they are already familiar with the information, it can make your job easier. However, be careful that you're not telling them what they already know, so you don't insult or bore them. For example, if you are writing a paper for a literature class, you should keep in mind that your literature teacher has read the assigned literature. In your paper you would therefore be careful not to just summarize the plot of an assigned novel, since your teacher would already know the plot. What the teacher doesn't yet know is your *interpretation* of the events. In most other classes, also, you should not merely regurgitate what was said in class or in the textbook. One of the dilemmas of writing for college classes is that you are usually writing to people who know even more about the given subject than you do, yet you must avoid simply telling them what they already know. One solution to this dilemma is to concentrate on *persuading* the reader that your own interpretation, idea, or conclusion is correct. The first section of Chapter 15, "Assume an Intelligent Reader who Disagrees with You," offers tips for writing such papers.

2. Is Your Audience Already Interested in the Subject or Idea?

No?

If they aren't interested to start with, one of your tasks as a writer will be to cultivate their interest. Thackeray believed authors not only need to make "new things familiar" but also need to make "familiar things new." Making "familiar things new"—or seem new—is one way of developing your reader's interest. Other ways are suggested throughout Chapter 13.

Yes?

If they are already interested, fine. It means you won't have to work at developing their interest. In fact, doing so might strike the reader as corny.

3. Does Your Reader Already Agree With You?

No?

If your reader does not already agree with you, your challenge is clear: persuade the reader. If you're trying to change people's values or behavior—whether you want them to stop smoking, pay a delinquent bill, try a new way of doing things, or switch to your political beliefs—you'll find tact and diplomacy are called for. Chapter 14 offers suggestions to help you. If it's a strong dose of logic and reason that the situation and audience demand, see Chapter 15 for help. As noted earlier, when writing papers for college classes, it's often best to make believe your instructor disagrees with your ideas but can be persuaded through reason and evidence. That forces you to include persuasive evidence.

Yes?

If your reader agrees with you at the start, your writing task might seem simple, and in many cases is. However, be careful you are not "preaching to the choir." If your readers already agree with you, do they really need to read what you have to say? This problem frequently occurs when we write about social issues. For example, if conservationists write to those who are *already* concerned about depleted parklands, energy reserves, or wildlife, they may be wasting their words, unless they have new information to offer.

Not Applicable?

Not all writing expresses an opinion or debatable idea. The question "Does your reader already agree with you?" is therefore not always relevant. For instance, in some informative writing the author is merely explaining a process or reporting facts, not arguing a particular point of view. Therefore this third question should be answered "yes," "no," or "not applicable."

The above questions concerning audience and purpose play a vital role in the worksheets provided in Chapter 11. Each time you have something to write, you can use a worksheet to guide yourself through the writing process. And remember, Chapters 12 to 15 offer tips on how to revise so that your reader will find your writing clearer, more interesting, or more persuasive.

The Relationship Between Audience and Purpose

Your intended audience and your purpose are intimately connected. The answers to the three questions about your audience can help you see that relationship. In general, whenever you answer a question with *no,* your writing challenge and purpose become clear. If the intended readers are not yet knowledgeable about your subject, your purpose is to write clearly and informatively. If they are not yet interested in your subject, your purpose and challenge include giving them a reason to read. If they are not yet persuaded of your point of view, your purpose is to persuade them tactfully and logically. If you answer "no" to more than one question, you have more than one reason to write.

What if the answers to all three questions are *yes?* That means your intended audience is already familiar with the information, is already interested, and already agrees with you. In such a situation, there is usually no reason to write.

Consistency of Audience

Occasionally the main difficulty with a rough draft is that the intended reader changes with each paragraph. For instance, one paragraph may assume the reader has extensive background information, while the next paragraph may assume the reader knows nothing about the subject.

Sometimes drafts seem to change readers entirely. For instance, in a draft of a paper on elementary school discipline, one paragraph might seem to be written to parents, another to the children themselves, and a third to the school board.

If you suspect that a rough draft shifts from one audience to another, check each of the paragraphs separately. Ask the three audience questions of each paragraph, jotting down your answers. This will enable you to see and eliminate any inconsistencies.

Revising for Audience and Purpose

When you have asked yourself the three basic questions about your intended audience and have reread your draft as your intended readers would, you're ready to begin revising. You'll see where your writing needs to be clearer, more interesting, more tactful, or more logically persuasive. Part III offers techniques that will help you with these revisions:

You may want to just browse through those chapters, selecting whatever techniques will help you the most with your specific writing situation. On the other hand, if you know exactly what technique you are looking for, the alphabetical index at the back of the book will help you locate it quickly.

In Chapter 4 you read the rough draft of "How to Have It Your Way" by Frances Katano. Reread the rough draft now, asking yourself how you might revise it to make it more effective if your purpose were to persuade readers who, like you, eat out, but who, unlike you, don't do anything about it when they have a bad experience. After rereading the draft, read Frances' final version. The side notes indicate some of the important changes Frances made.

HOW TO HAVE IT YOUR WAY

You have probably been out to dinner at one time or another. Dining out is fun, but sometimes little problems with the service, if not handled correctly, can ruin an evening.

Appeals to reader - see Chapter 13

These problems often seem to involve the waiters or waitresses. Even if the problem is with ill-prepared food, your waiter or waitress is your main line of communication to the kitchen. Therefore these people hold an important position. They will be a key factor in your having a pleasant or unpleasant evening out.

Anticipates reader's question See Chapters 8 and 14

Let's say you're dining out in a restaurant that has waiters. I believe the waiter should be at your table to help you feel welcome. A smile or a hello can make your day brighter. If he is too busy, at the moment, to take your order, he should at least be there to acknowledge your presence. Even then, he should take your order in a reasonable amount of time. It's up to you to judge how long is reasonable. I waited half an hour once. I was so angry when the waiter arrived, I couldn't enjoy my meal.

Gives example See Chapter 12

Has your steak come to your table rare when you asked for it well done? Or have you received only the lobster of a steak and lobster dinner? If you have, you have probably been through what I feel is an all too frequent occurrence. It's not funny when you receive something completely different from your order. I used to think it was rude to return the dinner, but I've recently grown tired of eating restaurants' mistakes. I now politely refuse to eat what they give me and request my original order. Sometimes, all it takes is a customer (you) to complain to the waiter or waitress that there's been a mistake. "I ordered a rare steak and I received it well done. Please exchange this." You might inquire, "Has the restaurant run out of steak for the steak and lobster dinner?" Since such comments need not be offensive, they work well. The main thing to remember is that you, as a customer, should enjoy the meal you are paying for.

Asks questions. See Chapters 7, 13 and 14

Gives example. See Chapter 12

Appeals to reader — see chapter 13

You may on occasion be seated in a cute little booth in a dark corner next to the busboys' cart, where you can dine to the music of clattering dishes. If this annoys you, then by all means ask to be seated elsewhere. I had dinner in a classy English restaurant, seated in a cramped booth next to the kitchen. The prices on my menu weren't any different than the prices on the menu of the people sitting in the large spacious booth next to the piano bar; but I paid a high price by having a miserable evening when I didn't ask the head waiter for another table. The restaurant has a wonderful English comic who sits at the piano bar. Unfortunately, I was unable to see or hear him.

Tipping can be another problem. The general rule on tipping is to tip approximately 15 percent of your bill. However, in my experience, the quality of the service and the price of the meal haven't always been directly related. A 15 percent tip may be a good guideline, but it's just that, a guideline. You may go to a very expensive restaurant and receive the worst service you ever had--or have very good service at a coffee shop. In my opinion, you should base your tip on the quality of service received.

Transition. See Chapter 7

All in all restaurants can be a source of many pleasurable experiences, but only if you make it that way. So, have it your way and enjoy.

Ends with a "call to action." See Chapter 14

ACTIVITIES: REVISING FOR AUDIENCE AND PURPOSE

I. Below are two versions of a form letter to new store employees. One was written by a student named Janet Fuller and has been adopted for use in the store where she works. The other was written just for fun, as a comparison with Janet's letter.

Janet's letter has two purposes: (1) To inform employees what their duties will be, and (2) to motivate the employees to perform those duties conscientiously.

A. Paragraph by paragraph, which of the two versions do you feel would be more effective in informing and motivating the employees? Why? What assumptions does each version of the letter seem to make about the employees? Are the assumptions wise ones to make?

B. If you don't think either version of the letter would be effective for the purpose, write a revised version of your own.

Version A

Dear Heather,

The following will be your duties as a new worker in Bigman's Snack Bar. I expect you to perform these duties in addition to carrying out the rules and regulations of Bigman's as set forth in other documents.

You will keep the Snack Bar clean. If you don't, the department heads will see the dirt when they come in for coffee.

Don't forget to restock all the goods too. You must refill the supplies when they are low.

You must also take the customers' food orders and ring them up on the cash register. If there's a shortage, you'll be held responsible. Count the cash at the end of your shift.

I'm your trainer. I'll let you know what else to do as part of your duties. If you have any questions, please ask them.

Sincerely yours,

Janet

Version B

Dear Heather,

Welcome to Bigman's. By now you will have been given many general rules and regulations of the company. Please don't let them scare you off. After a while, you'll find them easy to apply. As your trainer, I've been asked to give you an overview of the work to be learned for your specific department: The Snack Bar.

Because customers like to eat in clean surroundings, Bigman's stresses cleanliness. Inspections of the Snack Bar come when we least expect them. So the first job to be done when you come in will be to wipe all the tables not occupied with customers. Also you must wipe all counter tops and used trays. Wiping tables and trays will also be your last job of the evening before you leave. The first customers in the morning are the head bosses of the whole store. They expect the Snack Bar to be clean.

Restocking all goods is also important to the department. The night shift that you will be working must refill all the dry goods, such as forks and spoons and napkins for the next day. (The extra supplies are located in their own section of the storage room.) The reason we restock at night is that the day shift workers have to set up the actual food service for the customers. They can't also find time to refill forks and napkins. The most important reason is the customer. I'm sure you wouldn't like to wait longer to eat because you didn't have a fork.

The most important point in any business is the money accumulated during the work shift and work day. In addition to learning how to take the customers' food orders, you will also learn to run the cash register and count the cash profit of your shift. You and the cook are responsible for the shortages and overages in the change fund and profit money count. Like most companies, Bigman's is in business to make a profit. The bosses don't take kindly to shortages. Shortages are rare in our department, though, so don't worry every time you use the register.

This has been a broad overview of the procedures in our department. I'm sure you will find the work not difficult and your new co-workers a pleasure to work with. I look forward to working with you soon.

Sincerely yours,

Janet

II. In Chapter 5, you read two drafts of a paper by Allison Clough. Reread Allison's second draft. Then reread Allison's first draft and imagine it leading to a totally different type of writing than appears in the later draft. What other audiences might Allison have chosen to write to? For what other purposes? In specific terms, how would a second draft written for one of these other audiences and purposes be different from the later draft Allison actually wrote? (You might try writing a different "later draft" of Allison's paper, making it appropriate for an audience and purpose of your own choice.)

III. Reread a draft of something you have written yourself. Who is (or should be) your audience? What is (or should be) your purpose? How should your draft be changed so that it will do what you want it to do in terms of your audience and purpose?

ORGANIZE WITH SCISSORS AND TAPE

With a clear idea of your audience and purpose, you can read your draft as your intended reader would. As you do, you may want to work on the organization of your writing.

As you read in Chapter 3, a reader expects writing to have a beginning, middle, and end. The beginning should be an introduction that catches the reader's interest and lets him or her know what the paper will be about. The middle should answer the reader's questions, stick to the subject, and provide adequate explanation and details. The end should be a clear conclusion that leaves the reader satisfied.

In addition to providing a beginning, middle, and end, writers must also be careful to exclude information that is irrelevant to their thesis or purpose. If a writer goes off on tangents, the reader will become confused and wonder what the point really is. Likewise, repetitious writing can leave the reader wondering, "Haven't I already read this?"

If you used only one side of the paper to write your draft, you'll find that scissors and tape may now be your best friends. Paragraphs that seem irrelevant, ill-advised, or repetitious can be cut out. Paragraphs that seem out of order can be cut, rearranged, and taped in place. If introductory paragraphs now seem windy or irrelevant, as is often the case, you can simply snip them off, write a more appropriate introduction, and tape it in place. This last bit of advice may seem out of order, but writers often write their first paragraphs last. The reason, of course, is simply that they can't know for sure what they're introducing, or how to introduce it, until after they see what they've said.

The time saved by using scissors and tape is just one advantage of the technique. Another advantage is that you can visually try out various arrangements to see what works best. Two final tips: Don't try to tape little strips of paper to each other. Instead tape everything to a fresh sheet. Also, using the paragraph sign, ¶, is sometimes the quickest way to indicate where a new paragraph begins.

PARAGRAPH WITH YOUR READER IN MIND

People don't talk in paragraphs, and rough drafts aren't always written in them. Sometimes a draft looks as though it is one long paragraph; other times it looks as though every sentence begins a new paragraph. This is natural. Yet readers need paragraph divisions to help them read. Dividing material into appropriate paragraphs is thus an important part of revision.

Paragraph Length

How long should paragraphs be? This is a tricky question. As was explained in Chapter 3, paragraphing is a visual aid for readers. They are attracted to relatively short first and last paragraphs and appreciate occasional short paragraphs scattered throughout the text. In addition, paragraph length is affected by the eventual print size and formality of the writing. Because newspaper print is small and hard to read, newswriters keep the paragraphs short. Business letters, too, have short paragraphs to enable people to read them faster.

Repeatedly short paragraphs are not appropriate for most formal writing, however. Longer paragraphs seem more "solid" to the reader and promise a fuller development of ideas. In general, double-spaced typewritten reports look about right to readers when most of the paragraphs are about 3 to 4 inches long. (Of course, the first and last paragraphs still look more enticing when they're shorter, and the reader will still want a short paragraph for an occasional break.)

But 3 to 4 inches of double-spaced typing is not 3 to 4 inches of handwriting. This can create problems for people who write longhand drafts. What to do? Either type a draft, to get a better feel for the paragraphing, or learn to adjust for the difference between handwritten and typed length. Following are handwritten and typed samples of this paragraph. Notice the difference in the visual impact of the paragraph.

But 3 to 4 inches of doublespaced typing is not 3 to 4 inches of handwriting. This can create problems for people who write longhand drafts. What to do? Either type a draft, to get a better feel for the paragraphing, or learn to adjust for the difference between handwritten and typed length. Below are handwritten and typed samples of this paragraph. Notice the differences in the visual impact of the paragraph.

But 3 to 4 inches of double-spaced typing is not 3 to 4 inches of handwriting. This can create problems for people who write longhand drafts. What to do? Either type a draft, to get a better feel for the paragraphing, or learn to adjust for the difference between handwritten and typed length. Below are handwritten and typed samples of this paragraph. Notice the differences in the visual impact of the paragraph.

Paragraph Logic

Of course paragraphing is not totally visual. It's also logical. Readers expect paragraphs to have a *focus* or central idea. For instance, to keep the paragraph length appealing, a writer may divide one long paragraph into two or three shorter ones. This is logically possible because each short paragraph can still have a unified focus or central idea. However, two or three short paragraphs can not always be combined into one longer one. Why not? Because the one longer paragraph might then lack a clear focus. Thus paragraph logic is largely a matter of making each paragraph focus on a central idea or subject.

One way some writers improve their paragraphs is to include a sentence that clearly states the paragraph's focus or central idea. Not *all* logically divided paragraphs contain such a sentence, but the majority do. By spotlighting the paragraph's focus, such a sentence helps both the reader and the writer.

The following letter was written by a student, Marlene Graham, to her sister-in-law. It's very clearly organized despite the many pieces of information it contains. As you read Marlene's letter, mark the focus of each paragraph in the margin. In addition, if there is a sentence within the paragraph that clearly states the focus, underline that sentence.

Dear Sandy:

I hear you're coming for a visit. You probably are anxious to find out what there is to do and see in Hawaii, so let me give you a brief description of the main attractions.

The first thing people usually think of when you mention "Hawaii" is the beach. If you just want to lie in the sun, there is no problem; swimming is a challenge at some beaches. People don't realize just how strong the waves are and sometimes end up needing help. Unless you are an expert swimmer, I'd suggest using caution, especially if you are by yourself.

If you're like me and like to spend money, you can find plenty of places to shop. There are several malls made up of brand name stores along with a number of foreign import shops. The merchandise is as varied as the cultures and background of the people who live here. Beautiful jewelry and trinkets made from seashells can be found at stands located throughout the island. Of course, there are also many Hawaiian souvenir and clothing shops where a tourist can "go wild."

Speaking of tourists, let me name a few of the sights to see while you are here. Pearl Harbor, of course, is one you shouldn't miss. Waimea Falls Park has some beautiful scenic trails to hike on. I hear the Polynesian Cultural Center is very worthwhile. The Kahuku Sugar Mill gives tours daily. Also, Sea Life Park has a lot of exhibits and shows to offer.

After all that sight-seeing you should be ready for something to eat. What would you care for: French, German, Mexican, Italian, Greek, Japanese, Korean, Hawaiian, or maybe just American food? Whatever your craving, I'm sure we can find something to satisfy it. I would highly recommend a sunset dinner cruise on the ocean. A Hawaiian luau can also be a lot of fun.

As for the "night life," there are a number of discos and dinner shows to see. I will try to get some recommendations on them before you come.

Keep in mind that although the tourist attractions and restaurants can be fun, they can be quite expensive. But at least you won't have to rent a car. You can ride the bus almost anywhere you want to go; transportation should be no problem. We can make plans when you arrive. Meanwhile, this will give you some idea of what there is to do. Bob and I look forward to your arrival. See you soon.

aloha,
Marlene

For more experience with the way others divide paragraphs, reread the following: Coleman McCarthy's article on page 19, Janet Fuller's letter on page 93 (Version B), and Frances Katano's article on page 28. As you read them, mark each paragraph's focus in the margin. If there is a sentence that clearly states the paragraph's focus, underline the sentence.

USE TRANSITIONS TO LINK YOUR PARAGRAPHS

As was noted in Chapter 3, readers look for links between paragraphs. For example, they need to know if the paragraph they've just begun reading will continue the focus of the last paragraph, will go on to a new focus, or will summarize the writing so far. The same is true of sentences: readers need to know what the connection is between one sentence and the next, and between two parts of the same sentence. As Chapter 3 indicated, readers can sometimes read between the lines to see the connections between various ideas. However, readers are not mind readers. To help them understand the connection between paragraphs, writers frequently use one or more of the following transitional techniques.

Sometimes these techniques are used at the end of a paragraph, sometimes at the beginning of the next, and sometimes in both places.

Six Transitional Techniques

1. Give your reader "marching orders" by using standard transitional words:

. . . Hang gliding is thus a sport that gives the thrill of soaring high over the landscape. With only the wind for an engine, one has the power, freedom, and tranquility of a bird in flight.

> *In addition*, the cost of the sport is relatively low. . . .

The phrase *in addition* prepares your reader for a continuation of the previous idea. In the above example, the first paragraph obviously discussed the benefits of hang gliding; the second paragraph will discuss still another benefit: the low cost.

Here are some other transitional phrases you may find useful:

TO INTRODUCE:	USE:
An addition or continuation of a previously stated idea	*also, in addition, furthermore*
An example	*for instance, for example, to illustrate*
A change in direction	*but, however*
A result	*therefore, thus*
A summary or conclusion	*in brief, in short, in conclusion, to summarize*

The advantage of such transitional words is their clarity. They're hard to miss. The disadvantage is their lack of subtlety. When overused, they have the delicacy of a drill sergeant barking orders.

2. Repeat key words from one paragraph to another:

. . . Hang gliding is thus a sport that gives the thrill of soaring high over the landscape. With only the wind for an engine, one has *the power,* freedom, and tranquility of a bird in flight.

> *The power,* of course, is partly illusory. Although the hang glider is not dependent on a mechanical engine that can break, he or she is dependent on friendly wind currents. . . .

The advantage of repeating key words is that it's a fairly natural way of giving your readers a bit of extra help. (For instance, in Example 1, the writer could help the reader even more by writing: "Another benefit of the sport is the relatively low cost. . . .") The disadvantage of repeating key words is that *too much* repetition can actually make writing harder to read.

3. Use synonyms or other words that you know your intended reader will automatically associate with words you've already used:

. . . Hang gliding is thus a sport that gives the thrill of soaring high over the landscape. With only the wind for an engine, one has the power, freedom, and *tranquility* of a bird in flight.

The *peacefulness* is partly due to the quiet. . . .

The above example assumes the reader recognizes *peacefulness* as a synonym for *tranquility*. Now let's look at an example of association:

. . . Hang gliding is thus a sport that gives the thrill of soaring high over the landscape. With only the wind for an engine, one has the power, freedom, and tranquility of a *bird* in flight.

Of course *hawks, seagulls, and eagles* don't worry about mortality rates and safety records. Humans do. . . .

This example assumes that the reader recognizes that hawks, seagulls, and eagles are birds—probably a safe assumption. But what if the second paragraph began "Of course plovers, scissortails, and puffin don't worry about mortality rates and safety records. . . ." Would it be safe to assume that the reader would recognize these as birds? If not, the transition would confuse rather than help the reader. When you use synonyms and associations, be sure they'll be as clear to your readers as they are to you.

4. Use pronouns such as "he" or "they" and adjectives such as *these, this,* or *that* to direct your reader's attention back to a phrase or idea in the previous paragraph:

. . . Hang gliding is thus a sport that gives the thrill of soaring high over the landscape.

This thrill is being experienced by more and more people each year. Hang gliding clubs are now. . . .

This transitional technique is very graceful. Do, however, beware of using the word *this* without a supporting noun such as "this idea," or "this problem." A free-floating *this* can leave the reader wondering "This what?"

5. Use questions to signal a new subject or change in direction:

. . . Hang gliding is thus a sport that gives the thrill of soaring high over the landscape. With only the wind for an engine, one has the power, freedom, and tranquility of a bird in flight.

But what about the training? Is it hard to master hang gliding? That depends on. . . .

6. In long papers, use headings to link entire groups of paragraphs. In this chapter, for instance, the paragraphs on organization were grouped under the heading: "Organize with Scissors and Tape." This heading was designed to let the reader know what to expect in the paragraphs following.

One final note about transitions: They work best unobtrusively. The reader should be guided by them without being consciously aware of the guidance.

CHECK EACH PARAGRAPH'S LINK TO YOUR MAIN IDEA

In addition to establishing clear links between your paragraphs, you should also establish a clear link between each paragraph and your main idea. One way of doing this is to ask yourself of each paragraph: "What's the connection between this paragraph and my main idea or purpose?" If there is no clear connection, the paragraph should probably be omitted. If there is a connection, ask yourself if that connection will be clear to your intended readers. If not, make the connection clearer.

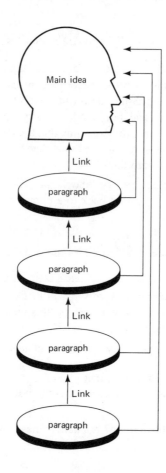

Although the links may range from the very obviously stated to the very subtly suggested, they should always be easy for the intended reader to follow.

Sometimes the writer must make the link between each paragraph and the main idea very explicit indeed. For instance, in *Will We Let Pollution Nibble Us to Death*, Colman McCarthy repeats the key words *adaptation* or *adapting* at the beginning of almost every paragraph. If you reread that article (page 19) and mark those words with a colored pen, you'll see quite clearly how each paragraph is clearly linked to McCarthy's main idea.

ACTIVITIES: PARAGRAPHS, TRANSITIONS, AND ORGANIZATION

I. A. Reread the following examples of student writing, circling the transitional devices used *between paragraphs*. (When the transitional device can't actually be circled, just make a marginal note of what the device is.) Do: Marlene's letter (p. 97), Version B of Janet Fuller's letter (p. 93), and Allison Clough's second draft (p. 78).

   B. Reread the above three pieces of writing. Circle any techniques which create links between *each paragraph and the main idea or purpose*.

II. Make a photocopy of a short magazine article you have *not* yet read, choosing one on a subject you're familiar with. Use scissors to cut apart the paragraphs of the copy. Without looking at the magazine original, see how close you can come to reassembling the paragraphs in their "correct" order. The stronger the transitions, the easier this will usually be. If you find it very easy, note what transitions the author used. If you find it very difficult, read the article as it appears in the magazine. Is it easy to follow? (It might be that the transitions are simply too subtle for this particular exercise. Or the author may have written for an audience that knows more about the subject than you do. You and your classmates can decide which is the case.)

III. Now it's time to tackle your own writing. Locate the draft you wrote at the end of Chapter 5, or write another draft now, and then follow these steps:

   A. Reread your draft, asking yourself what your real purpose, thesis, and audience are or should be. When you're satisfied with your answer, fill in the audience and purpose questions in part B of the Writing Process Worksheet in Chapter 11.

   B. Use scissors to cut your draft apart into separate paragraphs, or what could be paragraphs. Decide which ones to use, and in what order. Does each paragraph have a clear focus? Write whatever additional sentences or paragraphs are necessary, adding transitions and other links where they would help the reader. (Remember to keep your intended audience in mind. A transition that would be perfect for one type of audience might be confusing or too heavy-handed for a different audience.)

chapter 8

How to Share Your Drafts with Others—and Why

Joe Ceremony was very short.

When he entered a room, everyone had to be warned not to stand on Ceremony.

HAHAHAHA!

I'M A GREAT ADMIRER OF MY OWN WRITING

© 1980 United Feature syndicate, Inc.

After snipping and taping and rewriting parts of the draft, it's time to share the draft with others. Professional writers seek the opinion of their spouse, a friend, or another writer. Beginning writers should too. To help your reader feel free to make suggestions, your draft should look like something you're still working on. On the other hand, too many cross-outs, arrows, and tiny writing sandwiched between lines can defeat even those most willing to help. Therefore, before asking someone to read it, be sure your draft is readable. Also, be sure to let your readers know at what stage the draft is. You may still be working on the ideas and organization and want their reaction to those. On the other hand, you may feel satisfied with the ideas and want their reaction to the sentence style.

BE NONDEFENSIVE

When someone does read your draft, it's important that you not react defensively. This is easier said than done, but there are some strategies that will help you. First, remember that it *is* a draft. Second, remember that you asked for help. Third, try to adopt the "tell me more" attitude.

"Tell me more" is a mature reaction to almost any type of criticism. For instance, if your boss mentions that you seem irritable with the customers, you can reply: "I'm not irritable. They cause all the problems." Or, you can reply: "Tell me more. Does it seem to happen at a particular time of day? With a particular type of customer?" The defensive posture ends communication; the "tell me more" approach begins it. Thus when others offer suggestions for your draft, ask them to tell you more. Besides demonstrating your reasonableness, it will put you in charge of the situation.

Ironically, another time the "tell me more" approach helps is with readers who simply say that your rough draft is "fine" or "okay." Such a response may be sincere, but more likely it's the response of someone reluctant to criticize. If you encourage such people to tell you more, to tell you, perhaps, what paragraph isn't quite as good as the others, you can break the ice.

HAVE YOUR READER ROLE-PLAY

When you ask someone to read your draft, describe your intended audience first. (If you're working with a classmate, have him or her read the "audience" section of your Writing Process Worksheet.) Your helper can then read *as the intended audience would*, letting you know where the writing might be made clearer, more interesting, or more persuasive. This will help you both. It's easier for many people to tell a writer what the intended audience might say about the writing than to say what they themselves think about it. Also it's easier for many writers to hear that the intended audience might find the third paragraph repetitious than to hear that the person with whom they're speaking finds it so.

ASK WHAT YOUR MAIN IDEA IS

Another way that people can help you is by telling you what they think your main idea is. Often the reader of a draft will think the thesis or main idea is one thing while the writer intended it to be another. Sometimes this results from poor reading, but more often it means that the writer is sending wrong signals. A tip: When you're asking someone to help you see if the thesis is clear, be certain that you don't tell the person in advance what the thesis is.

READ ALOUD, AND BE READ TO

Reading aloud can help with both the content and the style of your work. To have someone help you with your ideas, try the following "question" technique. Read your draft out loud. After each paragraph, stop and ask your listener what question is in her or his mind. Helpful questions for your listener to ask during this type of reading are:

"What does that have to do with anything else?"
"What's your point?"
"Could you give an example?"
"Why?"
"But what about . . . ?"
"So what?"

This is a valuable way of seeing where additions, deletions, or rearrangements are needed in your writing. You can make notes of the questions, or you can answer the question then and there, making notes of what you say. This technique is especially helpful in the early stages of a draft, and a bonus is that the draft can be as messy as you like, since you'll be the one reading it aloud.

A different technique, asking "How does it sound?", can help polish your style. This time your helper reads your draft aloud while you follow along on a copy. Listen for places where the reader has difficulty making it "sound right." You'll hear your reader pause, or back up, or get the information wrong. On your own copy, put a check mark at each spot where this happens, to indicate that something about the style is confusing the reader. You can later polish those spots, making them easier to read.

ACTIVITIES: SHARING DRAFTS WITH OTHERS

I. Share one of your own rough drafts with a classmate, asking him or her to read as your intended reader would and to fill in the "Helper's Reaction to Draft" portion of the Writing Process Worksheet found in Chapter 11. Concentrate on reacting nondefensively as you and your helper discuss his or her suggestions and reactions.

II. With a different classmate, use the "question" technique.

III. If your rough draft is fairly close to being a final copy, use the "How does it sound?" technique with still a different classmate.

chapter 9

How to Polish Your Sentences

If readers have trouble understanding a writer's sentences, nothing else about the writing matters. If the readers can't, or won't, read the sentences, they can't appreciate the writer's thoughtful organization or clever ideas. Thus some writers spend considerable time polishing their sentences. Hemingway, for example, rewrote one page of *A Farewell to Arms* 39 times. Another novelist, Colette, spent an entire day revising just 20 lines of one draft. Fortunately, it's not necessary, or even a good idea, for most of us to do that much polishing.

How much polishing we should do depends on our total writing situation: our purpose, audience, subject, setting, and time limits. As we polish, we should ask ourselves if our intended readers would find our sentences clear or confusing. Concise or wordy. Smooth or awkward. Grammatically adequate or not. We should then revise with our readers in mind.

READING YOUR WRITING OUT LOUD

In the last chapter you learned how to detect rough spots by listening to someone else read your writing aloud. You can also read it aloud yourself. Does it sound unnatural? Confusing? Is it hard to read? If so, look away from your paper and imagine yourself talking to someone. How would you express the ideas if you were face to face with your reader? Say your ideas out loud, then write down what you said. The chances are your spoken words will be clearer, and less awkward, than the words that you found troublesome in your draft.

RECOGNIZE THE INEVITABLE WORDINESS

When we don't know what we want to say, we take many words to say it. Thus rough drafts are almost inevitably wordy. Remember the "Those years in Paris" Snoopy cartoon in Chapter 5?

The difficulty, of course, is that except when reading love letters or good news, most readers aren't willing to slog their way through wordy, repetitious sentences. It's easier to simply stop reading. This means that if we want to be read, we must take time to reduce the wordiness in our drafts.

Wordiness does not refer just to the number of words or the length of the writing. A very short paragraph can be wordy; a long one can be concise. Rather, writing is wordy when the writer has used more words than necessary to accomplish a particular purpose. A concise dictionary definition of *electricity* can be very brief indeed. But the author of a college physics text could take a chapter or more to explain—without being wordy—what electricity is and how it works. The purpose of a textbook is simply different from the purpose of a dictionary. Similarly, a dictionary description of *honeysuckle* could be just ten words long and be complete, while a writer wishing to share the honeysuckle's nostalgically sweet fragrance and the busy humming of bees around the vine might take fifteen sentences and still not be wordy.

If you can't judge wordiness by the number of words, how then can you judge it? Listen to your writing read out loud. Does it sound flabby? Padded? Meandering? If so, it's probably wordy. For example, read the following wordy (and also ungrammatical) passage out loud:

This course was taken under the instruction of Dr. Fisk, by whose encouragement and zeal have stimulated within me a well-based appreciation of man's religious endeavor on earth and throughout time, be it in the past, present, or future.

Simply take a break from your writing. On rereading, does the writing seem repetitious or too long for what it says? If so, it's probably wordy. Try typing the draft. If it looks too informal or rough, wordiness may be the problem. Judith Krantz, author of several best sellers, suggests that writers type drafts. Longhand, she says, "is impossible to judge because you have to see the words 'in print' before you know if they're any good or not."

Look at your prepositions. Too many prepositions (those little words like *by, with, for, of, up,* and *down*) can be a sign of wordiness. Reread the "encouragement and zeal" passage above, underlining all the prepositions.

Writing concisely is just one way writers polish their writing. Often writers also need to use more specific words or change the word order to make their sentences clearer. (You'll find tips for writing clearer sentences in Chapter 12.) Sometimes, too, writers need to use parallelism or other techniques to make their sentences more vivid or emphatic. (You'll find tips for writing vivid and emphatic sentences in Chapter 13.) Still, writing concisely is often the main challenge in revision. Wordiness left unchecked can sabotage both clarity and interest.

REDUCE THE WORDINESS

Once you recognize wordiness in your draft, the next job is to prune it. Often this is simply a matter of making the effort. Still, the following tips may help you:

TIPS FOR REDUCING WORDINESS

1. *Avoid stating the obvious.* If everybody knows it, does it need to be stated?

2. *Eliminate mindless repetitions.* "The modern world of today," "red in color," "big in size," are repetitious. Also, check your writing to be sure you're not repeating an idea or example in different paragraphs. (It's easy to fool yourself by using different words the second—or third—time around.)

3. *Find just the right word, using a thesaurus or dictionary to jog your memory.* For instance, you could write "coffee pot" instead of "utensil used to make coffee." Or "Crime suspect" instead of "person who is thought to have possibly committed a crime." Of course you must be sure your intended readers will understand the words you use. Thus it might sometimes be better to write "instrument that measures wind speed" rather than the shorter "anemometer."

4. *As a general rule, rephrase sentences that begin with such deadwood as "It seems to be the case that . . ."* or *"There are . . ."* "It seems to be the case that my writing is wordy" can become, "My writing is wordy," "My writing seems wordy," or even "My writing, it seems, is wordy."

5. *Rewrite sentences that have too many prepositions such as* **in, by, of, to,** *or* **for.** For example, "It was decided *by* the committee *to* recommend *for* approving the new contract" could become, "The committee recommends that the new contract be approved." Or, if appropriate, "The committee approved the new contract."

6. *Rephrase sentences to eliminate words that contribute nothing.* Imagine that you are going to pay 10 cents for every word you use, but you're not on such a tight budget that you have to write in curt or "telegram" style. "A dancer has to make dancing look easy because someone who shows he is straining doesn't look graceful" could become, "To look graceful, a dancer must look at ease." The second version is itself more graceful, and the writer saved 90 cents. "This will not only ensure the safety of the employees, but will also help reduce the chances of robberies" could become, "This will ensure the safety of employees while reducing the chance of robberies." That's a saving of 60 cents.

ACTIVITY: WORDINESS

I. The following sentences are wordy. Read them out loud, then rewrite them, using the Tips for Reducing Wordiness. Since wordy writing is often vague and confusing, feel free to "interpret" the sentences and invent details as necessary. Do not, however, change what you understand to be the sentence's basic meaning.

   As you work these excercises, your goal should be to make the sentences graceful and easy to read, not telegraphically abrupt. Realize also that in real writing, sentences must be written so that they are appropriate for the intended reader and blend well with the surrounding sentences.

1. There were approximately two hundred students in attendance at the seminar.
2. Meaning was found by the philosopher in things as small as the grains of sand in the ocean and the leaves of the trees in the forest.
3. When you clear your mind of what you were thinking, you will often find that it is easier to listen to what the speaker has to say.
4. It has been decided by this office that beginning with the next month after this one, the occupants of this building will be required to participate in the practice sessions for procedures should there be a fire.
5. It is said that going too fast in doing something can turn out to be a waste of one's time, if it causes mistakes.
6. There are exceptions to all of the rules that we learn.
7. Regarding the future, it is not to be supposed by people that the supply of oil in the ground will last forever.
8. The elimination of wordiness in a paper one is writing can have the effect of making the writing look easy, when the fact of the matter is that it's hard work.
9. In an article in *Consumer Reports* it is pointed out that, "Many dealers prefer to sell an item that's in stock rather than take a special order."
10. The players on the field were very warm and hot from the sun that was beating down on them while they played the last two innings.

II. There is no "right" way to revise the above sentences, but some revisions will be more effective than others. Exchange your revisions with a friend or classmate and discuss them. Which ones are shorter? Are smoother? Give more information? To what extent do you need to know more about the intended audience to decide which versions are better?

III. Locate something you drafted earlier. Check it for wordiness by reading it out loud. How does it sound? If it's not typed, try typing a paragraph or two to see if it looks wordy. After taking a break from it, whether it's typed or in longhand, check it for prepositions. Do you have too many?

IV. Select the wordiest paragraph in something you've written. Rewrite the paragraph, eliminating as much wordiness as you can without sounding curt or abrupt.

CORRECT THE GRAMMAR

Eliminating wordiness is the first step in correcting grammar. Why? Because once the wordiness is gone, you can see your sentences more clearly. Let's look again at an earlier example:

This course was taken under the instruction of Dr. Fisk, by whose encouragement and zeal have stimulated within me a well-based appreciation of man's religious endeavor on earth and throughout time, be it in the past, present, or future.

This passage is not a grammatical sentence. What went wrong? Probably the student who wrote it was so awash in words that he forgot what he'd written in one part by the time he got to the next part.

Memory research indicates that when writers write, their last six to nine words can be stored clearly in their memory; further back than that the writers are more likely to remember the idea than the exact words. This helps explain why even writers who know all the grammar rules still make grammatical mistakes, especially in rough drafts. For example, a writer who forgets that a sentence started with the word *because,* may write an unintentional sentence fragment, such as "Because the committee has not yet met to discuss the proposal." A writer who forgets that she began a sentence with "The causes" may later use *is* instead of the correct *are* as the verb. The student who wrote about Dr. Fisk's encouragement and zeal may have forgotten that he had written "*by* whose."

The moral of this is *not* that you should write short sentences. (Short sentences may be grammatically easier, but when overdone they can also strike the reader as immature or monotonous.) The moral is that you should first eliminate the wordiness from your writing and then reread what you have written, consciously checking to see that the parts of each sentence fit together. If you're concerned that you won't recognize what is grammatically correct and what isn't, or if you want extra help with grammar, check the Grammar Guide in Appendix A. For now, however, here are three quick techniques to help you check your grammar.

QUICK GRAMMAR TIPS

1. To check if something is a complete sentence, use the "I think that . . ." test. Most of the time, complete sentences will make sense when read after that phrase. Most sentence fragments won't, especially if the words "I think that . . ." are said quickly and without emphasis.

FRAGMENTS: Because of the rain.
                         Reading about a place where you've never been.
SENTENCES: The game was called because of the rain.
                         Reading about a place where you've never been is one way to travel.

The sentences above would make sense following the words "I think that." The sentence fragments would not, although "I think that because of the rain" could make sense if you emphasized the word *think* or *that.* Still, read quickly and without emphasis, the test works. Try it.

2. To check if you've run two sentences together as though they were one, read your sentences out loud, noticing where you pause or stop. You can often hear when one long passage needs to be divided by something stronger than a comma.

RUN-TOGETHER SENTENCE: TV news presents vivid pictures, newspaper news presents detailed information.

APPROPRIATELY DIVIDED SENTENCES:

TV news presents vivid pictures. Newspaper news presents detailed information.
TV news presents vivid pictures; newspaper news presents detailed information.
TV news presents vivid pictures, but newspaper news presents detailed information.

3. To check if your subjects and verbs agree, mentally erase interrupters such as prepositional phrases. ("Up the street," "to the office," and "of the workers" are examples of prepositional phrases.) This will often enable you to see the grammatical subject and verb more clearly.

INCORRECT SUBJECT–VERB AGREEMENT:

The shirts in our new line is selling well.
One of the electricians are here.

PREPOSITIONAL PHRASES MENTALLY ERASED:

The shirts . . . is selling well.
One . . . are here.

CORRECTED SUBJECT–VERB AGREEMENT:

The *shirts* in our new line *are* selling well.
One of the electricians *is* here.

When the interrupting phrases are mentally erased, it's easier to see that the subject of the first sentence is *shirts,* not *line,* and the subject of the second is *one,* not *electricians.* Of course, "line are" and "electricians is" sound wrong when taken out of context and read by themselves. Remember: To see if the parts of your sentence fit together, you have to look at the entire sentence, not just the words that come close together. (This same quick test of mentally erasing interrupters can also help you check whether your pronouns should be singular or plural.)

Use Your Judgment

One final word about checking your grammar. At some point you may have learned a set of rules, such as "Never use the words *but* or *and* to begin a sentence"; "Never use contractions"; "Never use sentence fragments"; "Never use *I* or *you* in writing." These are really guidelines to formal writing, not rules for all writing. And even in formal writing, there are some exceptions.

For example, there's nothing wrong with beginning a sentence with *but* or *and.* But one has to be careful not to overdo it. Contractions also call for judgment: Too many and your writing'll seem offhandedly casual; too few can render it ceremonially stiff. Sentence fragments can, on occasion, be effective—provided they're clearly appropriate, intentional, and not overdone.

Using *I* and *you* isn't simple. When *I* is used too often, the writer seems concerned only with him or herself. On the other hand, writers who never use *I* run the risk of appearing phony or pompous. Likewise, the word *you* must be used with care. For example, in writing for a teacher, it would be inappropriate to write, "When you assassinate someone, you. . . ." (The teacher, we assume, has not assassinated anyone—and has no plans to.)

Perhaps guidelines such as those above should be rewritten: "Don't overuse *but* or *and* to begin sentences"; "Use neither too few nor too many contractions"; "Use sentence fragments with the greatest of care"; "When you write *I* and *you*, be sure their use is appropriate." In short, use your judgment when you write, letting your audience and purpose be your guide.

ACTIVITY: GRAMMAR

I. The following passages, taken from rough drafts, contain grammar mistakes. Rewrite them, reducing the wordiness and using the Quick Grammar Tips. Assume that sentence fragments are not appropriate for the writer's purpose or audience.

1. When purchasing a new car, be ready to bargain with the salesperson. As most salespeople and dealers plan to make a profit from the sale.
2. This course was taken under the instruction of Dr. X, by whose encouragement and zeal have stimulated within me a well-based appreciation of man's religious endeavor on earth and throughout time, be it in the past, present, or future.
3. One by one the band learns each drill. Working for precision, style, and snap. Just like the football team that works a certain play until it becomes second nature.
4. Often the cars displayed in a dealer's window is equipped with options you don't need.
5. Because of our geographical location, there is no earthquakes to worry about.
6. I remember hearing a special on TV last fall on promising careers in the United States, preventive medicine was one of the most needed.
7. Throughout his first year at law school, Turow finds time-consuming and hard work.
8. The new committee member found he had to master piles of statistics. Which he found tough, complicated and at times discomforting.
9. The number of parked cars limit the visibility tremendously.
10. Further examples of this can be found in the graphs the author takes from *Time* and *Fortune* magazines. Although they are relevant to the information being presented. But it would have been more logical to introduce them earlier.

II. Exchange your rewritten sentences with a friend or classmate. Are your rewritten sentences grammatically correct?

III. Use the Quick Grammar Tips to correct the grammar in one of your own rough drafts. But remember: Reducing wordiness is the first step to correcting grammar.

chapter 10

When—and How—to Wrap It Up

KNOW WHEN YOU HAVE REVISED ENOUGH

Most writing has a deadline. A letter or report that's six months overdue is often too late: the semester may have ended, the legislature may have adjourned, or the business may have folded. Professional writers too must meet deadlines: an article on Christmas can hardly appear in the August issue of a magazine, and one on income tax preparation won't be welcomed by readers in May.

So we must be practical about knowing when we've rewritten and polished enough. The writing itself sometimes tells us: it stubbornly becomes worse instead of better with every change we make. Other times the deadline itself arrives. One writer has described her reaction to approaching deadlines very graphically: "I feel like Con Edison cutting off certain states to keep the generators going during a power shortage. In first and second drafts I try to cut off as much as I can of my editing generator, and in my third draft I try to cut off some of my idea generators, so I can make sure that I will actually finish the essay."[1] Flaubert, author of *Madame Bovary,* wrote, "Writing is never finished; it's merely abandoned." Both writers are saying that since a writer's words and ideas could always be different, rewriting could be a never-ending process. It's part of the writer's job to know when to stop. In other words, "Don't strip the wax."

CHECK THE SPELLING AND APPEARANCE

Are you a poor speller? Many fine thinkers and writers are. The difficulty is that most people in the business and college communities equate poor spelling with poor thinking. They shouldn't, but they do. This means that whenever you write in an academic or business situation, you should be very careful to check your spelling. In rough drafts

---

[1] Anonymous writer quoted by Nancy Sommers, "Revision Strategies," College Composition and Communication, 31 (December 1980), 386–87.

your spelling doesn't matter. In final copies your spelling usually matters a great deal. It affects the total impression that you make on your reader.

A few tricks may help you look up spellings faster. First, make sure you have an up-to-date paperback dictionary that includes all the forms of a word. For example, when you look up *hire,* you should also find *hired* and *hiring.* Second, if you're a very poor speller, buy a small "spelling dictionary" to carry with you at all times. Although not as complete as a regular dictionary, it can be faster and less conspicuous to use. Third, keep a *Roget's Thesaurus* (a book that lists synonyms) handy. When your spelling of a word is way off, it can be almost impossible to locate the word in a dictionary. However, you can look up an easy-to-spell synonym in the *Thesaurus* and often find the word you want listed there. (Buy a *Thesaurus* that's arranged alphabetically; it's much easier to use than ones arranged by code numbers.)

In addition to the spelling, the graphic layout or appearance of your writing makes an impression on the reader. Appendix D is a brief format guide showing what most readers expect letters, reports, and other writing to look like. Follow it. In addition, ask yourself if subheadings would help make your message clear. Subheadings (such as "Check the Spelling and Appearance" and "Type and Proofread the Painless Way") break long reports into more manageable chunks and help the reader keep track of the organization. In general, the longer your writing, the more your reader will appreciate subheadings. Consider, too, the possibility of using charts or tables to present your ideas more graphically.

TYPE AND PROOFREAD THE PAINLESS WAY

We're now nearing the end of the writing process. All that's left is to type, proofread, and finally use what you've written.

If you don't know how to type, and if you can't always count on having someone to do your typing for you, learn how to type now. Handwritten work is not acceptable in most college reports or business situations. Save handwriting for friendly letters, invitations, and thank you notes, where it's appropriate. In other situations, give your reader the courtesy of typed material.

Here are a few tips to make the typing go as quickly as possible: (1) Check your typing ribbon. It should be neither too new nor too old. If it's brand new, it will smudge; if it's too old, it won't be sufficiently legible. (2) Use the right paper. Erasable typing paper is easy to erase but also tends to smudge easily. It's thus often better in the long run to use regular (not onionskin) typing paper and a bottle of liquid correction fluid. (3) Use a photocopy machine to make your final copy. Sometimes this isn't appropriate: some teachers won't accept copies, and business letters should obviously be originals. But often a photocopy is acceptable. When it is, you can save time by retyping just the portion of the page that needs it, taping it in place with transparent tape, and copying the whole thing on a photocopy machine. The tape won't show.

Once your paper is typed, you must proofread it for typing mistakes and spelling or punctuation errors. This final proofreading shouldn't be omitted: if you've spent untold hours writing something, why spoil it at the last minute with careless mistakes? There are two painless ways to proofread: (1) Read your paragraphs in reverse order, starting with the last and working forward. That way you won't be reading the content, just the sentences and words. (2) Trade proofreading chores with a friend. (One reason proofreading is so painful is that we're always afraid we won't like what we've written and will want to start all over.) Keep in mind, however, that if your friend misses mistakes, you can't blame him or her. It's your paper. You—not your typist and not your friend—are responsible for what it looks like and says.

Finally, always keep a carbon or photocopy of your work. Things get lost in the mail. Teachers lose papers. Writing is hard work. Don't take a chance on someone's losing the only copy you have.

HAVE COURAGE AND USE YOUR WRITING

The last step of writing is using it. Handing it in. Mailing it. The type of writing discussed in this book is meant to be used. It's meant to communicate something to someone else. Not using it would be like giving a speech in an empty room.

This last step can be as hard as the first step of getting started. Both, in a way, involve facing the unknown. When we start writing, we don't know where we'll end up. When we use our writing, we don't know how others will react.

If our readers react as we want them to, we've accomplished our purpose in writing. But what if they don't? Ask yourself what's the worst thing that could happen. Would you lose your job? Your health? Your friend? If not, take courage and put your writing to work for you. Mail the letter of complaint. Deliver the report you've written. Submit the article for publication. Do it. If you get the results you want, you've accomplished something. If you get results you don't want, you've learned something you can put to use the next time you write. Either way, you win.

Suppose you're all set to use your writing but don't know where to send it. Fortunately, most reference librarians are happy to help people locate the addresses of organizations, politicians, and businesses. In large libraries it would usually be the social science reference librarian who would help you. If you've written an article for publication, a book such as *Writer's Market* will help you decide where and how to submit the article.

If you've written something to be read by others, let them read it. Take courage and do it.

chapter 11

Worksheets

On the following pages you'll find samples of two different worksheets designed to help you as you write. They are the *Writing Process Worksheet* and the *Checklist for Effective Writing*. Because there is just one copy of each worksheet, you may make as many photocopies as you need for your own use. It's best to make the copies in advance, so you won't be tempted to mark in the sample itself.

WRITING PROCESS WORKSHEET

As you work on a writing project, you should keep a Writing Process Worksheet with you, checking off the various writing steps and answering questions as you go. The worksheet can help you in four ways:

1. It will remind you of the various steps *possible* in the writing process. (You won't necessarily do all the steps or follow the same order each time you write.)

2. It will help clarify why you are writing, and to whom.

3. It will refer you to other chapters of this book.

4. It will help you when you share your draft with others. If you exchange drafts with a classmate, you can have the classmate fill in Section C. If someone who is not a classmate reads your draft, you can ask that person the questions in Section C. (When you look at the worksheets, you'll notice that whoever reads your draft must know who your intended readers are and why you are writing to them. You can either tell them or let them read that information in Section B. You might also mention any special length limits imposed on your paper.)

5. Your teacher may ask you to hand in the worksheet along with your writing. If so, it will help your teacher know who your intended reader is, why you are writing to that reader, what changes you've made in your drafts, and what you feel best about in your writing.

Name _____ Date or subject _____

WRITING PROCESS WORKSHEET

Keep this guide with your writing so you can check off steps and answer questions as you go. You won't always need to do all of the steps, and sometimes you'll return to a step several times.

A. THE PRELIMINARY DOODLE, DRAFT, AND BREAK

_____ Decide what you want to write about or to whom you wish to write. (See Chapter 4 for help.)

_____ Brainstorm. Organize the brainstorming. Gather other information as necessary. (See Chapter 4 and Appendix B.)

_____ Do some freewriting. (See Chapter 4.)

_____ Plan a tentative thesis and audience. (See Chapter 4.)

_____ Write a messy preliminary draft to get your ideas straight. (See Chapter 5.)

_____ Take a break from your writing. (See Chapter 6.)

B. REREADING AND REVISING THE DRAFT

_____ Reread the draft; clarify your thesis, audience, and purpose.

_____ Answer the following questions:

1. My reader will be _____
   (give name and/or description)

2. This reader knows me _____
   (well, slightly, not at all)

   This reader and I are probably _____
   (similar/different)

   If different, in what ways? _____

3. This reader is probably:

   _____ already knowledgeable about my subject or idea.
   (yes/no)   (If no, see Chapter 12 for tips and techniques to use in your writing.)

   _____ already interested in the idea or subject.
   (yes/no)   (If no, see Chapter 13 for tips and techniques to use in your writing.)

   _____ already in agreement with me.
   (yes/no/N.A.) (If no, see Chapters 14 and 15 for tips and techniques.)

   (Note: If all three answers are yes, there's probably no reason to write.)

4. My purpose or reason for writing will be to _____

   _____

The setting will be _____

(letter, magazine article, school paper, etc. See Chapter 2.)

_____ Revise your draft with the above reader, purpose, and setting in mind.

C. HELPER'S REACTION TO DRAFT

(Questions to be answered by someone else.) (See Chapter 8.)

1. What seems to be the draft's thesis or main idea?

   _____

2. Considering *the intended reader, purpose, and setting,* what seems especially

   good in the draft? _____

   _____

3. What might *the intended reader* find unclear? Dull? Tactless?

   Annoying? Illogical or unpersuasive? _____

   _____

4. What changes might the writer make? _____

   _____

Helper's name _____

(optional)

D. THE FINAL COPY

_____ Revise your draft, using whichever of the above comments will help. (See also the Checklist for Effective Writing.)

_____ Polish your sentences. (See Chapter 9, 12, or 13.)

_____ Correct the grammar. (See Appendix A.)

_____ Type the final copy, following the samples in Appendix D. Make a copy to retain.

_____ Proofread the paper as a courtesy to your reader. (See Chapter 10.)

E. NOTES ON YOUR FINAL COPY

1. If you've changed your audience from the rough draft,

   describe your new audience. _____

2. What have you changed most since the draft and why? _____

   _____

3. What are you most pleased with in this writing? _____

   _____

CHECKLISTS FOR EFFECTIVE WRITING

You may wish to use this checklist as you revise rough drafts or review the final copy of your writing. In addition, your teacher may use it to evaluate your writing.

The items on the checklist are divided into four categories. The first category applies to almost all writing and refers to techniques you learned in earlier chapters of this book. The next three categories focus on a particular writing purpose: writing to inform, interest, or persuade the reader. Tips and techniques for each of these purposes are included in the next part of this book and the checklist refers you to those chapters that will help you most.

First, check all your writing against the items in the first category. If one of the items isn't appropriate to your specific audience or purpose, check the "not applicable" box.

Next, check your writing against the items in the category that best describes your purpose: informative, interesting, or persuasive. Once again, if a given item doesn't fit your particular purpose or audience, simply check the "not applicable" box. (Be careful, however, that you don't use "not applicable" as a rationalization to avoid work.)

Finally, keep in mind that effective writing depends on the entire writing situation: why you're writing, to whom, about what, and under what special time, length, or other limits. You'll therefore have to combine techniques to suit yourself, your audience, and your purpose in writing. The checklist is a guide, not a recipe.

Name _____ Title or # _____

CHECKLIST FOR EFFECTIVE WRITING

INTENDED READER: _____

PURPOSE: _____

SETTING: _____

(if applicable)

Yes	No	N.A.	A. *ALL WRITING:* (See Chapters 1–10.)
			1. The thesis is clear, specific, and appropriate to the intended reader. (See pages 18–22; 65–70; 79–83.)
			2. The writing's purpose is clear and appropriate to the intended reader. (See pages 13–17; 87–90.)
			3. The assumptions regarding the intended reader are consistent and reasonable. (See pages 7–9; 87–90.)
			4. The organization has a clear beginning, middle, and end. (See pages 35–38; if appropriate, 144–148.)
			5. The organization and transitions will be easy for the intended reader to follow. (See pages 32–42; 95–101.)
			6. The sentences are concise and easy for the intended reader to understand. (See pages 42–45; 105–107.)
			7. The writing has been proofread and grammatical errors corrected as appropriate for the intended reader and situation. (See pages 112–114.)
			8. _____ (Item to be added by student or instructor.)
			B. *WRITING INFORMATIVELY:* (See Chapter 12.)
			1. The writing explains something the intended reader probably does not yet know. (See page 88.)

Yes	No	N.A.	
			2. There are enough examples, comparisons, definitions, or details to answer the intended reader's questions. (See pages 133–144.)
			3. The details and examples are sufficiently specific. (See pages 127–128.)
			4. _____ (Item to be added by student or instructor.)
			5. Considering the intended reader and purpose, this writing: *(is also/needs to be more)* interesting. (See below.) (circle one) *(is also/needs to be more)* persuasive. (See p. 121.) (circle one)
			C. WRITING INTERESTINGLY: (See Chapter 13.)
			1. The opening paragraphs give the intended reader a reason to read. (See pages 156–166.)
			2. The intended reader would find the examples, details, or comparisons especially interesting. (See pages 171–173.)
			3. The descriptions are vivid. (See pages 167–171.)
			4. The writing builds the reader's curiosity or suspense. (See pages 163–166.)
			5. The intended reader would find the sentences polished and appealing. (See pages 173–182.)
			6. _____ (Item to be added by student or instructor.)
			7. Considering the intended reader and purpose, this writing: *(is also/needs to be more)* informative. (See above.) *(is also/needs to be more)* persuasive. (See p. 121.)

Yes	No	N.A.	D. *WRITING PERSUASIVELY:* (See Chapters 14 and 15.)
			1. The thesis is one that the intended reader could or does disagree with before reading the paper. (See pages 89–90; 205–208.)
			2. The writing shows tactful consideration for the intended reader's ideas and feelings. (See pages 186–192; 195–201.)
			3. There is sufficient evidence to persuade the reader. (See pages 205–207.)
			4. The evidence is sufficiently explained. (See pages 217–218.)
			5. The writing anticipates and answers the intended reader's questions and objections. (See pages 192–195.)
			6. The writing is logical and the tone responsible. (See pages 209–219.)
			7. The sources are appropriately documented. (See pages 219–223.)
			8. _____ (Item to be added by student or instructor.)
			9. Considering the intended reader and purpose, this writing: *(is also/needs to be more)* interesting. (See p. 120.) *(is also/needs to be more)* informative. (See p. 120.)

part III

WHEN WRITERS WRITE: THEIR PURPOSES AND TECHNIQUES

In the last section you learned about the writing process in general—how writers write. In this section you'll become familiar with the techniques writers use to make their writing effective in various situations. For the sake of convenience, we'll consider four common writing situations. The writer may want to:

> help the reader understand.
> build the reader's interest.
> tactfully persuade the reader.
> rationally persuade the reader.

These four situations are not, of course, mutually exclusive. Often we need to be both entertaining and tactfully persuasive. Or both clear and rational. Or all four.

In addition, we have to consider not only our overall strategy, but also what strategies to use at particular points in the writing. For example, when we're finally ready to rewrite the opening paragraph of a draft, we have to consider which of the four strategies is appropriate there. Is our main concern at that point to help our reader understand us? If so, and we're writing a letter, we may begin with a clear reference to the situation that has prompted us to write. If we're writing a paper for a history course, we may begin with the thesis itself. Are we most interested in using the introduction to attract our reader's attention? Then we might begin with a provocative question, witty quotation, or amusing story. Do we feel we must, above all, begin tactfully? Then we'll want to establish rapport so our reader will feel comfortable and not threatened by what we have to say. Do we need to persuade our reader rationally? Then, once again, we might begin with the thesis itself, or perhaps with a brief summary of the question or problem we're discussing.

If all of this sounds a bit too consciously controlled, take heart. Recall your first driving lessons: Remember the confusing array of strategies and decisions involved? Remember having to decide when and how to brake? When and how to accelerate? How to maintain an even speed? If you learned on a manual shift, remember having to decide when to shift gears? When to apply the clutch? And how, with only two feet, to keep track of three foot pedals? Remember the frustration of having to remember all those procedures while at the same time having to watch the cars in front of you, the white line, the speedometer, *and* the rear-view mirror? All that while also having to remember to give a left-hand turn signal before turning left?

It's a wonder any of us learned to drive at all. While we're learning, driving seems most unnatural; after a few weeks or months, however, it usually becomes second nature. Unless we're driving in a strange city, we soon find that we automatically maintain an even speed, shift, check the rear-view mirror, the speedometer, the gas indicator, the side-view mirror, and the cars in front of us, without giving any of it a thought. We don't even "see" the white line; we instinctively know where it is.

So it is with writing. When people are first learning to write, they must consciously make decisions and use techniques. After a while, however, the process and techniques become automatic—unless, of course, the writer is faced with a new or unusual writing situation. Then, like a driver in a strange city, the writer once again becomes consciously aware of the strategies to be used and decisions to be made.

chapter 12

To Write Informatively and Clearly, Anticipate Your Readers' Questions

When is it most important to write clearly and informatively? Clarity is important in all writing, but especially so whenever your readers know significantly less than you do about the topic under discussion; that's when they need extra help to understand what you're saying.

Popularizations (writing that explains a complex or technical subject in terms that ordinary readers can understand) are an obvious example of writing where clarity is important. Books such as *I'm O.K.—You're O.K.* and Isaac Asimov's *The Universe* are popularizations that explain psychological and astronomical concepts clearly enough so that those of us who are not psychologists or astronomers can easily understand them. Attorneys explaining legal concepts in letters to their clients and students writing history papers that their classmates can understand are all writing popularizations.

Another type of writing that requires great clarity is "how to" instructions. Whether writers are explaining how to use a newly purchased videotape recorder, raise orchids, or develop photographs, they must remember that the reader does not yet "know how." If the writing is ambiguous or misleading, the reader may end up with high blood pressure, dead orchids, or ruined pictures.

In addition, much of the routine correspondence of life, such as letters announcing meetings, ordering merchandise, or requesting corrections in billings, require attention to clarity. Meetings can be spoiled if the announcement gives the date and time but omits the place. People can receive the wrong mail order merchandise if their order isn't clearly written.

Readers are not mind readers. When your purpose is writing to inform, don't assume your readers will read between the lines or automatically know what you mean. They won't.

Although the reader isn't a mind reader, you, the writer, should be. To write clearly, you must anticipate your reader's questions. The main questions that might occur to a reader are:

"Huh? What do you mean?"

"What's that? Could you define that word?"

"What's it like or similar too?"

"Such as? For example?"

"Did you forget something?"

"What do I do now?"

"How does it work?"

"What's your point, anyway?"

The first and last questions can be prevented through effective writing. One or more of the middle six questions may always occur to readers. It's the writer's job to know when they'll occur and to answer them as they arise. As one student writer put it, "When I'm writing to explain something to my reader, I make believe I have only this one chance to explain it."

This chapter will present ways of responding to each of the above questions. First you'll learn how to write *clear sentences*, then how to use *definitions, comparisons, examples,* and *details,* to make your writing clear. You'll also learn how to *give directions* and *describe a process.* Finally, you'll read about ways to *organize your writing* so that your main idea is evident throughout. The activities are all together at the end of the chapter.

Sometimes you'll be able to apply these tips as you draft. Most of the time, however, you'll find that they help as you rewrite the draft, anticipating and answering your reader's questions.

Your Reader's Not a Mind Reader

"I have a pet at home"   *"Oh, what kind of a pet?"*

"It is a dog."   *"What kind of a dog?"*

"It is a St. Bernard."

"Grown up or a puppy?"

"It is full grown."

"What color is it?"

"It is brown and white."

"Why didn't you say you had a full-grown, brown and white St. Bernard as a pet in the first place?"

"Why doesn't anybody understand me?"

Reprinted courtesy Kaiser Aluminum & Chemical Corp. © 1965.

"HUH?" (FOUR WAYS TO WRITE CLEARER SENTENCES)

1. Be Specific: Your Reader Is Not a Mind Reader.

The miscommunication in the cartoon results from the use of vague words. Words such as *pet,* and *dog* may seem fairly specific, but they aren't. As a general rule, the greater the chance that people can "picture" a word differently, the more vague or abstract the word is. On the other hand, the greater the chance that people will draw the same mental picture from a word they know, the more specific the word is.

The word *pet* is abstract because it includes so many different kinds of pets: goldfish, dogs, cats, monkeys, lizards, and even birds. *Dog* is much less abstract, because poodles, St. Bernards, and fox terriers are more similar than are poodles and snakes. But still, people can picture different kinds of dogs, and so *dog* is, to some extent, still abstract. *St. Bernard* is much more specific, since St. Bernards all resemble each other. But no two St. Bernards are exactly alike—just ask their owners. So, the most precise way of identifying a specific St. Bernard would be by using the dog's name: "Brandy."

But, you may be saying to yourself, suppose my reader doesn't know that "Brandy" is my St. Bernard's name? Or suppose I want to discuss St. Bernards in general, not just Brandy? Or suppose I want to discuss dogs in general? These are excellent questions. You can't use very specific words all the time. You can, however, use the most specific word that conveys what you do have in mind. "Brandy, my three-year-old St. Bernard, had to be carried over the river" tells the reader much more than does the sentence "My dog had to be carried over the river."

To see if you are using vague words when you write, reread something you've written, circling the words that are as vague as *dog*. Then ask yourself if the words you've circled are as specific as they can be. For example, if you had circled the word *music,* you could ask yourself if you meant all types of music, including pop, jazz, rock, disco, western, and classical. It might be that you did mean all types of music, but it might also be that you really meant jazz. If so, you could then ask yourself if you really meant all types of jazz. After all, what's true of Dixieland isn't necessarily true of progressive jazz, and vice versa.

Even in conversation, vague words can cause problems. How often have we heard people groan, "Oh no, I didn't mean *that* big." Or *that* short. Or *that* expensive. Such words get us into trouble because they, too, are vague. They ask that our audience be mind readers. The same is true of writing. If a doctor wrote an order for a "big dose of insulin" to be given to a diabetic patient, the patient—and undoubtedly the doctor— would be in trouble. The nurse would need to know exactly how much insulin to administer. If a sales representative receives a memo instructing her to call on a particular store "periodically," she might interpret "periodically" to mean once every three or four months while her boss might have meant once every three or four days.

As writers we must therefore develop the habit of using words that say precisely what we mean. One way to develop this habit is to work on our spoken as well as written language. For example, in conversation, many of us use the word *thing* when we can't readily think of the precise word we want. "That thing is growing well." What's growing well? The rose bush? The tall weed behind it? The elm tree behind them both? "Hand me the thing, please." What thing? The Phillips head screwdriver? The drill? The wrench? The direction booklet? Force yourself to think of the precise word you want in place of the catchall word *thing,* or a vague word such as *long* or *short.* The habit of being specific will carry over into your writing.

(See practice activities at the end of this Chapter.)

2. Check Word Order

Readers can be easily confused by careless word order. Each of the following sentences can be interpreted in two ways:

SENTENCE	READER'S QUESTIONS
Chuck asked Diane to write down what the senators said after having many dinners together.	*Who had dinner together?*
As our representative in the Senate, I urge you to back this plan.	*Who's the representative?*
Sitting on top of the electric wires, we saw a row of birds.	*What were you doing sitting on top of electric wires?*
The teacher will accept papers from students of any length.	*Students of any length?*

The general strategy for improving sentences like these is to put descriptions as close to the words they describe as possible. The word order has been revised in the sentences below.

CLEARER WORD ORDER

After having *many dinners together, Chuck asked* Diane to write down what the senators said.

I urge *you, as our representative* in the Senate, to back this plan.

We saw *a row of birds sitting* on top of the electric wires.

The teacher will accept *papers of any length* from students. (Are the words *from students* really necessary?)

The above revisions were easy to make; just the word order had to be changed. Other types of sentences, however, may require the addition of a word or two.

SENTENCES WITH WORDS MISSING	READER'S QUESTIONS
On November 19, while waiting to catch the bus, two dogs were barking and snapping at me.	*The dogs were waiting for the bus?*
Sitting at my desk one day, the boss approached.	*The boss was sitting at your desk? Why?*
By watching the last act carefully, the play takes on new meaning.	*By whose watching the last act carefully?*

Assuming that the dogs weren't waiting for the bus, the boss wasn't sitting at your desk, and the play wasn't watching itself, these sentences could be made clearer by the addition of a word or two in the right spot:

On November 19, *while I was* waiting to catch the bus, two dogs were barking and snapping at me.

Sitting at my desk one day, *I saw* the boss approaching.

If you watch the last act carefully, this play takes on new meaning.

(See practice activities at the end of this chapter.)

3. Use Clear Pronouns

Pronouns can muddle communication if they seem to refer to the wrong word.[1] Can you see how the pronouns in the following sentences could cause confusion?

SENTENCES	READER'S QUESTIONS
Jim told Mike he was working too hard.	*Who was working too hard? Jim or Mike?*
Today's parents are more concerned that their children are secure and happy than that the children live out their fantasies.	*Whose fantasies? The parents' or the kids'?*
Christmas time is rough on sales clerks. The mall stays open late, even though for the last hour or so there are very few customers. They get exhausted.	*Who gets exhausted? The customers, the sales clerks, or both?*

Sometimes the easiest way to improve sentences like these is to replace the pronoun with another word. The first sentence, for example, could be revised to read:

Jim told Mike that *Mike* was working too hard.

The second sentence would be clearer if the word *parents* replaced the ambiguous pronoun *their:*

Today's parents are more concerned that their children are secure and happy than that the children live out *the parents'* fantasies.

The third sentence would be improved if we changed the word order as well as the pronoun. In this case, another pronoun, *who,* replaces the ambiguous word *they:*

---

[1]Grammatical pronoun agreement and sexism in pronouns are discussed in the Grammar Guide, Appendix A.

The mall stays open late during the Christmas season, even though there are very few customers during the last hour or so. These late hours are rough *on the sales clerks, who* become exhausted.

One other confusing use of pronouns should be mentioned. Consider the following sentence:

Because I'm studying engineering, I hope there's a good job market for them when I graduate.

After pausing a second or two, most readers would, of course, figure out that *them* must refer to *engineers*. But the word *engineers* is not in the sentence, and clear writing should not make readers slow down to figure such things out. The sentence might more clearly be written:

Because I'm studying engineering, I hope there's a good job market for engineers when I graduate.

As we hurriedly write rough drafts, we forget precisely what words we have or haven't used earlier in a sentence. Thus when we revise, it's important to check our sentences to make sure there's a written word or group of words for each pronoun to refer to. Otherwise, once again, we may be asking our readers to become mind readers.

(See practice activities at the end of this chapter.)

4. Avoid Gobbledygook

As the Air Force tells its officers, "Communication is never having to say 'Huh?'" Unfortunately, "Huh?" is about the only response possible to a type of writing that's called "gobbledygook." (It's called that because, like a turkey's gobble, it sounds loud and important but says little.) Below are some examples of gobbledygook with their English translations.

HUH?	ENGLISH
No vehicle shall be turned so as to proceed in the opposite direction upon the approach to, or near the crest of, a grade.	Don't make U-turns near or on hills.
We concur with your recommendation to disseminate the available data regarding increased remuneration.	We agree. It's time to tell people about the pay raises.
Respondents must ascertain that all requested information has been provided.	Please answer all questions.
I am experiencing a meaningful psychological attachment of a romantic nature.	I'm in love.

Gobbledygook, you'll notice, is not only garbled, it's also wordy. (See Chapter 9 for help with wordiness.) Why do people write gobbledygook? Sometimes, it's a mistaken attempt to impress others. (This attempt often backfires.) Other times, it shows that the writer isn't sure of what he or she is saying. Sometimes it's an out-and-out attempt to prevent the reader from understanding what's really being said. In all cases, it blocks communication.

How can you know if you're writing gobbledygook? The easiest way is to ask someone. If that's not possible, select a piece of your writing and circle all the words with three or more syllables. If you average three or more such words per line, you may be writing gobbledygook. To test if you are, try rewriting the passage using shorter, simpler words. If you can, chances are you were writing gobbledygook. Another test is the one for wordiness discussed in Chapter 9. Circle the prepositional phrases and read your writing out loud. If your writing sounds wordy, it may also be gobbledygook.

Eliminating the gobbledygook from your writing does not, of course, mean eliminating all of the technical or long words. It does mean eliminating many of them. Gobbledygook is often a matter of density. Even when a reader understands what every word in the sentence means, if there are too many long or unusual words, the reader will have to plod slowly through the sentence. So keep it simple!

Some simpler words to use if you're writing gobbledygook:

HUH?	ENGLISH
Instead of:	*Try:*
accordingly	so
advantageous	helpful
an appreciable number	many
ascertain	find out
concur	agree
consequently	so
demonstrates	shows, proves
endeavor	try
enumerate	list
finalize	finish, complete
fundamental	basic
magnitude	size
maximize	increase (to the maximum)
operational	working
optimum	most, best, greatest
prioritize	rank, list in order
recapitulate	sum up, summarize
usage	use

For practice in writing clear sentences, please see activities I to III at the end of this chapter.

"WHAT'S THAT?" (A DEFINITION CAN HELP)

Occasionally there is no short, simple synonym for a technical or difficult word. The word *parachute* is a good example. We all know what a parachute is, but suppose you were writing for someone who didn't know the word *parachute?* You would then have two choices. You could, to avoid using the word, constantly write, "a large, umbrellalike device of fabric that opens in midair and allows a person or object to descend at a safe rate of speed, as from an airplane." Or, you could define the word the first time you used it and thereafter simply use the word *parachute.* Obviously this second choice would be more sensible.

Once again, however, you would have to be careful not to overburden your readers. How many new words can you expect readers to retain while reading your writing? Is there some simple synonym you could use?

Let's say the technical word is really the best, or perhaps the only, word for what you mean. How can you write a clear, straightforward definition of it? The first step is to ask yourself what your reader really needs to know. Don't launch into a discussion of how the poison ivy plant evolved, or a technical discussion of its botanical family, if all your reader needs to know is what it looks like and where it grows. To take another example, if you're writing about calories, ask yourself if your reader needs to know that a calorie is "the amount of heat needed to raise one gram of water one degree Centigrade." If you're writing on physics, that may be exactly what your reader needs to know. But if you're writing on nutrition, your reader may need to know only that a calorie is a measure of the amount of energy contained in food. Or, perhaps, if you're writing about diets, your reader may need to know that "every 3,500 excess calories we consume is converted into one extra pound of body fat." A definition of *calorie* that involves heating one gram of water one degree Centigrade isn't going to help most dieters. Once you've decided what your reader needs to know, you can tailor your definition to that need.

Classification

A traditional way of defining something is to "classify" it. For example, if you wanted to define what a *hammer* is, you could first say it is "a tool." That would let your reader know what general category or type of thing a *hammer* is. Next, you could explain how a hammer is different from other tools: "It's used primarily for driving nails." By explaining what general category of objects a hammer belongs to, and then explaining how the hammer differs from other objects of the same general type, you would have "classified" it for your reader. Your complete definition might read: "A hammer is a tool used primarily for driving nails."

Let's take another example. Suppose you were writing about the brain and wanted to define *cerebral cortex* for your reader. You might first classify it as part of the brain: "The cerebral cortex is the large, outermost layer of the brain." You could then distinguish it from other parts of the brain by adding, "It's the part of the brain responsible for our 'higher' abilities, such as thought, art, music, and math." Or consider the definition of *parachute* given earlier. It also was a classification: The reader was first told that a parachute was "a large umbrellalike device" and was then told how it differed from other large, umbrellalike devices.

Other Methods of Defining

Classification is not the only way to define something. Quite often a *comparison* will help: "An Arabian horse is to other horses what a Siamese cat is to other cats: more graceful, sleek, and elegant." Or an *example* can help clarify what's meant: "The 'social sciences' include subjects such as sociology, economics, political science, and psychology." Other times, the best definition simply tells *"who, what, why, when, or where"* — whichever is most important for the reader to know. For example, one "definition" of Franklin Roosevelt might be that he was "president of the United States during World War II."

In a way, however, all of these definitions still depend on classification. The Arabian horse is distinguished from other horses; the social sciences are distinguished from other subjects of study; and Franklin Roosevelt is distinguished from other presidents. Thus when writing definitions, don't worry about *which* technique you are using. It doesn't matter; what matters is clearly telling your reader what he or she needs to know.

What to Avoid

There are two types of definitions that do not help readers. Here's an example of the first type: "To define something means to give its definition." The problem is that a reader who doesn't know the word *define* also won't know the word *definition*. Such definitions are called "circular" since they can keep going in circles. Another example of a circular definition: "A dermatologist is someone who specializes in dermatology."

The second type of definition that can exasperate readers is the one that uses words as technical or difficult as the word being defined. For example, most people who don't know what a *will* is won't be helped much by reading that it's "a legal declaration of the disposition to be made of an estate after death." "After death" would be clear, but would the rest of it?

You may be wondering if it isn't easier and safer to copy dictionary definitions than to write your own. Sometimes it is. Often, however, dictionary definitions read like the definition of *will* above. If you're tempted to use a dictionary definition, ask yourself if it will tell your readers what they need to know, and if they'll understand it. Even then, quoting from the dictionary, and giving proper credit, may make the definition stand our awkwardly from the rest of your writing.

For practice writing definitions, see activity IV at the end of this chapter.

"WHAT'S IT LIKE?" (COMPARISONS: THE LONG AND SHORT OF IT)

Brief Comparisons

Let's say you want to describe the blue whale's size to someone who has never seen a whale. You could say that the adult blue whale weighs almost 150 tons and is almost 100 feet long. But such tonnage and footage might be difficult for your reader to picture. A brief comparison might make the whale's size clearer.[2] For example, you could say that the whale can weigh as much as 50 good-sized elephants, and that it's as long as 5 elephants standing trunk-to-tail in a chain. Or you could simply say that whales are larger than dinosaurs ever were. However, if your reader were more familiar with football than with elephants or dinosaurs, you might say that the blue whale weighs as much as 150 teams of football players and is as long as a third of the length of a football field.

The point is that comparisons such as the above can be especially useful in helping readers visualize a size, shape, distance, or time span. For example, Carl Sagan devised a comparative "cosmic calendar" to help readers of *The Dragons of Eden* visualize the great lengths of time involved in the formation of the earth and life on it. He asks his reader to "imagine the fifteen-billion-year lifetime of the universe . . . compressed into the span of a single year. Every billion years of Earth history would correspond to about 24 days of our cosmic year."[3] On such a one-year calendar, the "big bang" that started our present universe would occur on January 1. In September the Earth would be formed. By October, algae would have appeared. But not until December 26 would the first mammals appear, and not until the last day of the year, December 31, would humans evolve. To focus on December 31, humans would not evolve until nightfall and, as Sagan points out, not until 10 seconds before midnight would recorded history begin. Such a comparison lets most readers comprehend cosmic time in a way they otherwise could not.

If cosmic time seems a bit unreal to you, consider money. "One billion dollars" is difficult for most of us to really understand. Just how much is it? A writer could say it has nine zeros: $1,000,000,000. But if a billion dollars is explained as being the same amount of money as would be earned by one person making $20,000 a year for 50,000 years, it becomes easier to understand. Or, if it's described as being roughly $4.00 for every man, woman, and child in the United States, it makes sense in a different way.

Of course, comparisons are useful in describing things other than size. Imagine writing directions for a paste mixture to be used in applying wallpaper. You might give the exact measurements of water and dry paste to use: 1 pound of paste for each 10 pints of water. But what if your readers make a mistake? An additional description of the desired consistency would help them recognize their mistake. How thick should the mixture be? As thick as mashed potatoes? As pancake batter? As maple syrup? Let's say

---

[2]Brief comparisons used to make a specific point are often called *analogies*. In this book, however, we will simply use the word *comparison*.

[3]*The Dragons of Eden* (New York: Random House, Inc., 1977).

it should be as thick as pancake batter. Will your reader know how thick pancake batter is? If not, a different comparison would be necessary.

Earlier in this book I compared learning to write to learning to drive. In doing so, I assumed that most people know how to drive cars. If you don't, the comparison probably didn't work for you. What comparison might have worked better in your case?

For practice with brief comparisons, see activity V at the end of this chapter.

Longer Comparisons

Many times in both academic and personal writing situations, longer comparisons of the similarities and differences between two things can be used to help a writer explain an idea more clearly.[4] For instance, let's say you wanted to describe the complexity of a homemaker's job. If you were writing for an audience of businesspeople, you might write a detailed comparison of the similarities and differences between managing a smoothly run home and managing a smoothly run business. For instance, you could discuss the supply, budgeting, logistics, and communications functions of each. You could also discuss the extent to which the business manager and the homemaker have support personnel to help them. Such an extended comparison could be very helpful in making the point that homemaking can be a demanding, challenging job. However, it will work only if the reader is already familiar with the business world and only if you, the writer, know enough about both business and homemaking to write with accuracy and authority.

When writing long comparisons a writer must give extra attention to clear organization. When you're writing about two different things at the same time, it's important that the reader be able to follow the comparison point by point. Let's say that you've been asked to write a report recommending one of two possible locations for your volunteer organization's new office. Let's further say that you visit the two sites, gather all the essential information about them, and decide to recommend the office above the health food store. Here's what your notes from each visit might look like:

OFFICE ABOVE HEALTH FOOD STORE	OFFICE IN JOE'S SPARE ROOM
500 sq. ft	Free!
Hot	Cool and pleasant
No parking	Needs furniture
Close to where most volunteers live	Pretty far from town
On bus line	In suburbs
Duplicating service next door	Lots of parking
Business-like image for fund raising	Joe's preschool kids make a lot of noise and get into things
Furnished with desks, etc.	Far from duplicating services, etc.
$175/month rent	600 sq. ft.
	Couldn't work there all hours of night

---

[4]In essay exams and some other writing, *compare* usually means to discuss similarities, and *contrast* means to discuss differences. In this book, however, *compare* means to show differences as well as similarities.

How would you write the report? You could write a glowing description of the convenience and businesslike image of the office above the health food store, saying nothing about Joe's spare room in the report. If you did, however, the members of your organization would wonder why you weren't giving them the information on Joe's room. On the other hand, you could describe the inconvenience and unbusinesslike setup at Joe's, saying nothing about the $175 office except that you recommend it despite its cost. But if you did that, the organization members would wonder why they should go along with your recommendation, since you would have told them nothing about the commercial office. Obviously, in a situation like this one your readers expect, and deserve, a comparison of the two office sites. The question becomes how to organize the comparison. Basically, there are two ways of doing it. Here's one way:

Format 1

INTRODUCTION:	Your recommendation of the commercial space over Joe's spare room.
JOE'S ROOM:	Cost Pleasantness Degree of convenience Lack of businesslike atmosphere
COMMERCIAL SPACE:	Cost Unpleasantness Degree of convenience Businesslike atmosphere
CONCLUSION:	Brief statement as to why the convenience and businesslike atmosphere of the commercial space are more important than the pleasantness and low cost of Joe's spare room.

The important point to note in this format is that the order is the same for the discussion of Joe's room and the commercial office space. This is the main trick to writing clear comparisons: keep the order of your points the same. The reader expects it.

The other format for comparisons, and the one I prefer, looks like this:

Format 2

INTRODUCTION:	Your recommendation of the commercial space over Joe's room.
COST:	Joe's Commercial space
PLEASANTNESS:	Joe's Commercial space

CONVENIENCE:	Joe's Commercial space
BUSINESSLIKE ATMOSPHERE:	Joe's Commercial space
CONCLUSION:	Brief statement as to why the convenience and businesslike atmosphere of the commercial space outweigh the pleasantness and low cost of Joe's spare room.

Once again, it's essential that the order be the same. In this case, once the order is established—Joe's versus commercial space—it must be maintained throughout the report. Rather like a spectator at a tennis match, the reader expects the ball to pass back and forth between one court and the other in predictable fashion. The advantage of format #2 is that it makes it easier for the reader to follow the comparison point by point. Format #1 requires that the reader remember everything said in the first half of the report (about Joe's room) while reading the second half (about the commercial space).

With either format, the writer must be very careful to use clear pronouns. In the sample report we've been using, if the writer referred to both office locations as "it," the reader could quickly become confused.

Often it's easier to "see" something when it is compared with something else. The disadvantages of Joe's spare room might be difficult to see if the commercial space could not be used for comparison: The inconvenience of not being near duplicating services and of not being able to work until midnight might be overlooked. Ironically, sometimes the better we know something, the harder it is to see it except by comparison to something else. Just as a quick comparison can help make something that's new seem familiar to a reader, a longer comparison can give both writer and reader new insight into the familiar.

What to Avoid

There are two types of comparisons that confuse rather than help the reader. The first we've already mentioned: the comparison that draws on a subject the reader isn't familiar with. Explaining soccer in terms of football isn't going to make soccer any clearer to a reader who doesn't understand football either.

The second type of comparison to avoid is one that is potentially misleading. For example, electricity flowing in a wire is often explained as being similar to "water running in a pipe." This comparison allows a simple explanation of amps: they are like gallons per minute. The difficulty with the comparison is that electricity is like water in only very limited ways. For example, gravity does not affect the flow of electricity, but it has a pronounced effect on the flow of water.

Since no two things are exactly identical, all comparisons are limited. This doesn't, of course, mean they shouldn't be used to illustrate a point. It does mean that careful writers will indicate the limitations. For example, a writer might write, "*In some ways* electricity flowing in a wire is similar to water running in a pipe."

It also means that comparisons can only help make points clear or vivid: they cannot prove anything. For example, a student might note certain similarities between two periods of history, say the Renaissance in Europe and the twentieth century in most of the world: Both periods are marked by increased communications (The Gutenberg Press then and satellite communications and copying machines now), exploration of new territories (the Indies of the New World then; the planets now), scientific discoveries (Copernicus then; Einstein now), and increased trade between nations. Yet because of the vast differences between the two periods, the comparison could not be used to demonstrate anything about our future, or what the nations of the world "should" or "could" be doing now. The comparison could be used to help *explain* the writer's point about our contemporary world, but the actual proof would have to come from elsewhere.

This confusion between using a comparison to explain and to prove something can be seen in a statement such as, "If you can give up smoking, you should be able to give up drinking." Or, "If we can put a man on the moon, we should be able to find a cure for the common cold." The difficulty with this type of "proof" is that although smoking and drinking have much in common, they are also different in many ways. The same is true of the technologies and difficulties involved in rocketry and biochemistry.

For practice with longer comparisons, see activity VI at the end of this chapter.

"SUCH AS?" (EXAMPLES TO THE RESCUE)

When we're trying to explain something to someone face to face, we know when we're not getting our message across clearly. The puzzled expression on our listener's face may prompt us to add a specific example. When we're writing, we have to anticipate when these examples may be necessary.

For instance, if we were to write a general statement such as, "Some musical instruments can be purchased new for under $100," our readers might want examples. The easiest way to include quick examples is to make them part of the original sentence. For instance: "Some musical instruments, *such as recorders and guitars,* can be purchased new for under $100." Similarly, if we were writing about sports that can be enjoyed alone, we might write, "Some sports, *such as jogging, weight lifting, and ice skating,* don't require a team or even a partner."

Often, however, the reader needs more than quick examples. For instance, if you were writing about zoos, you might at some point write, "Most zoos include some 'worry activities' to keep the animals alert." Your reader might well be puzzled by this unless you gave an example. You might add, "For instance, since animals in the wild aren't assured of a meal every day, zoos sometimes skip an animal's feeding one day out of seven. By providing normal stress, this uncertainty or 'worry' helps keep the animal healthy." This addition not only includes an example, it *explains* the example as well.

Such an explanation is frequently necessary if examples are to serve their purpose. Consider the following statement: "Some musical instruments, such as the guitar, are considered easier to play than others, such as the violin." The statement contains examples, but it's still not clear. Why is the guitar easier? Is it because the guitarist doesn't use a bow? Is it because the music written for the guitar is easier? No, it's neither of these. The writer would therefore do well to add another sentence explaining the example: "The guitar's fingerboard has 'frets,' or metal ridges, to help guide the guitarist's fingers; the violin has no such aids."

What to Avoid

An example that's not specific enough won't help your reader. For instance, in the sentence, "Some sports, *such as noncompetitive ones,* don't require a team or even a partner," the "example" might leave the reader wondering, "What's an example of a noncompetitive sport?"

An example that raises new questions might not help your reader either. In general, you should avoid examples that are emotional or controversial unless the emotion or controversy is part of your point. Remember, examples should help your reader understand you; they shouldn't get in the way of clear communication.

Finally, don't use an example to "prove" a generalization. For instance, if you were writing that college students are subjected to many pressures, you might use yourself and a few of your school friends as examples. Indeed, you and your friends might be very good examples of students subjected to financial, emotional, and time pressures. But demonstrating that four or five students are subjected to pressures doesn't prove that all, or even most, students are subjected to those pressures. Examples can only illustrate and explain a generalization; they can't prove it.

Despite the warnings above, carefully chosen examples are essential to effective writing. Examples that are specific, well explained, and appropriate to your intended reader can make your writing clear and easy to read. Activity VII at the end of this chapter will help you use examples.

"DID YOU FORGET SOMETHING?" (DETAILS)

It would seem that the better we know something, the easier it should be to write about. Indeed, common advice to writers is, "Write about something you know." Yet, ironically, those things we know best can sometimes be the hardest to communicate clearly to others. Why? Simply because the more we know, the harder it is to remember how much our readers don't know. When the details are obvious to us, we forget they're not obvious to others.

Who, What, Where, When, Why, and How

Consider the following letter:

Jake's Records
18 South Street
Boston, Mass. 02106

Dear Mr. Myers:

I'm writing to say that I won't pay my bill until you correct it. It's wrong. You only sent two records, not three, and one of them was warped when I received it. Furthermore, I want it replaced.

Sincerely yours,

Trudy Dela Cruz

Trudy Dela Cruz

Trudy knows all the details of her purchase. The problem is that, even after reading her letter, Mr. Myers doesn't. Journalists have long been taught to check their stories to see if they have included the basic information of who, what, where, when, why, and how. Let's use this technique to check Trudy's letter. Mr. Myers knows "who" is involved, but he doesn't know exactly "what" is. (Which record was warped? Which record was ordered but not received? What's the account number?) Nor does he know much about "when." (When did Trudy place her order? When did she receive the bill?) Also, he doesn't know exactly "how" to help her. (How can he adjust her bill when he doesn't have the information he needs? Also, how should he replace the warped record? Does she plan to return the defective one?)

Here is a different letter Trudy could have written, telling Mr. Myers what he needs to know.

344 Trinity Street
Providence, R.I. 02901
March 19, 1982

Jake's Records
18 South Street
Boston, Mass. 02106

Dear Mr. Myers:

I've always been pleased with your mail order records in the past. However, the bill for my last order presents problems.

On February 11, 1982, I ordered the following three records from you:

Album Title	Your Order #	Your Price
1 - Best of Chopin	CL-201	$4.99
1 - Blues on Jazz	J-419	$5.99
1 - French Music for Harp	CL-304	$4.99

Early this month, I received the Chopin record and the Blues on Jazz. However, when I played these records for the first time, I discovered that the Chopin record is badly warped.

In addition, I have not yet received the French Music for Harp, although I did, last week, receive the enclosed bill for all three records.

You can see my difficulty. Enclosed is a check for the Blues on Jazz. I would still like to receive the French Music for Harp but naturally do not wish to be billed for it until I've received it.

As to the Chopin, I'm not paying for the defective record. However, despite the inconvenience to me, I'm willing to return the record to you, at your expense, if you so wish. In your reply, please let me know if you have good copies of the Chopin in stock, should I wish to reorder the record.

Sincerely,

Trudy Dela Cruz

Trudy Dela Cruz

In this second letter, Trudy has told Mr. Myers what he needs to know, has clearly paid what she feels is due to Jake's records, has enclosed the bill for his reference, and has opened the possibility of ordering a replacement for the defective record. She has, in short, provided him with all the details he needs to understand precisely what she is trying to tell him.

For practice in using details, see activity VII at the end of this chapter.

"WHAT DO I DO NOW?" (EXPLAINING "HOW TO")

When the doctor or X-ray technician says, "Take a deep breath. Hold it," many of us do just that. We wait to hear, "You can breathe now," before breathing again. When writing instructions or directions we, like the doctor, must remember small details. Furthermore, we must be sure that we put the details and steps in the right order. If a detail or step is omitted in directions for repairing a leaky faucet, making stained glass, or changing a baby's diaper, the consequences could be, at the least, unpleasant. Consider the consequences if someone were to leave out a single step while writing directions for engineers at a nuclear power plant.

The best way to write clear directions is to constantly ask yourself, "What do my readers need to know before they can understand or do the next step?" If the water supply has to be turned off at the main valve before repairs on the faucet can begin, tell your readers that first. Don't assume they'll know it. Of course, once you've written "Turn off the water at the main valve," you'll have to ask yourself, "What do my readers need to know to do that?" Obviously, they need to know where the main valve is. If it were likely that the reader might not know, you'd have to include a description of what the main valve looks like and where it's typically located.

A second tip for writing clear directions is to remember that if something can be misunderstood, it will be. Reread what you've written, asking yourself, "If someone really wanted to misunderstand this, how could they?" For example, if you began a description of how to fix leaky faucets by writing, "Turn off the water," your reader might do just that: turn off the water faucet.

A third step is to follow your own directions, doing nothing that the writing does not tell you to do. If you find yourself perched on a ladder, holding a ceiling fan in place, unable to let go because the electric wires have already been connected, but unable to secure the fan in place because the screws you need are in the next room and your helper just left . . . you may suddenly see ways to improve your directions. You might add a few details. Or you might change the order of the steps. (Perhaps the fan should really be secured in place before the wires are connected.) The correct order for details and steps in "how-to" writing is simply the order in which your reader needs the information. Often, for example, the thoughtful writer will list all the necessary materials (and sometimes the time required to complete a project) at the beginning of the directions.

Finally, here are some tips on the *style* of "how-to" directions. First, keep your sentences short. Second, use the present tense. Third, address your reader directly, either implying the word *you,* as in this paragraph, or writing the *you* out.

Implied "You":

"Keep your sentences short."

"You" Directly Stated:

"You should keep your sentences short."

Such a style may not win literary prizes, but it's ideal for letting a reader know "how to" do something.

For practice explaining "how to," see activity VII at the end of this chapter.

"HOW DOES IT WORK?" (EXPLAINING A PROCESS)

Sometimes we need to describe "how something works" rather than "how to do it." For example we might want to explain how athletes are selected for the Olympics, or how evolution works, or how a particular government was overthrown. Such descriptions are similar to "how-to's" in that a process is being described and the writer must remember to include all the details and steps that the reader needs to know.

The two types of writing serve different purposes, however. Whereas the purpose of "how-to" writing is to enable the reader to *do* something, the purpose of "how it works" writing is to enable the reader to *understand* something. For instance, a well-written set of directions telling me how to change my car's spark plugs might enable me to change them but not enable me to understand what a spark plug really is or how it works. A well-written explanation of how a car engine works might enable me to understand how the engine and its parts—including spark plugs—work but not enable me to maintain or fix my own car.

This difference in purpose causes two other differences between "how-to" and "how it works" writing. First, especially in writing that's only a few pages long, the scope may be different. A writer who plans to explain how to build a thermometer at home may need several pages to do it clearly, while a writer who merely wants to explain how a thermometer works may be able to explain it in less than a page. Thus, when you're explaining how to do something, you must usually narrow the subject more than when you're explaining how it works. Of course, to avoid superficiality, you must also limit the subject of "how it works" writing. Considering your intended readers, how much of the subject can you clearly describe or explain—using the necessary definitions, comparisons, examples, and details—in the number of pages you're prepared to write?

Another difference between the two types of writing is the style. When you're explaining how to do something, you can address the reader directly. But when you're explaining how something works, addressing the reader becomes tricky. For instance, in explaining how a particular government was overthrown, it would be inappropriate to write, "First, you arrange a supply of weapons." That's "how-to" writing. "How it works" writing would read, "As is often the case, the revolutionaries' first step was to arrange a supply of weapons."

Once in a while the two types of writing are combined. For example, a writer may feel that someone who understands how thermometers work will have an easier time following the directions for making one. Should you find yourself tempted to combine the two types of writing, ask yourself what your reader really needs to know. Resist the temptation to turn a recipe for making pie crust into a chemistry lesson.

See activity VII at the end of this chapter for practice in describing a process.

"WHAT'S YOUR POINT?" (ORGANIZATION PAYS)

Clear organization is essential if you want your readers to know what your main point is. Let's assume that you've finished drafting something. You've revised, you've added examples, details, and perhaps a brief comparison or two. You've deleted passages that are clearly irrelevant. Now you're ready to reorganize your material. How can you do so *in a way that will emphasize your main idea?* Let's begin where the reader does, at the beginning.

Openings

"Make your last line your first line" is standard advice to writers who wish to write clearly. It's fine advice. Put the conclusion of your rough draft (or a polished version of it) at the beginning of your final copy. If your strategy is to write clearly, don't make a mystery out of what you have to say. Say it in the first paragraph.

The following examples of opening paragraphs may lack pizzazz, but they leave little room for the reader to wonder what the point is going to be.

Opening Paragragh from a Letter:

Our latest phone bill, dated February 19, contains two errors. First, we are charged for three long-distance calls we did not make. Second, we are incorrectly charged for an extension phone. At the request of your service representative, Mr. John Bane, I'm writing to provide details of both situations.

Opening Paragraph from a Literature Paper:

In Margaret Craven's *I Heard the Owl Call My Name,* many similarities exist between Mark and the salmon. Although these similarities may at first seem coincidental, they eventually help the reader better understand Mark's life and death.

Even before the first paragraph, there's often an opportunity for writers to let their readers know exactly what they'll be reading about. Business memos, for instance, have a "subject" line near the top, to prepare the reader for what follows. This saves time and prevents misunderstandings.

Sample Subject Lines:

To:	Norman DeMello	*Date:*	Feb. 1, 1982
From:	Jane Lum		
Subject:	1983 Vacation Schedule		

To:	Elaine Nakayama	*Date:*	Nov. 11, 1982
From:	William Berry		
Subject:	Changes in our Profit-Sharing Plan		

Titles are another opportunity to let the reader know exactly what to expect. Below is a list of magazine articles. The articles could have all had the same title—"Television"— but these titles are much more precise:

Sample Titles:

"Four Arguments for the Elimination of Television"

"How Soaps Help You Cope"

"What Happened When Five Families Stopped Watching TV?"

"Design Jobs in Public Television"

"Cameras in the Courtroom"

"Educational TV Gets Failing Marks"

Many writers try not to *depend* on titles to make their subjects or ideas clear. For one thing, a very clear title is often dull. For another, readers often skip titles or read them hastily. Finally, if you write for publication, you can't count on the publication's using the same title you wrote. Editors frequently change titles to something that will "sell" better. Newspaper headlines, too, are usually written by a special headline writer, not by the reporter who wrote the story. (Have you noticed that news headlines occasionally fit the available space better than they fit the content of the story?) Thus your message should be clear without the title. Make the title an added bonus.

Middles

Throughout the middle, or body, of your writing, you can focus your reader's attention on your main idea in at least four different ways.

First, you can make sure that each paragraph really does pertain to your thesis. As you go through your rough draft, simply stop at every paragraph and ask yourself, "How is this paragraph relevant to my main idea?" If it isn't relevant, the paragraph should probably be omitted. If it is relevant, make the relevance or connection clear to your readers.

The second technique for focusing your reader's attention on your main idea has already been introduced in Chapter 7. It's using logical transitions—and lots of them. The following skeleton shows just the transitions from a piece of writing. Despite our having only the transitional words to read, the writing seems, in an eerie way, to make sense; we can follow the writer's main idea from beginning to end.[5]

There are three _____.

In the first place _____

_____. For example _____

_____. In

addition, _____

_____. In the second place _____

_____. For

instance _____. Furthermore

_____

_____. The third feature _____

_____. This feature

_____

_____. As a result, _____

_____

In conclusion, the features _____

_____. These features

_____

Imagine how transitions can help a reader focus on the main point when there's actually a point being made!

---

[5]Courtesy of Norman Roberts, from his unpublished booklet of model essays.

A third way to keep the reader's attention on the main idea, at least in long papers, is to use subheadings. Let's say you're recognized as being good at chairing committees and getting people to work well together. As a result, the head of an organization you belong to has asked you to write a report on "how to be an effective committee chairperson." If your report is only two or three pages long, it might not need subheadings to be clear. But if you discuss five different management principles, giving examples and explanations of each, your report might grow to ten or more pages. In this case, your reader would need subheadings to keep track of your ideas. Here, in much condensed form, is what your report might look like with subheadings:

HOW TO BE AN EFFECTIVE CHAIRPERSON

_____

_____

_____

_____

Establish Realistic Goals

_____

_____

_____

Know the Needs and Strengths of Your Committee Members

_____

_____

_____

Delegate Work

_____

_____

_____

Stick to Schedules

_____

_____

Let the Committee Members Take the Credit—You Take the Blame

Without the subheadings, your reader might become confused and think that your main point is "delegate work." The subheading lets the reader know that "delegate work" is only one of five points.

Finally, in addition to subheadings, occasional summaries can be used to help organize long reports. At the end of a given section, it's especially helpful if the writer briefly summarizes what has been said so far, emphasizing its connection to the main idea. In the case of the "effective chairperson," the writer could conclude the section on realistic goals something like this:

So, the first principle in chairing an efficient committee is to establish realistic objectives. With no goals, the committee can wander aimlessly. Faced with overly ambitious goals, committee members will become frustrated. However, with reasonable goals, agreed on by all, a committee can be successful—and have a yardstick by which to measure that success. Of course the success of the committee still depends on its members working together in harmony—and that brings us to our next point.

Such a paragraph summarizes what has been said about realistic goals, relates it to the main idea of being a successful chairperson, and prepares the reader for the next section of the report.

Conclusions

When your main concern is writing clearly, your concluding paragraphs should include a clear reference to your thesis. In addition, if the writing is more than a page or two long, you may want to include a brief summary of the main points you've covered.

For practice in organization, see Activity VIII.

SUMMARY OF CHAPTER

What are the chief points covered in this rather long chapter on how to write clearly and informatively? The main point is that when it comes to informative writing, "readers are not mind readers." This means you, the writer, must write clear sentences, using words that are as direct and specific as the situation allows. You must also tell your readers what they need to know, when they need to know it. This means anticipating their questions and including the definitions, comparisons, examples, or details they may need. Finally, to write clearly, you must organize the whole so that your reader never becomes so lost in your details as to lose sight of your main idea. This does not mean that you must do all these things consciously. With experience, many of them will become as automatic and natural as tying a shoelace or driving a car.

ACTIVITIES: WRITING CLEARLY

I. Clear sentences: being specific

A. The following sentences are vague. Rewrite them so they are more specific. Don't look at anyone else's rewrites until you've finished all five.

Example: Because of his sickness, he felt bad.

Because of his flu, he felt nauseous yesterday.

1. Stores are good places to get jobs.

    _____.

2. She writes good books.

    _____.

3. Painting is difficult.

    _____.

4. Marie is active in sports.

    _____.

5. I plan to double my insurance.

    _____.

B. Exchange your sentences with someone else who has done the exercise above. Note which sentences the two of you interpreted differently. Since the sentences were vague to start with, different interpretations are natural—and they show why it's important to be specific.

C. When you exchange the above sentences, note which sentences the two of you interpreted in similar ways. What accounts for the similarity? In general, what type of audience would interpret the original sentence(s) the same way you did? Could the writer count on that?

II. Clear Sentences: clear word order and clear pronouns

A. In the sentences below, either the pronouns, the word order, or both, are confusing. Rewrite each sentence so that its probable meaning is clear and direct. (You'll have to decide for yourself what the original writer meant.)

1. On Friday the Campus Cinema Club is showing a movie about sex in Stewart Hall.

   _____

   _____.

2. Leaping gracefully across the stage, I enjoyed watching the ballet dancers.

   _____

   _____.

3. The young restaurant owner told the banker that he was a successful person.

   _____

   _____.

4. I selected a book, took out my wallet, and handed it to the salesperson.

   _____

   _____.

5. Grinning broadly, the letter was held tightly in John's hand.

   _____

   _____.

6. Being in line for a promotion, the work seems more enjoyable.

   _____

   _____.

7. Being a student who works full time, a movie is a rare treat.

   _____

   _____.

8. He decided to devote his life to research, which is a good thing.

   _____

   _____.

9. Computers fascinate many people who feel they should be able to solve problems quickly.

   _____

   _____.

10. He only broke the typewriter.

   _____

   _____.

B. Read over something you've written, looking specifically for confusing word order and ambiguous pronouns. Revise whatever unclear sentences you find, then ask someone else to check your revisions. Are the sentences clearer?

III. Clear sentences: avoid gobbledygook

A. Translate the following sentences into clear, simple English:

1. Responsive personality types demonstrate behaviors such as smiling.

   _____

   _____.

2. We request that you advise this office as to your capacity for videotaping *The Sunday Night Movie* this weekend.

   _____

   _____.

3. It's incumbent upon those who utilize this library to conduct themselves in such a manner as not to distract those engaged in quiet study.

   _____

   _____.

4. The governor's action alleviated the anticipated noncompliance with the newly promulgated regulation.

   _____

   _____.

5. Preparatory to selecting a university at which to matriculate, one should prioritize one's objectives in undertaking said matriculation.

   _____

   _____.

6. Too many ponderous words render a sentence difficult to comprehend, even when the reader is cognizant of the definition of each individual word.

   _____

   _____.

B. Look for the gobbledygook in books, magazine articles, and even the letters and memos you receive. Bring the "worst" examples to class to translate and share with others. Try to decide why the writer wrote in gobbledygook rather than English.

C. Review several samples of your own writing, looking for occasional streaks of gobbledygook. If you find some, ask yourself why you wrote them. For example, are you more likely to respond with gobbledygook in some writing situations than others? Which ones? Why? Does the audience make a difference?

D. Translate passages of your own gobbledygook into clear, simple English. Share your translations with others. Are the revised versions clearer and easier to read?

IV. Definitions

A. Just for fun, try writing short, simple definitions of the following words. Assume your reader doesn't know what the words mean. Do not use a dictionary.

Typewriter: _____

_____

Boat: _____

_____

Explanation: _____

_____

Laugh: _____

_____

B. Exchange your definitions with someone else. Did you write circular definitions? Did you use words more difficult than the word you were defining?

C. Look the four words up in two or three different dictionaries. Compare the definitions given and, in each case, decide which dictionary's definition is the clearest.

D. As you read newspapers, magazines, and books, become aware of the definitions that writers have included either in the body of their writing or in footnotes. Ask yourself who the intended reader is and whether the definition has been included for that reader or for someone else. If someone else, who? Why?

E. Reread something you've written on a technical or difficult subject. Are there any words in your writing that your intended reader would not understand? Which words should you simply change, and which words should you define? Change words and write definitions where appropriate.

V. Brief comparisons

A. Think of a friend or relative who lives in a different city or state. Now imagine that in a letter you're writing to that person, you happen to mention the various distances, weights, and so forth, listed below. What brief comparison could you use to make each item graphically clear to your reader? (*Hint:* A fact book, such as the *Information Please Almanac,* might help you.)

Friend or relative you're writing to: _____

ITEM	BRIEF COMPARISON
Marathon distance of 26 miles, 385 yards	<u>606</u> times around a tennis court
Distance between your home and the classroom (__miles)	
15 pounds	
Your own weight (___pounds)	
The color of a friend's hair	
4 seconds	
speed of light (186,000 miles/sec.)	

B. Reread something you've written, looking for places where quick comparisons like those above would help your reader. Write whatever comparisons would make the writing clearer.

VI. Longer comparisons

Comparisons are useful not only to explain something clearly, but also to come to a better understanding of it ourselves. These activities will help you see how comparisons can give you new ideas:

A. WARMUP

   1. Assume that you want to understand the effect of television news coverage on viewers. To better understand that effect, you might compare TV news with newspaper news in the following way: (a) Either freewrite or brainstorm ideas on both TV news and newspaper news. (b) Review your freewriting or brainstormed lists to see what interesting similarities and differences you note. (c) Freewrite or brainstorm a list of *other* significant or interesting similarities and differences. (d) Ask yourself what really characterizes TV news—in other words, what has the comparison showed you about TV news?

   2. Follow the above directions with one or more of the comparisons below. This time you can decide which of the two items you really want to discover more about:
      school and work
      writing and talking
      golf and fishing (or any other two sports)
      being married and being single
      a movie version of a book and the book itself
      a book (or author or movie) you enjoyed and one you didn't

The reasons you stop listening to others and the reasons they stop listening to you

B. WRITING

1. Write a rough draft on any one of the ideas from Activity VI.A. You can find an audience and purpose for the draft by asking: "Who should be interested in hearing this?" or "Who would benefit by hearing this?"

2. One of the most common (and frustrating) contrasts in life is often the contrast between what someone or something appears to be and what that person or thing is really like. A musician's performance, for instance, may seem effortlessly easy when in fact it takes a great deal of practice, energy, and discipline. A person who seems self-confident and boisterous may in fact be nervous and riddled with self-doubt.

   Brainstorm a list of activities, people, and things that appear to be different from what they are. Select one or two items from your list and brainstorm details concerning both the appearance and the reality. Take as your audience either someone who would be interested in learning what you have to say or someone who could profit by it. Draft and revise an appropriate article, letter, or report. (If you select a writing situation that will call for tactful writing, read Chapter 16.)

3. Stereotypes of various groups of people (ethnic groups, the elderly, the young, for example) are often based on superficial appearances rather than reality. Brainstorm a list of stereotypes that you feel are false. Select one or two and then follow the directions in 2 above.

4. Brainstorm a list of things you feel have changed significantly over time. (For example: Word processors compared to conventional typewriters, new generation computers compared to the original ones, or sports training methods today compared to those 25 years ago.) Select one item from your list to write about, explaining the change to someone who would otherwise not be aware of it. (Note: Once again, if you select an emotional or controversial subject, you'll need to write persuasively (see Chapters 16 and 17) as well as clearly.

C. READING

As you read newspapers, magazines, and books, look for long comparisons. (For example, writers frequently compare what things are like with what they used to be like, or with what the writer feels they should be like.) When you find comparisons, ask yourself if the comparison helps the intended audience understand the writer's ideas. If so, how?

VII. Examples, details, and "how to."

A.

1. If you have a job or do volunteer work, imagine that you've been promoted and asked to write a set of "how-to" directions for your replacement.

Limiting yourself to a part of your job that can be fully explained in three pages or less, write the directions.

2. Now imagine that your organization puts out a newsletter that is mailed to customers or to the public. Further imagine that your supervisor has asked you to write a one- or two-page description of your job to be included in the next isssue. Unlike the "how to" that you wrote for your replacement, this description will be designed to give outsiders an idea of what you do. The two pieces of writing should therefore be quite different.

B.
1. If you have a hobby, imagine that you've been asked to write a series of "how-to" columns for beginners. Select a process that you can fully explain in three pages or less, and write a sample column.

2. Now imagine that you've been asked to write a general interest article on your hobby. This time you're to explain what people with your hobby "do," but you're to write it for outsiders. Instead of explaining how to, this time you'll be explaining how it works.

C. As you read various manuals and textbooks, notice the "how-to" and "how it works" writing. Locate some examples that seem clearly written and others that seem confusing. Compare the two sets, asking yourself what makes the difference.

VIII.   Organization

A. Reread something you've written recently. Did you make your last line your first line? Should you have?

B. Make a copy of something you've written, and then cut the paragraphs apart with scissors. Ask someone who has not read that piece of writing before to see if they can reassemble the paragraphs in the original order. (Be sure your scissor cuts don't give them clues.) Repeat the experiment with a second person. If both people can reassemble your writing in its original order, your transitions and organization were probably clear. If one could and one couldn't, the problem *might* be in your writing. If neither of them could judge the original order, the problem is most likely with your writing.

C. If you've written something longer than five typed pages, check to see if you used subheadings. If you didn't, try adding some.

D. Locate a magazine or newspaper article you think is clearly written. Ask yourself what devices the writer has used to make the organization clear.

chapter 13

To Write Interestingly, Give Your Readers a Reason to Read

When do you need to write interestingly? Whenever the intended reader has no natural need or desire to read what you have written.

To take a very practical example, let's say one of your friends has started a small "instant copy" business near the university and he has asked you to help with the advertising. Your first draft of the ad tells the readers what they need to know: the business's name, location, phone, and operating hours. It also contains the line:

Try Copious Copies the next time you need copies made.

After a break, you reread your draft and decide that it's dull. The student audience you want to attract wouldn't read it. Even if they did, they wouldn't remember it. In short, you need to make your ad more interesting to the potential customers.

Just as potential customers don't have to read ads, no one has to read anything you write. Some people, such as teachers, may have to skim your writing, but no one has to read it attentively. Making them *want* to is up to you.

This chapter presents six techniques you can use to give your readers a reason to read:

Appeal to the readers' self-interest
Establish common ground
Build curiosity or suspense
Write vivid descriptions
Polish your sentence style
Use clever quotations and titles

The exercises are all at the end of the chapter.

ESTABLISH COMMON GROUND

Common ground is like a handshake. It's a reference to something the reader and writer have in common: a shared feeling, interest, or belief. When public speakers begin with a joke or two, they're really establishing common ground with the audience. In addition to being funny, the joke says: "Hey, we all have a shared sense of humor. We're the same kind of people."

Writers sometimes begin with a touch of humor for this same reason. There are also other ways of establishing common ground with the reader. One way is to begin with some aspect of the subject that you both find interesting. For example, Jodi Baba, a student, wanted to describe the planning and effort that go into the band performances put on during halftime at football games. Her intended audience was football fans who don't bother to watch the halftime entertainment. In her draft, she began with her main idea:

LACKS COMMON GROUND

Many football fans take the halftime entertainment of the marching band for granted. They don't realize all the time, effort, and hard work that go into the production of a halftime show. . . .

This beginning may say what Jodi has in mind, but it neglects her intended audience. There's nothing for them to relate to in such a beginning. Therefore in revising her draft, Jodi wrote a new introductory paragraph:

ESTABLISHES COMMON GROUND

The score is 21 to 14. It's the fourth down with five yards to go and twelve seconds left on the clock for the second quarter. The play is made, but it is interrupted by the gun that signifies the end of the first half. As you rush to the nearest concession stand for a hot dog and a coke, you are surrounded by the sounds of a drum cadence as the marching band takes the field. You get back to your seat just in time to see the final number of the show. As the band marches off the field, you turn to your friend and simply say, "I forgot the mustard!"

This paragraph begins with common ground. It shows that Jodi knows what halftime is like for a football fan. Reassured by such a beginning, football fans—Jodi's intended audience—are more likely to read the rest of Jodi's writing. By the way, Jodi's revised conclusion makes a full circle to her introduction:

ENDING WITH COMMON GROUND

So, the next time you're at a football game and halftime rolls around, rush back to your seat after getting your hot dog and coke. Then sit back, relax, and enjoy the halftime entertainment. Oh, and don't forget the mustard!

Common ground can also be seen at work in the following professionally written newspaper column. The author, Dr. Leonard Reiffel, is primarily explaining why birds fly in V formations, but he seems to assume that his readers aren't interested in bird aerodynamics. What does he assume they are interested in? Where else, besides at the opening, does Dr. Reiffel establish a common ground of interest or information with his readers?

WHY BIRDS FLY IN V-FORMATION[1]

. . . One of the most stirring sights of the fall is the migrational flight of birds flying south in majectic V formation. Almost everyone gets a special thrill out of seeing a gaggle of geese passing overhead in their beautiful V formations.

The common sense explanation as to why birds fly in V formation is that there is a lead bird and that the other birds fly in a V around the lead bird to see exactly where he is going. Then they can all keep together and get to the same place. This explanation turns out to be wrong.

Upon a little reflection, you will see that there are many other kinds of formations in which the birds could maintain visual contact with each other and could tell that they are going in the same direction. So why do many different species of birds all characteristically fly in V's?

This question once interested scientists at Cal Tech in Pasadena, California. Cal Tech has a large crew of aerodynamics experts. A couple of them got together and, with a computer and other kinds of sophisticated analysis techniques, finally figured out why birds fly in V formation. The answer is this: The birds are lazy and that is the easiest way to fly. If a group of 25 birds flies in a V formation, they can fly about 70 per cent further as compared to flying alone.

The reason is that the formation acts together and equally distributes wind drag across all the birds. This reduces the wind drag on each individual bird by a corresponding amount.

One other thing that we might expect based on common sense also turns out to be wrong on the basis of this analysis. One would think that the lead bird had the toughest time. If the birds get help from flying in a V, one would think that the help would come from the birds ahead to the birds behind.

However, since the whole formation acts together more or less like a single wing, the lead bird is not working any harder than any other birds. He achieves this by falling slightly behind where he should be to make a perfect V.

According to the computer calculations, a close look at a V formation shows that the bird at the tip and the birds at the very back end of the V are a little off position. This gives each bird an equal amount of drag and distributes the load uniformly.

---

[1]Dr. Leonard Reiffel, "Why Birds Fly in V-Formation." Courtesy of the author.

The birds presumably have a social organization that prevents any one bird from lagging so far behind that he rides in the wake of everybody else. Thus, all the birds do equal work.

Calculations show also that the V does not have to be equal on both sides. You no doubt have seen many occasions in which the V is much longer on one leg than on the other. The birds are really being quite smart because this doesn't change the drag. . . .

Dr. Leonard Reiffel

We'll discuss Dr. Reiffel's column in more detail later. First let's look at two examples of common ground you've already read: Frances Katano's article on dining out (Chapter 2) and Janet Fuller's letter of instruction to Heather, the new employee at Bigman's store (Chapter 7). Frances' intended audience is people who eat out and meekly leave tips even when the service is poor. To avoid alienating them, Frances began with common ground, something her readers could agree with. In her draft, the common ground was a bit long-winded:

In our busy society, eating out has become America's favorite pastime. Many of us enjoy eating out as a form of recreation, a stopping point in our busy lives, or just a necessary part of human existence.

In her final copy, she retains the idea of the common ground but softens it and makes it apply more directly to her readers. She then introduces her main idea—but quietly:

You have probably been out to dinner at one time or another. Dining out is fun, but sometimes little problems with the service, if not handled correctly, can ruin an evening.

Later in her final copy Frances adds another piece of common ground: "I used to think it was rude to return the dinner." This is a way of saying to her readers: "I know that you don't want to be rude; I don't either. We agree on that. But returning poorly prepared food isn't rude."

Janet's letter of instructions to Heather also begins (and ends) with common ground:

Dear Heather,

Welcome to Bigman's. By now you will have been given many general rules and regulations of the company. Please don't let them scare you off. After a while you'll find them easy to apply. As your trainer, I've been asked to give you an overview of the work to be learned for your specific department: The Snack Bar. . . .

This has been a broad overview of the procedures in our department. I'm sure you will find the work not difficult and your new co-workers a pleasure to work with. I look forward to working with you soon.

Sincerely yours,
Janet

The beginning is like a friendly handshake. As Heather reads it, she sees that even though Janet is her trainer, they have something in common: Janet understands Heather's dismay at the pages of regulations and instructions she's already received. The ending, too, is like a tactful handshake, reassuring Heather that the common ground established at the beginning wasn't just a gimmick.

Janet's letter, however, brings us to the question of when to use common ground. In a slightly different situation, perhaps one where Heather was already very motivated to read the instructions carefully, such attention to establishing common ground might not be necessary.

The common ground in Dr. Reiffel's article on birds is also necessary because of the audience: people who are more interested in birds than in science. How would Dr. Reiffel have to change the article if he were writing for a scientifically minded audience?

In general, the more you and your intended reader are alike, the less you have to worry about establishing common ground; the greater the difference between you and your intended audience, the more desirable it may be to establish common ground. Once again, let your responses to the Writing Process Worksheet in Chapter 11 be your guide.

Occasionally, you'll find that you have a split audience: part of the audience is interested in one thing, while others are interested in something else. This type of audience can be very difficult to write for. Still, if you must write for a split audience, establishing common ground with each faction of the audience can help. That's what Selma Lynch, a student, did in a travel article she wrote on Hawaii. In her article, she wanted to describe both the hustle-bustle of Waikiki and the quiet pleasures of the rural areas. Here's the beginning of her final copy:

Hawaii is the best of many worlds. Whether you enjoy feeling the disco beat on a Friday night or singing along with the soft strum of a guitar on a hot Sunday afternoon, then Waikiki is the place to be. From the hustling city life to the slow, mellow style of the country, this island paradise offers more than its share of attractions. The streets of Waikiki, with their elegant hotels, cosmopolitan men and women, and bar-hopping, disco-dancing night life, contribute to the fast-moving city environment. But Hawaii also has country towns such as Haleiwa, with its houses on the shores and horses in the pasture. Along the main road of Haleiwa you'll find the old community church and a "shave ice" store as well as a new, but wood-structured, shopping complex.

And here's her conclusion:

The island of Oahu, along with the other islands of Hawaii, offers something for everyone. So whether it's the city life, country life, or just mere relaxation you're looking for, head over to Hawaii and enjoy it all.

You may notice that Selma's introduction, and especially her conclusion, not only establish common ground—they also appeal to the reader's self-interest. (See Activity I at the end of this chapter for practice with common ground and appealing to the reader's self-interest.)

APPEAL TO THE READERS' SELF-INTEREST

An honest appeal to your reader's self-interest is another useful technique. For example, you might begin revising the Copious Copies ad referred to earlier by asking yourself, "Why should students who need copies made read this ad?" Your first response might be something like "Because my friend needs the business." However, that's not looking at it from the reader's point of view. Ask yourself, "What's in it for the reader?" The answer to that question, you might decide, is that Copious Copies is cheaper than the library copies and faster than the popular Quick-Fix copies down the street. You can now add that information to the ad itself:

Need copies made quick and cheap? Price at the library too high? Lines at your old copy service too long? Save yourself time and money. Try the new one. Try Copious Copies.

Appeals to the reader's self-interest aren't limited to advertising. Whenever we ask someone to do something—whether it's to replace defective merchandise, to contribute to the local Community Fund, or to vote for our choice of candidate—an appeal to the reader's self-interest can be an effective way to begin. Consider the two letters below. Which would you be more likely to continue reading if you were a merchant and had little or no interest in the local baseball team?

Version A

Dear Mr. Skinflint:

Our baseball team needs uniforms. Our present uniforms are old and worn out. Besides, the current uniforms don't fit our new players. . . .

Version B

Dear Mr. Skinflint:

How would you like to see the Skinflint Drugstore advertised all over town during every baseball season? Our baseball team's uniforms can carry the Skinflint Drugstore name and logo everywhere the players go: into the crowded Beefy Burgers after the games, into the supermarket, into the shopping center, and, of course, onto the playing field. . . .

The difference between the two versions? One is concerned with the team's self-interest while the other is concerned with Mr. Skinflint's. If you find that your own drafts read more like Version A than Version B, you may want to add another step to your revising process. Simply make a list of all the advantages your reader can gain by reading what you have to say. Then select one or two of them and revise your draft to appeal to your reader's self-interest. Such an appeal will not only motivate your reader to read, it can also persuade him or her to accept your idea.

To be effective, of course, appeals to the reader's self-interest must be honest. For instance, if the lines at Copious Copy are as long as the lines at Quick-Fix, or would be when readers responded to the ad, then the appeal would succeed only once. A reader who is enticed by an opening such as "You too can make a million dollars a year using borrowed money" may well stop reading when it becomes clear that the opening was a fraud. When you begin with an appeal to your reader's self-interest, you have to deliver what you promise.

Sometimes, however, being honest isn't enough. A bit of tact may also be necessary. For instance, a student wrote the following opening paragraph for an article on alcoholism:

In the United States, drinking has become a major problem. So, too, has alcoholism. But most problem drinkers either don't realize they're alcoholics, or they just can't face the fact that they are. So who are these alcoholics? What is alcoholism, really? How serious is it?

Wesley Ando, student

Wesley's audience are people who might, without realizing it, either be alcoholic themselves or have an alcoholic friend or relative. Obviously this intended audience would benefit from reading the article. But a direct appeal to their self-interest might not be a good idea. Something like, "Are *you* an alcoholic? Is your spouse?" might scare off the very readers Wesley had in mind. Therefore Wesley wisely chose to omit the word *you* from his introduction. That tactful omission permits the reader to read on without having admitted anything. An indirect appeal such as this is often best when the subject is touchy or the reader might take offense.

What to Avoid

Consider the following opening paragraph from a memo an employee wrote to Mrs. Waters, the manager of a fast food restaurant:

Since beginning work at Beefy Burgers seven months ago, I've been impressed by the emphasis placed on happy, satisfied customers. A satisfied customer will not only return, but may spread the word about Beefy Burgers. That's why I think you will be interested in considering a procedure that will provide our customers with even faster service during rush hours. . . .

This paragraph appeals to Mrs. Waters' self-interest: the more customers Beefy Burgers has, the better off Mrs. Waters will be. But is the paragraph appropriate? That depends on Mrs. Waters. If, for example, she requested a report on ways to improve service, then the appeal to her self-interest is embarrassingly overdone. A general rule of thumb might be: If your reader has requested a report or has already shown interest in what you have to say, don't belabor the obvious with an appeal to his or her self-interest. Let your answers to the "audience" questions on the Writing Process Worksheet (Chapter 11) help you decide whether to appeal to your reader's self-interest.

Dishonesty is another pitfall to avoid in appeals to the reader's self-interest. One must be careful not to be so carried away with enthusiasm as to stretch the truth or cynically manipulate the reader. Either one can quickly undermine a writer's credibility and self-respect. Remember, effective appeals to the reader's self-interest call attention to *genuine* advantages to the reader.

BUILD CURIOSITY OR SUSPENSE

You're at the movies. The opening shot is of a cemetery in late autumn. Only the gray tombstones relieve the brownness of the once-green grass. The trees are starkly bare, their last leaves now mottled lumps on the ground. The camera slowly focuses on a young woman in her mid-twenties. The woman is obviously grieving.

After this opening shot, the movie jumps back to the woman's wedding day five years earlier and picks up the thread of the story from there. The flashforward at the beginning has let you and the rest of the audience know that someone close to the woman is going to die. But who? Her husband? A child? Someone else? And why? And how? You watch the rest of the movie to find out. The opening scene has piqued your curiosity—and built suspense.

The opening scene has also used a technique that, in its more subtle forms, is called *foreshadowing*. This technique not only builds a reader's interest in how something happened, it also invites the reader to "think along" with the movie or author.

The following paragraph, for example, is taken from a student letter to a campus newspaper. (You may remember it from Chapter 3.) The writer invites readers to think along with her as she explores the healthfulness of the food offered for sale on campus:

Today for lunch I had a Pepsi, a package of nuts layered in salt, and a burrito supreme. I'll have something similar tomorrow. Am I becoming a junk food addict? Yes, it appears that way, at least for as long as I attend Shelton College. Certainly, among Shelton's four dining options I should find something nutritionally wholesome. Let's visit each of the four and see if I can.

Although the writer has already said it "appears" that Shelton College is turning her into a junk food addict, the reader reads on to see if, indeed, there is no healthful food to be found in the lunch wagons, the cafeteria, the vending machines, or the Gourmet Dining Room. Just as with a mystery movie or novel, the reader is thinking along with the author.

Raise Questions

Using questions is perhaps the easiest way to invite the reader to think along with you. For example, Wesly Ando uses questions in the opening paragraph of his report on alcoholism. When we looked at that paragraph a few pages back, we were concerned with Wesley's appeal to his reader's self-interest. But note that the paragraph also builds the reader's curiosity.

In the United States, drinking has become a major problem. So, too, has alcoholism. But most problem drinkers either don't realize they're alcoholics, or they just can't face the fact that they are. So who are these alcoholics? What is alcoholism, really? How serious is it?

We can also see questions at work in the following passage by Isaac Asimov, a well-known professional writer. The passage is an excerpt from Asimov's book, *The Universe*.[2]

There must have been in the ancient empires those who occupied themselves with what might be considered the first cosmological problem facing scholars: Is there an end to the Earth? *question*

To be sure, no man in ancient times, however far he traveled, ever came to any actual end of the Earth. At most, he reached the shore of an ocean whose limits were beyond the horizon. If he transferred to a ship and sailed outward, he never succeeded in reaching the end either.

Did that mean there was no end? *question*

The answer to that question depended on the general shape one assumed for the Earth.

All men, before the time of the Greeks, made the assumption that the Earth was flat, as indeed it appears to be, barring the minor irregularities of the mountains and valleys. If any pre-Greek ancient thought otherwise, his name has not come down to us and the record of his thinking has not survived.

Yet if the Earth were indeed flat, an end of some sort would seem an almost foregone conclusion. The alternative would be a flat surface that would go on forever and forever—one that would be infinite in extent, in other words. This is a most uncomfortable concept; throughout history, men have tended to avoid the concept of endlessness in either space or time as something impossible to grasp and understand and therefore something that cannot easily be worked with or reasoned about.

On the other hand, if the Earth does have an end—if it is finite—there are other difficulties. Would not people fall off if they approached that end too closely? *question*

Of course, it might be that the dry land was surrounded by ocean on all sides so that people could not approach the end unless they deliberately boarded a ship and sailed out of sight of land; far out of sight. As late as the time of Columbus, in fact, this was indeed a very real fear for many seamen.

The thought of such a watery protection of mankind raised another point, however. What was to prevent the ocean from pouring off the ends and draining away from the Earth? *question*

One way out of this dilemma was to suppose that the sky above was a solid shield as, indeed, it appears to be[1], and that it came down to meet the Earth on all sides, as it appears to do. In that case, the entire Universe might be thought to consist of a kind of box, with the sky making up the curved top and sides, while the flat bottom is the sea and dry land on which man and all other things live and move.

[2]From *The Universe: From Flat Earth to Black Holes and Beyond* by Isaac Asimov. Copyright © 1966 by Isaac Asimov. Used with permission from the publisher, Walker and Company.

What might the shape and size of such a "box-Universe" be? *question*

To many, it seemed a rectangular slab. It is an interesting accident of history and geography that the first civilizations on the Nile, the Tigris-Euphrates, and the Indus Rivers were separated east and west, rather than north and south. Moreover, the Mediterranean Sea runs east and west. The dim geographical knowledge of early civilized man therefore expanded more easily east and west than north and south. It seems reasonable to picture the "box-Universe" then as considerably longer east-west than north-south.

¹ The biblical term "firmament" attests to the primitive belief of the sky as a "firm" object, a solid substance.

Reading a passage like this is rather like going on an adventure with the writer. Asimov clearly leads the reader from question to question. A tentative answer to one question immediately gives rise to a new question. The suspense keeps the readers reading even though they already know that the earth is round, not flat. In fact, knowing that the earth is round provides a kind of foreshadowing that makes this passage even more suspenseful: How did the ancient thinkers figure it out?

This movement from a wrong answer to a right one is another technique for building curiosity. In his article on birds Dr. Reiffel twice uses a "wrong" idea as the introduction to the "right" idea:

The common sense explanation as to why birds fly in V formation is that there is a lead bird and that the other birds fly in a V around the lead bird to see exactly where he is going. Then they can all keep together and get to the same place. This explanation turns out to be wrong. *wrong explanation*

Upon a little reflection, you will see that there are many other kinds of formations in which the birds could maintain usual contact with each other and could tell that they are going in the same direction. So why do many different species of birds all characteristically fly in V's? *why it's wrong*

This question once interested scientists at Cal Tech in Pasadena, California. Cal Tech has a large crew of aerodynamics experts. A couple of them got together and with a computer and other kinds of sophisticated analysis techniques, finally figured out why birds fly in V formation. The answer is this: The birds are lazy and that is the easiest way to fly. If a group of 25 birds flies in a V formation, they can fly about 70 percent further as compared to flying alone. *the correct explanation*

One other thing that we might expect based on common sense also turns out to be wrong on the basis of this analysis. One

165

```
would think that the lead bird had the toughest time.  If the
birds get help from flying in a V, one would think that the help
would come from the birds ahead to the birds behind.
```
wrong explanation

```
     However, since the whole formation acts together more or less
like a single wing, the lead bird is not working any harder than
any other birds.  He achieves this by falling slightly behind
where he should be to make a perfect V.
```
correct explanation

Note the tactful way Dr. Reiffel introduces the "wrong" idea: "The common sense explanation . . ." and "One other thing that we might expect based on common sense. . . ." (He doesn't write "You may be mistakenly thinking. . . .") Note also that in both cases he quickly lets his readers know that the common sense explanation "turns out to be wrong." The reader then becomes curious to know what the right explanation might be.

Another way to build your readers' curiosity and invite them to think along with you is to imply rather than state your thesis. Dr. Reiffel, you'll note, withholds the real reason that birds fly in V formation until almost halfway through his article. Sometimes writers go further and don't state the thesis at all. On page 78, for example, you read a description of the changes that have occurred in fireman. The author, Allison Clough, clearly states half of this thesis: changes have occurred. But he doesn't spell out the other half: he doesn't like the changes very much. Instead, he describes the changes in such a way that his readers will know how he feels without having to be told. How does he do this? Largely by using positive, emotional words to describe the firemen of old and neutral words to describe modern firefighters. The technique is clearly seen in the last paragraph:

```
     Of course we still ride on fire trucks, light and sirens
pulsing, but the fire trucks I remember from childhood were ex-
quisitely large and shiny red.  Today the fire trucks are still
large, and with an extreme amount of hard work, they do shine.
But they're no longer red.  Now they are "high visibility" yellow.
True, yellow is more readily seen.  But yellow is yellow, not
glorious red.
```
lets us know how he feels

Allison doesn't have to add: "I prefer red and don't like the new changes."

Finally, a writer can create interest and build curiosity by beginning with a provocative statement. It need not be the writer's main idea. For example, one student began an article this way: "I can tell you more about my mother's childhood than my own." The sentence intrigues the reader, who immediately wants to know why. Curiosity is aroused.

WRITE VIVID DESCRIPTIONS

The crowd stands at the graveside: a funeral is taking place. Suddenly one of the onlookers, a boy, bursts into uncontrollable laughter. The mourners are shocked at first, then realize something strange has happened. He is led away. It turns out that a blood-vessel in his brain has burst, flooding the third ventricle—the open space in the centre of the brain. An event known to doctors as a subarachnoid haemorrhage.

Now the scene is a railway train. One of the passengers in the carriage is a girl, returning home after her day's work. She begins to laugh uproariously. The other passengers stare. She becomes intensely embarrassed, but continues to rock with laughter, tears running down her cheeks. As the passengers begin to mutter, the train stops. Although it is not her destination, the girl staggers from the train and clings to the railings, laughing frantically. Two months later she develops a severe paralysis of her left side.

Gordon Rattray Taylor

These are the first two paragraphs of Gordon Rattray Taylor's book, *The Natural History of the Mind*.[3] The book is scientific, yet it begins more like a short story or novel. Why? Because Taylor is writing for nonscientists and wants to make them curious enough to read on. His technique for arousing their curiosity is simply to begin with an anecdote that contains a conflict. In this case the conflict is the incompatibility of laughter with gravesides and trains. The reader wants to learn more, wants to know what causes the laughter.

In addition to the conflict, Taylor uses another technique: in describing the scene, he *shows* his reader what happens. He doesn't just *tell* them. He chooses vivid words so the readers can see the girl "*rock* with laughter," as she "*staggers* from the train and *clings* to the *railings*." Also he uses the present tense to put the reader right in the middle of the action. Compare Taylor's actual opening paragraphs with the less descriptive version below:

There was a boy who suffered a subarachnoid haemorrhage at a funeral. It caused him to laugh uncontrollably. In another example of a similar phenomenon, a girl was incapacitated with laughter on a railway train. She later developed a paralysis of one side.

In Taylor's own version we see the scenes for ourselves. In the version above we've merely been told about them. Which is more interesting? Which gives us a reason to continue reading?

Sensory Details

The real question, of course, is how to bring a passage such as the one above to life. One way is to use more details. Taylor's passage tells us about the crowd as well as the boy. It also tells us more about the girl: the girl is returning home from work, she feels

---

embarrassed by her laughter, she gets off at a stop that's not her destination. Details permit the reader to see the scene. Indeed, Taylor could have used even more details to help us: How did the boy behave when he was being led away? Who was being buried? What color was the girl's dress? Her hair? What did she do for a living? Details could go on endlessly: Where was the funeral? What did the other mourners look like? What time of year was it? What was the weather like? What did the other people on the train look like? What was the inside of the train like?

The writer must decide what's important to the scene and concentrate on creating that impression. In *The Natural History of the Mind,* Taylor used the opening scenes as examples to illustrate a point about brain functions. He therefore wanted the reader's attention focused on the behavior of the boy and girl, and he selected details to accomplish that. A more detailed description of the setting—or even of what the boy and girl looked like—wasn't necessary for his purpose and might distract the reader.

Let's turn to another example. The following passage is not very descriptive, even though the writer's purpose is to let the reader know exactly what her boss looks like. It's an early draft.

I had always been afraid of my boss. He wasn't really tall, but he seemed tall. He was heavy, with big shoulders and a pot belly. I usually saw him wearing a bathing suit. He was a very nervous man who moved around a lot.

The first sentence is great: The word *had* provokes curiosity. But on rereading this draft, the writer, Linda Hee, asked herself: "What does my boss really look like? What does his face look like? His shoulders? What does he look like when he's nervously moving around? Her answers provided her with enough details to substantially revise the draft, which eventually contained the following paragraphs. You may recognize them from Chapter 2.

I had always been afraid of my boss. He was not tall, but his extremely large girth made him seem so. His wide meaty shoulders supported a large head that spouted thick, dark hair in constant disarray. His face was partially hidden by a wiry mustache that curved downward at the ends, giving him an appearance of a constant scowl. Underneath his shoulders a massive paunch bulged over his bathing suit--his only attire in the two years we worked together in his palatial home.

describes his face and body

He was a very nervous, aggressive man, constantly moving in circles, always puffing on an endless chain of cigarettes. Great clouds of smoke billowed from underneath his mustache, punctuated by an incessant smoker's cough. The more nervous and excited he became, the faster he would twirl in circles, his elbow working like a motorized hinge pumping cigarettes to his mouth while keeping pace with his feet.

describes motion and energy

How can you include details as rich as Linda's? The first step is not in the writing, or even the rewriting. It's in the observing. If you don't see that the boss twirls in circles, for example, or that his mustache is like wire and curves downward at the ends, you can't include those details in your writing. To write descriptively, you need a rich store of details from which to draw. We call these details *sensory* because they come to us through our five senses: we see, hear, smell, taste, and touch them.

But learning to see—and hear, smell, taste, and touch—details can take some practice. We have all learned to filter out background noises and sights in order to avoid sensory overload. To become a descriptive writer, you must practice unfiltering a bit. Here's a procedure to help: Whenever you're waiting for class to begin, or for the bus to come, or for the light to change, select a sense and concentrate on it. What exactly do you see, for instance? What shapes? Textures? Colors? Motion? Or what do you hear? As each sound registers, listen for others that you had filtered out without even realizing it. What about touch? What does the steering wheel, pen, or inside of your pocket feel like to your fingertips? Rough or smooth? Cold or warm? What do you smell? Taste?

It's impossible to concentrate on information from all of the senses at once. And its impossible to be aware of sensory details when you're preoccupied with thoughts. An exercise like this reminds you to stop thinking and start seeing, hearing, smelling, tasting, or touching. Best of all, you can do it with time you might otherwise waste.

When you use sensory detail in your descriptions, be certain to select details that will work together to create the impression you want. For example, all of the details Linda uses contribute to the single impression she's trying to create: her boss is a fearsome man.

Vivid Verbs

Of course, sensory details alone don't create vivid descriptions. Vivid verbs also play a role, especially if we include verbs that end in *-ing* or *-ed* and act like adjectives. Reread Linda's paragraphs, studying the italicized words:

I had always been afraid of my boss. He was not tall, but his extremely large girth made him seem so. His wide, meaty shoulders *supported* a large head that *sprouted* thick, dark hair in constant disarray. His face was partially *hidden* by a wiry mustache that *curved* downward at the ends, giving him an appearance of a constant scowl. Underneath his shoulders a massive paunch *bulged* over his bathing suit—his only attire in the two years we worked together in his palatial home.

He was a very nervous, aggressive man, constantly *moving* in circles, always *puffing* on an endless chain of cigarettes. Great clouds of smoke *billowed* from underneath his mustache, *punctuated* by an incessant smoker's cough. The more nervous and excited he became, the faster he would *twirl* in circles, his elbow *working* like a motorized hinge *pumping* cigarettes to his mouth while keeping pace with his feet.

The verbs Linda chose to use create an overwhelming impression of motion and vitality. Compare them with the verbs in the early draft: *wasn't, seemed, was, saw, wearing, was, moved.* How did Linda think of the more vivid verbs? Partly by concentrating on the details of what her boss really looked like. Partly by concentrating on the verbs, asking herself what verbs would create the impression she wanted. And partly by using a thesaurus.

A thesaurus is a handy collection of synonyms, words that mean roughly the same thing. Most book stores carry the oldest and best-known thesaurus, Roget's, which is available in a paperback edition that's arranged alphabetically and is very convenient to use. There's a trick to using a thesaurus wisely: It should be used to jog your memory, not to find a "new" word to use. The reason is that no two words ever have exactly the same meaning. Sometimes the difference is subtle and is in the feeling or context associated with the word rather than in the dictionary meaning.[4] For instance, let's say that Linda had originally written, "His face was partially covered by a mustache" and she wanted a more precise, more vivid word than *covered.* Looking in *Roget's Thesaurus in Dictionary Form,* she wouldn't find *cover,* but she would find *covering.* Part of that entry would include synonyms for *cover* and *covered:*

> **COVERING**—*N.* **covering,** cover, shelter, screen, coverture, integument, tegument; lid, top, coverlid; rug, carpet, runner, scatter rug, throw rug, carpeting; curtain, drape; blanket, bower, canopy, cap, caparison, cloak, mantle, muffler, pall, panoply, shelter, shroud, shutter, swathe, wraps, antimacassar, cozy.
>
> **hood,** bonnet, cowl, capote.
>
> **crust,** coating, coat, bloom, encrustation, incrustation, efflorescence (*chem.*), scale, scab, slough (*med.*), eschar (*med.*).
>
> **peel,** rind, bark, husk, shell, hull, cortex.
>
> **sheath,** sheathing, capsule, pod, casing, case, involucrum (*zool.*), wrapping, wrapper, jacket, envelope, vagina.
>
> **veneer,** facing, leaf, layer; paint, stain, varnish, gloss, enamel, wash, washing, whitewash, plaster, stucco; gilt, gilding, overlay.
>
> **horse blanket,** horsecloth, body cloth, blanket; caparison, housing, housings, trappings; harness, saddle.
>
> **roof,** ceiling, roofing, top, housetop; cupola, dome, vault, terrace, spire, thatched roof; canopy, marquee, awning; calash; attic, garret, loft; rafter, coaming, eaves.
>
> *V.* **cover,** superimpose, overlay, overspread, envelop, clothe, invest, wrap, incase; face, case, veneer, paper; clapboard, weatherboard, shingle; conceal, curtain, hide, cloak, hood, shelter, shield, screen, protect.
>
> **coat,** paint, stain, varnish, incrust, crust, cement, stucco, plas-

(handwritten annotations: nouns *— bracketing the first section;* verbs *— bracketing the* V. cover *section;* major differences in meaning *— pointing to* cover *and* coat*)*

---

[4] The feelings associated with words are called *connotations* and are discussed in more detail in Chapter 16.

semicolons separate sets of words with similar meanings

adjectives

If Linda were simply looking for a fancy new word, she could choose *veneer*. But to write that her boss's face was "partially veneered by a mustache" would be silly. Although both words mean "to cover," *veneer* is inappropriate because veneers are usually used to create a deceptively elegant appearance: fine wood veneers are typically applied over cheaper woods. *Veneer* doesn't seem to fit Linda's boss. In fact, of all the words given as synonyms for *cover* and *covered*, only a few would work in Linda's sentence. The bold-face type indicates special meanings: *coated, scaly, overlapping,* and *roofed*. These words are obviously inappropriate to Linda's sentence. And, as we've seen, even a synonym listed under the simple word *cover* could be treacherous if the writer were not already familiar with the word's normal use. That's why the thesaurus should never be used to provide a new word. As a memory aid, though, it can't be beat. Just for fun, look over the synonyms for *cover* and see if there are any others that would do as well as, or better than, the word *hide* in Linda's sentence. Remember, the dominant impression you create should be that the man is energetic and frightening.

Comparisons

In addition to sensory details and vivid verbs, writers can use interesting comparisons to bring a description to life. In the last chapter, for example, you read a comparison designed to give a specific reader a clear idea of the blue whale's length:

The blue whale is as long as one-third the length of a football field.

Seeing a similarity between two things that are otherwise different can give the reader a pleasant shock of recognition. In the above example the recognition depends upon the reader's being familiar with football fields. In the following draft, Mary E. Pollard, a writing student, draws a comparison that depends upon her reader's knowing a common childhood game:

```
Two wreckers were at the scene of the accident, one in front
of the truck and the other behind the silvery car.  Both wreckers
were driving in opposite directions, trying to pry the car and
truck apart.  The road was blocked off with spurting red flares,
directing all traffic to the left lane, to keep traffic flowing
steadily.  The way the wreckers were pulling the two cars
reminded me of people playing tug-of-war, with one group trying to    Comparison
get the rope from the other....
```

Later in this same description Mary used another comparison most readers would recognize: "The way the truck was being jacked up from behind made me think of a horse about to use his hind legs to kick someone."

Some writers prefer to draw comparisons that are closer to the subject under discussion than are football fields to whales or childhood games to traffic accidents. For example, to keep the imagery aquatic, one could say that the blue whale was "one-fifth the length of a luxury liner." Sometimes a comparison can be found within the scene or subject itself: "The old man was as thin as the fishing pole gripped in his hand." Or, "Their anger steamed as hot as the asphalt they had just poured." But the source of the comparison isn't as important as whether it fits the dominant impression the writer is trying to create. In the following paragraph from her description of her boss, Linda Hee uses two comparisons:

```
My desk was in the library; his was around the corner in the
living room.  Unfortunately, he chose to share my desk.  Every day
he sat across from me on one of the kitchen stools that he dragged
across his freshly vacuumed Chinese rugs, leaving tracks like skis
over newly fallen snow.  Smothering the stool with his large          Comparison
frame, he would bend over his work, hunched shoulders supported by
elbows resting on my desk.  He looked like a great vulture            Comparison
hovering above his prey.  Day after day we sat there, the vulture
and I, working at breakneck speed, shuffling our respective piles
of paper to and fro....
```

Do these two comparisons work equally well or is one more appropriate than the other?

The comparisons we've discussed so far are fairly forthright; they use the words *like* or *as*. Other comparisons may be more subtle. For example, Linda's phrase "a wiry mustache," is really a shortened comparison. In its longer form it might read: "The hairs of his mustache were like wires." But why put the reader to all that trouble when the comparison can be reduced to "his wiry mustache"? "Smothering the stool with his huge frame" is also a shortened comparison. The longer version might be: "His huge frame covered the stool as thoroughly as a pillow covers the face of a victim being smothered." In this case the long form is awkward and heavy-handed; the short form is just right.

   Such shortened comparisons (formally called *metaphors*) can add much to descriptive writing. Sometimes they seem just naturally to come to mind. Other times they have to be nudged into existence by the writer's first thinking of a longer comparison (_____ is like _____) and then shortening the whole thing to one or two words.

What to Avoid

In the following passage the writer has tried too hard. As a result, the passage sounds phony:

The tree danced in the winds as the mayor announced that the city's budget was like "lean hamburger." All the fat had been knifed out as ruthlessly as the praying mantis kills and eats its sex partner. To the merry tunes of the birds flying among the trees as though an air traffic controller were telling them what routes to take, the press conference adjourned.

   What's wrong with this paragraph is that comparisons and vivid writing seem to have become the author's goal rather than the means by which the author accomplishes the real goal: communicating a dominant impression or idea in an interesting way. The confusion of means and ends shows up in the clashing images: While trees "dance" and birds sing "merry tunes," we're asked to consider the praying mantis eating its partner and the mayor ruthlessly knifing fat out of the budget. The two sets of images contradict each other. In addition, the sudden likening of the birds to airplanes undercuts the natural imagery that had been used up to that point. Another difficulty can be seen in the basic comparison of the budget to "lean hamburger": the comparison is false. Lean hamburger is, in fact, more expensive than hamburger with a higher fat content.
   In truth, the "lean hamburger" paragraph was written to illustrate what can go wrong with comparisons. (That's why I can attack it so ruthlessly.) But the lesson is one we all need to be reminded of: comparisons and vivid language are means to an end. They aren't ends in themselves. (See Activity II at the end of the chapter for practice writing vivid descriptions and building curiousity.)

POLISH YOUR SENTENCE STYLE

The two most important elements of an attractive sentence style have been discussed earlier in this book. Chapter 9 offered tips on eliminating the wordiness that seems an inevitable part of rough drafts, and Chapter 12 presented ways to use more specific language. These two techniques of being concise and being specific help writers make sentences clearer to the reader. That's what polishing sentence style is all about: making the meaning—not just the words—glow.

Parallelism

Parallelism is a way of making the words and ideas in a sentence line up so the reader can easily see what goes with what. Just as the sides of parallel bars or railroad tracks are evenly spaced from each other, so parallel parts of a sentence travel along side by side. Consider the following sentence:

The rules state that <u>shoes</u>, a <u>tie</u>, and a <u>coat</u> must be worn. — *parallel*

Shoes, tie, and *coat* are parallel because they are in a list. They're all the same kind of words, in this case nouns. Another sentence might have parallel verbs:

On weekends, she <u>reads</u>, <u>hikes</u>, and <u>writes</u> letters. — *parallel*

Or the same sentence might be written with parallel *-ing* words:

On weekends, she enjoys <u>reading</u>, <u>hiking</u>, and <u>writing</u> letters. — *parallel*

The following sentence also contains parallel words and ideas:

The report was <u>thoughtful</u>, <u>concise</u>, and <u>interesting</u>. — *parallel*

In this sentence the italicized words don't all end the same way, but they do function as adjectives describing *report*. Now let's look at a sentence in which the parts are not parallel but could be:

At school I studied economics and how to do accounting.

This sentence is rather like parallel bars that have been bent out of shape: "economics" and "how to do accounting" don't fit together. Although we usually say we "studied" economics, math, or whatever, we don't usually say we "studied how to"; we usually write "learned" how to. Thus the sentence could be rewritten to read:

At school I studied *economics* and *accounting*.

or

At school I *studied* economics and *learned* how to do accounting.

In the first revision, *economics* and *accounting* are parallel. In the second, *studied* and *learned* are parallel.

Now let's look at another out-of-shape sentence:

> When Maria moved to another state, she became careless about her appearance and a sloppy worker.

At first this sentence may seem to be in order. But what two words are really joined by *and*? The sentence can be easily revised to make the parts parallel:

```
When Maria moved to another state, she became careless about her      parallel
appearance and sloppy in her work.
```

or

```
When Maria moved to another state, she became careless about her      parallel
appearance and work.
```

Let's look at another sentence,

> More and more people are beginning to understand acupuncture as a science rather than some backwoods, barefoot, needle-crazed witch doctor.

The words that the reader expects to be parallel are *science* and *doctor*. Both words are nouns, but it doesn't make sense to say "acupuncture as a . . . witch doctor." Therefore the student writer revised this sentence to make the meaning clearer:

```
More and more people are beginning to understand acupuncture as a     parallel
science rather than as the practice of some backwoods, barefoot,
needle-crazed witch doctor.
```

The words *science* and *practice* are parallel. (A word such as *hokum* or *magic* could be used instead, to make the meaning even clearer.)

Before you read any further, review some of your own writing to see if you've written sentences containing words that should be parallel but aren't. (If you don't find any, ask a friend to help you.) If you've written such sentences—and most people do—rewrite them so the parallel ideas are in parallel form.

Parallelism for Special Effect

Once you have acquired the knack of writing sentences with parallel elements, you can begin to play with parallelism for special effect. For example, a long series of rapid-fire parallel items can make details seem to pile up on top of each other, impressing the reader with their number or bulk:

> The gunshot awoke the hogs, cattle, chickens, geese, dogs, the horses on the farm . . . and immediately Mr. Brown ran out of the house to investigate the noise.

Compare this passage with the denuded version below:

> The gunshot awoke the animals . . . and immediately farmer Brown ran out of the house to investigate.

The first version, with its pile of parallel animals, communicates noise and confusion. The second version doesn't. But is the first version wordy? No. Writing is wordy when there are more words than necessary to do the job. The number of words alone doesn't determine wordiness.

Here's another example of parallelism at work:

> I love oven-toasted garlic bread, and pizza, and chewy fudge brownies.

And here's the same idea communicated without benefit of parallelism:

> I love to eat oven-toasted garlic bread. Pizza's another favorite of mine. And chewy fudge brownies are good.

There is nothing "wrong" with the second version. Grammatically it's correct. But it lacks the polish and the flow of the parallel version.

The Farmer Brown passage and the passage on pizza and chewy fudge brownies create two different effects. The first passage contains a rapid-fire list and sounds brisk. The second is more drawn out, both by adjectives and by the repetition of the word *and*. It therefore sounds slower, perhaps dreamy. You can create either effect. Try writing your own imitation of these two passages, choosing a different subject. (Perhaps you could describe an accident in the supermarket, or elsewhere, trying for a brisk effect, and describe types of relaxation you enjoy, trying for a slower, more dreamy effect.)

Parallelism can also be used to create suspense or a sense of increasing importance, as in the following examples:

1. As a result of the chairman's advice, he was first troubled, then disoriented, and finally unnerved, to the point of requiring psychiatric care.

2. She began by improving her grades, then she became more efficient at work, and finally she was promoted to manager.

Writers achieve this effect by carefully arranging the order of the parallel items and by giving the readers clues that more is to come: "first . . . ," "then . . . ," "and finally." Nonparallel—and less polished—versions of these sentences might be:

1. He was unnerved by the chairman's advice, after he was troubled and disoriented by it. Psychiatric care was finally required.
2. She improved her grades. They promoted her to manager because she was efficient at work.

Notice that not only are the parallel forms more polished, but their meaning is clearer. You can try imitating them now, choosing a different subject. Just remember to build in importance.

Finally, parallelism can be used to surprise the reader. Consider the following sentence, which contains parallelism but does not surprise the reader:

Mr. Greenshades, who was an inaccurate accountant, was slow and methodical.

Now read the following:

As an accountant, Mr. Greenshades was slow, methodical, and highly inaccurate.

This revised version surprises the reader with a punch line. Here are some other examples of this punch-line technique:

The children were rosy-cheeked, golden-haired, well dressed, and completely vicious.
The book is well organized, clearly written, and totally dull.

Now it's your turn to imitate these examples, choosing a subject of your own.

Emphasis Through Word Order

Parallelism is not the only way to emphasize certain words or ideas. Any words placed at the beginning or end of a sentence will receive special attention. They are the spots where your reader is most likely to be paying attention. The middle of a sentence, by contrast, does not receive as much attention. Thus another trick of polished writing is to be sure that these prime spots aren't wasted.

PRIME SPOT WASTED	PRIME SPOT USED
The operation was a success, I'm glad to say. (Emphasis on "say.")	The operation was, I'm glad to say, a success. (Emphasis changed to "success.")
After several months of looking for work, you learn what questions people will ask during interviews. (Emphasis on "After several months.")	You learn, after several months of looking for work, what questions will be asked during interviews. (Emphasis changed to "you learn.")
With regard to heredity, they discovered the double helix was the key. (Emphasis on "with regard" and "the key.")	The double helix, they discovered, was the key to heredity. (Emphasis changed to "double helix" and "heredity.")

These revisions were achieved by moving less important material to the middle of the sentence. Review some of your own writing and select one paragraph that seems weakly written. Try revising just one or two of the sentences to take more advantage of the prime spots. Don't try to rewrite all your sentences this way, however. That would be like using an exclamation mark at the end of every sentence.

Another way to take advantage of prime spots is to surprise the reader by reversing the normal word order. In English, readers normally expect the order to be sub-ject–verb–completer: "They went to work." By reversing the order, a writer can surprise the reader while still placing important words at the beginning and end: "To work they went." This technique must be used sparingly. Otherwise it can be both confusing and overly cute.

Polish with Punctuation

Punctuation marks don't just sit there on the paper; they send your reader all sorts of signals.

Periods

The period says, "That's that." It promises nothing about what's coming next. It simply separates one unit of thought from another. But in doing so, it emphasizes each unit. That's why sentence fragments are sometimes useful. They emphasize just a word or two. Consider the following passage:

> Sunshine. Constant sunshine. He woke to it early in the morning. *Intentional Fragments*
> Watched it linger outside his office window. Drove home through
> it at five P.M. And soon it would be gone.

Of course this passage is descriptive writing, where sentence fragments seem more appropriate than in other types of writing. But consider the following nondescriptive passage:

> He planned to become a researcher. Why? To help find solutions *Intentional Fragments*
> to medical problems. And to help ease the pain he'd so often seen
> as a child.

Here, too, the fragments create an emphasis that is lost when the passage is rewritten:

> He planned to become a researcher so that he could help find solutions to medical problems and ease the pain he'd so often seen as a child.

Still, sentence fragments must be used with care. Overdone, they become too gimmicky. Used in formal situations, they seem too casual and, even when intentional, look like mistakes.

Semicolons

Whereas periods emphasize each separate unit of thought, semicolons do just the opposite. They say, "Hey, hang on, something else is coming." In the following passage, for example, the period clearly separates one idea from the next:

Read the directions carefully. Incomplete application forms will be returned.

The same passage, rewritten with a semicolon, seems to say, "There's a connection between these two ideas":

Read the directions carefully; incomplete application forms will be returned.

When you use semicolons, do make sure the material on *each* side of the semicolon is equivalent to a complete sentence. Although sentence fragments can be used for special effect by themselves, they shouldn't be used with semicolons.

Colons

Another puncutation mark that says "something else is coming" is the colon. The difference between semicolons and colons is that colons are more forceful: they seem to say "You'd better read this." Also, colons can be used even when there isn't the equivalent of a full sentence on both sides:

Yes, Turow uses all the tools of a writer's trade. But he makes one glaring error: Turow treats the reader as if he were intellectually inferior.

Zabrina Giron, student

The elderly are in nursing homes or in senior citizens' communities or shut away in their homes. They are exactly where society wants them: segregated from the younger generation.

Evlyn Atkins, student

At this point the filler is mixed. A word of caution: read the instructions that come with the filler very carefully, for they will tell not only how much to mix the hardener with the resin, but also how much time you'll have to work with the filler before it hardens.

Rick Wagner, student

In general, colons are useful for alerting the reader that the material following the colon is either an example or an explanation of the preceding idea. When the equivalent of a complete sentence follows a colon, it can begin with either a small or a capital letter. A capital letter emphasizes the break between the two parts of the sentence, whereas a lower case letter deemphasizes the break:

Thus we come to the final irony: (The) more jealous we are, the [*break emphasized*]
less attractive we become to others.

```
Thus we come to the pain problem: (he's) a workaholic.  ⎤  break
                                                        ⎦  deemphasized
```

Dashes

Another puncutation mark that can be used for special effect is the dash. When used near the end of a sentence, as in the following passage, the dash blends a general idea with the specific examples that follow it.

Mabuhay! Your local Filipino Community Council appreciates your assistance with our Anniversary Pageant. As you know, we are in search of a young lady who will inspire our activities—a lady who exudes the beauty, intelligence, warmth, and charm typical of a Filipina. This special Filipina will be chosen to represent our community, reigning over the festivities of our Diamond Jubilee Pageant.

Lyddy Felipe, student

Ironically, although a dash can help blend ideas together, it can also be used to emphasize an idea:

After the votes were tallied, Yamada discovered she had won—by one vote.

When dashes are used in pairs, they usually emphasize the idea they set off:

Professor Young's car—and the student papers in it—was stolen over the weekend.

By the way, dashes are handwritten and typeset in books as one long line — like this. Most typewriters don't have a long dash, however, so in typed papers the hyphen is typed twice, with no spaces, -- like this. Of course, whether the material is handwritten, typed, or printed, the dash, like other special effects, should not be overused.

In sum, the choice of punctuation is often just that—a choice. Sometimes a colon will be just right. Other times a semicolon or dash may be better. Often the simple period, with or without a sentence fragment, is most effective. It all depends on the passage and the punctuation that has been used in the surrounding sentences. As you revise your drafts, try playing with the punctuation until it gives the emphasis and style that you want.

Rhythm

Rhythm isn't limited to poetry and music. Ordinary, everyday language has a rhythm too. Read the following sentence out loud, emphasizing the words that have a slash mark over them:

He wént to the stóre to búy a páir of shóes.

It's an ordinary sentence, but it has a beat or rhythm. When we say that writing "sounds good" or is "smooth," we're often referring to the fact that we can feel this rhythm.

When you read your own writing out loud, or listen to it read by others, listen for the rhythm. If your work sounds good when it's read naturally, without the beat being emphasized in any way, then leave it alone. If, however, your writing sounds awkward, or the emphasis seems to fall on unimportant words, or the words seem to fade away near the end of each sentence, you may want to work on the way your sentences sound.

One way to revise writing that sounds rough or weak is to look away from the paper and say what you have to say. Often the more we continue to look at what we've already written, the harder it becomes to change anything. Furthermore, people often speak with a more natural rhythm than they use when writing.

Another useful technique is parallelism. It contributes to rhythm by helping to eliminate wordiness, by emphasizing the right words, and, almost automatically, by affecting the sound.

Awkward Rhythm

May I say that in working at Big L's Customer Service as a Desk Clerk, I have gained excellent work experience. I realize that we have worked with a lot of money in cashing checks. Also, good public relations is gained in working as a Service Desk Clerk. I have learned to deal better and more efficiently with people, namely customers and money than I had ever been able to before working at Big L's Customer Service. I feel that public relations is a very important aspect in a job.

Rhythm Improved Through Parallelism

```
    May I say that in working as a desk clerk at Big L's
Customer Service, I have gained valuable experience in working
with both people and money.  The customer complaints I was         sentences
authorized to handle developed my tact and sense of public         parallel
relations.  The large sums of money I was permitted to handle      to each
while cashing checks developed my accuracy and attention to detail. other
```

The revision uses parallelism of a particular type: the parallel items are equally long. Here's another example of rhythmic parallelism:

He *read more books, wrote more papers,* and *drank more coffee* than he ever thought possible.

Another way to improve rhythm is to change the word order. For example, the following sentence is parallel, but the last word sounds tacked on:

The aisles were crowded with women, hundreds of joyous children, and men.

Besides the weak sound, the sentence suffers from ambiguity: are the men also joyous? A simple reordering of the sentence improves both the rhythm and the clarity:

The aisles were crowded with men, women, and hundreds of joyous children.

Rather often, as in this example, when a sentence has one parallel element that's longer or more complicated than the others, that element is best placed at the end.

Finally, contractions, or the lack of them, can affect the way writing sounds. Contractions such as *I'm, you're* or *it's* can make writing sound natural. However, too many contractions or ill-advised ones such as "The market'll improve next week" can make writing sound so casual that it actually becomes harder to read. To get the feel of contractions and how they affect the tone of your writing, read something you've already written. If you avoided contractions when you wrote it, revise it, using contractions where they sound natural. If, on the other hand, you find that you normally use many contractions, try revising so that some of the contractions are eliminated. Play with the sound of your writing until it seems not only smooth but appropriate for your subject and audience. (See Appendix A for the correct spelling of the contractions.) For more practice polishing sentence style, see Activity III at the end of the chapter.

USE CLEVER QUOTATIONS AND TITLES

"Next to being witty yourself, the best thing is being able to quote another's wit." Of course "wit" here means more than humor or cleverness: it means understanding or insight combined with a polished turn of phrase. And there's little doubt that such wit keeps readers reading.

Quotations

There are two ways writers find "quotable quotes." The method that might seem easiest is to look in a book of quotations. There are several traditional collections, such as Bartlett's and several newer collections such as *Peter's Quotations* by Dr. Laurence Peter, author of *The Peter Principle*. This latter book offers, for example, 31 quotations on the subject of "quoting." Among those 31 quotations is the one that begins this section. (It's a quotation from Christian N. Bovee.)

A book of quotations can be a great aid in borrowing another writer's wit. The difficulty is that one can be easily tempted to use a quotation that's not quite appropriate. Such a quotation usually betrays its source and the writing seems phony. To be effective, quotations must seem to spring naturally from what is being said.

For this reason, many writers make their own collections of "quotable quotes." It's not hard, especially if you limit yourself to just those subjects that you're most interested in and most likely to write about.

The most convenient way to collect quotations is to keep file cards and a pen handy whenever you read something on a subject that's important to you. That way you won't have to disturb your reading to go find pen and paper. (File cards are generally easier to file and keep track of than are slips of paper.) On the card, in addition to the quotation, you should copy the author's name and the other information in the sample below. If you take time to note the subject of the quotation, you will save time later when you arrange your cards by subject matter.

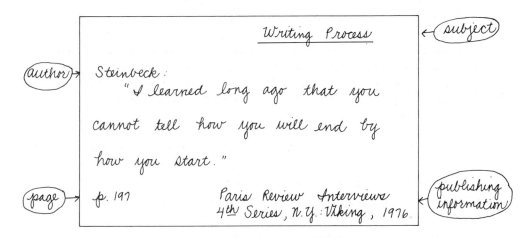

The advantage of collecting your own quotations is that they'll probably sound more natural in your writing than would quotations you find in a quotation book. In addition, the quotations you collect will probably come closer to reflecting your own ideas.

When you quote someone, remember to use quotation marks and give the author credit. Otherwise, you leave yourself open to charges of plagiarism—theft of another's material. When you borrow someone else's wit, borrow with credit; don't steal. Brief quotations often require only that you mention the author's name and perhaps the book or magazine the quotation came from. For instance, the above quotation might be used as follows:

> William Steinbeck once said, "I learned long ago that you can not tell how you will end by how you start."

Longer quotations, and even short ones used in academic papers, require more detailed documentation. For help with formal documentation, see Appendix C.

Also, be sure to punctuate the quotation correctly. If you don't know when to begin a quotation with a capital letter and when not to, or if you're not sure if periods go inside or outside the quotation marks, check Appendix D.

Titles

It goes without saying that a catchy title can motivate a reader to at least begin reading your writing. How do writers think of clever titles? One of the easiest ways is through comparisons. Consider the following titles:

1. Scrimmage in the Courtroom
2. Telling the News vs. Zapping the Cornea
3. TV's Star Wars; News from Above
4. Now You See It, Now You Don't
5. And on the Seventh Day He Was Still Talking

The titles have three things in common: First, they are all titles of articles about television. Second, the writers depend on the reader's having some idea of the subject either because of the place the article appears (such as *TV Guide*), the accompanying pictures, or a little blurb announcing the subject. Third, all five titles depend upon a comparison that the reader should perceive:

1. The legal action against XYZ network's sports coverage is compared to a football scrimmage.
2. XYZ's news coverage is compared with ZYX's.
3. Helicopter news competition between TV stations is compared to the battles in the movie *Star Wars*.
4. TV coverage of soccer games is compared to a magician's act.
5. A well-known sports commentator is compared to God.

The last three comparisons depend upon the reader's recognizing a reference to something else: the movie *Star Wars,* the magician's "Now you see it, Now you don't" line, and the Biblical line, "And on the seventh day he rested." Such references, sometimes called *allusions* since they "allude" to something else, cleverly build common ground with the reader and at the same time contain wit.

Other ways of writing clever titles are to use vivid language and to pay attention to the sound of words. "Zapping the Cornea" not only is more vivid than "showing pictures of the news," it also sounds more lively.

Perhaps the easiest, but not always the most effective, way to play with the sound of words in a title is to repeat the same initial sound in each word: "Camera Call for Carrie." This technique, called *alliteration,* should be used with care. When overdone it becomes a bad joke: "Bridge Brings Brisk Business Boom to Bridgeport Breweries."

SUMMARY OF CHAPTER

No one has to read a word you write, at least not carefully. You have to make people want to read it. How? By appealing to their self-interest, or establishing common ground with them, or luring them with a catchy title or opening paragraph.

But that alone won't be enough. Once you have their attention, you have to hold it by delivering whatever you promised in your opening paragraphs. In addition, you can build curiosity or suspense or you can delight them with polished sentences and witty quotations. You can, in short, capture and hold your readers' attention by giving them a reason to read.

Sometimes, of course, you'll be writing for an audience that's already interested in the subject. In that case, don't belabor the obvious. But don't take your reader for granted either. Even motivated readers can suddenly lose their interest.

ACTIVITIES: INTERESTING WRITING

I. Appeal to the Reader's Interest and Establish Common Ground.

A. Make a point of noticing what written material you read carefully, what you just glance at, and what you don't bother to read at all. Near the beginning of this book you analyzed why you sometimes "tune out" while others are talking to you. Now, in similar fashion, analyze what causes you to lose interest in someone else's writing. Are the reasons similar or different? Can you draw any generalizations to help you make your own writing more interesting?

B. Review material you have already written or drafted to see which of it was written for an audience that was either not interested in your subject or only minimally interested in it. Revise that writing now, using techniques from the first two sections of this chapter. Choose techniques appropriate to your subject, audience, and purpose.

II. Build Curiosity and Write Vivid Descriptions

A. If you've never written a description of a person, place, or experience, try one now. For instance, brainstorm a list of places you enjoy. (Try to think of specific places: that is, not San Francisco, but a specific street, a park, or even a room within the city.) From that list, select the person, place, or experience you would most like to describe to someone else. Finally, decide who you might write to: preferably someone who has no special interest in the person, place, or experience you're describing. Your challenge in this practice writing will be to describe the person, place, or experience vividly while attracting and holding your reader's curiosity. When you are finished, top off your description with a catchy title.

B. Exchange your descriptions in class. Which are most effective? Why?

C. Reread an informative paper you have written. Would the question-answer technique make it more interesting? If so, revise it.

III. Sentence Style

A. Reread something you wrote in the past. Select the one or two paragraphs in which the sentence style most needs work, then use the techniques in *Polish Your Sentence Style* to make the sentences more appealing.

B. Exchange your work with a classmate. Which sentences does your classmate think are most improved? Why?

C. If you did not do the parallelism exercise earlier in this chapter, do it now.

chapter 14

To Write Persuasively, Consider Your Readers' Point of View

When do you need to write persuasively? Whenever you are saying something your readers are likely to disagree with. Or whenever you're trying to talk your readers into doing something. For instance, in a friendly letter, a writer may attempt to persuade someone to come for a visit, change jobs, stop smoking, or agree to a reconciliation. In business correspondence, writers may wish to persuade others to make payment, make good on a guarantee, or improve a product. In magazine articles, writers may attempt to persuade people to visit Florida, see a recommended movie, or limit the amount of television watched by children.

When writers aren't attempting to persuade readers to do something, they may be attempting to influence the readers' thinking. For instance, someone writing a letter-to-the-editor is usually trying to persuade others to agree with certain ideas. A student writing a history paper needs to persuade the professor that the interpretation of events presented in the paper is valid—even though it differs from the professor's own interpretation. An article on public school education may be an attempt to persuade the intended readers that the public school system isn't as bad as some other writers say it is.

All persuasion requires tact: seeing things from the intended reader's point of view. People read with their emotions and feelings as well as with their intelligence and reading skills. As a general rule, the less your readers may agree with you to start with, the more important it is that you consider their point of view. This chapter offers five techniques you can use when you need to consider your readers' point of view:

Offer concessions

Anticipate and answer your readers' objections

Avoid negatively loaded language

Be tactful in little ways

End appropriately

OFFER CONCESSIONS

"Don't judge a man until you've walked a mile in his moccasins," is an old Indian saying. With a slight revision, it applies to writing also: "Don't try to persuade your reader until you know what it feels like to be in your reader's shoes." In the last chapter you read that one way to develop your reader's interest is to establish common ground by introducing subjects that both you and your reader find interesting or important. When you are trying to persuade your reader to do something or to agree with you, you can use a special type of common ground: mention ideas that both you and your reader agree on. This type of common ground is called a *concession* because a writer using it admits or "concedes" that certain of the reader's ideas make sense even though the ideas are in conflict with the writer's main point.

Sometimes people are afraid to admit that others are even partly right. They fear that doing so will weaken their own argument. Actually, the opposite is usually true: a reader is more willing to be persuaded when the writer first shows respect for the reader's ideas by conceding that some of those ideas make sense. See the two versions of a memo written to the employees of J. B. Witherspoon. If you were one of the employees addressed, which version would you find more acceptable?

Date: Feb. 17, 1982

To: All Employees
From: Norma G. Bones, Owner
Re: Women's Lib Name Badges

It has come to my attention that some of you would like the name badges that currently read "Miss" changed to "Ms." As a second choice, you say you want all titles dropped from the name badges. I will not go along with this immature, unprofessional request. Please remember that we are running a business and we're here to please our customers. It's not what you want but what our customers want that is important. And J. B. Witherspoon customers prefer "Miss" to the new-fangled "Ms." Therefore your name badges will continue to read "Miss."

Anyone who does not like being addressed as "Miss" can come and see me about it. I'm sure that the person hired with the money you are now making won't mind being addressed as "Miss."

Date: Feb. 17, 1982

To: All Employees
From: Norma G. Bones
Re: Name Badges

I understand some employees would like to see the name badges that currently read "Miss" changed to "Ms." I agree that "Ms." is growing in acceptance and is used by many other businesses. J. B. Witherspoon customers, however, seem to still prefer the more traditional "Miss." Since we're here to serve our customers, it would seem that a change in the name badges would not be appropriate at this time. Dropping the titles entirely is an interesting alternative; but, once again, the time is not right for such a change.

I know that many of you use "Ms." in your personal lives and can understand that you would prefer the same title at work. I appreciate your concern and regret that, at this time, I must decide against a change in the name badges.

Although some employees would find neither memo persuasive, most would find the second version more acceptable than the first. The reason is that the second version shows respect for the employees' request by making three concessions:

1. "Ms." is used in other businesses.
2. "Ms." is gaining in popularity.
3. The employees use "Ms." in their personal lives.

These concessions reflect an effort to see things from the employees' point of view and to agree with their ideas wherever possible.

One advantage of making concessions is that doing so forces writers to think things through from the opposite point of view. This helps the writers to see if their own ideas are indeed true or not. For instance, while considering "Ms." from the employees' point of view, Norma G. Bones would come to see that the use of "Ms." is indeed growing— and that even J. B. Witherspoon's customers might someday accept, or even prefer, it. (It's even possible that "walking around in the shoes" of her employees might have helped Norma Bones decide that poor employee morale could be more harmful to Witherspoons than a change in name badges would be.)

The following letter-to-the-editor also demonstrates the use of concessions:

```
Dear Editor,
        Much has been said recently concerning the proposed
Department of Education guide on abortion for senior high school
students.  To add to the other letters that have appeared in the
newspaper, I wish to voice my concerns regarding the proposal.
        The stated objectives of the new abortion guide are to
"interpret the complexity of the issues related to abortion," and
to aid the student in applying them "to the decision-making
process."  The objectives are worthy; however, the methodology     [concession
used to achieve them does not allow the student sufficient
familiarization with "the complexity of the issues" to adequately
perform the "decision-making process."
        If the teacher's guide is to be truly objective, it must   [implied
present the negative as well as the positive aspects of abortion.   concession
Medical hazards relating to abortion go completely unmentioned in
```

the text, as do negative psychological and sociological aspects of the issue.

The moral issue of abortion also appears to be given light consideration and the views of many religious groups receive poor representation throughout the guide.

The issue is a serious one to which our students deserve a more impartial guide.

Sincerely,

A. Reader

Consider the difference in the letter's effectiveness had the writer omitted the concessions and written something like this:

Dear Editor:

The proposed Department of Education guide on abortion is biased and I don't approve of it at all. It leaves out the medical hazards as well as the negative psychological and sociological aspects of abortion. The guide should not be used; it has no place in our schools.

Sincerely,

A. Reader

Few readers who did not already oppose the abortion guide would find such a letter persuasive.

Now let's see how someone writing a letter defending the abortion guide might use concessions.

Dear Editor:

There have recently been many letters from readers voicing concerns over the proposed school abortion guide. The most common concern seems to be that the guide does not address the moral issues of abortion. It is true that the moral issues are not *concession* addressed in the guide, except for a brief statement that "some religions believe that abortion is morally wrong." It's also true *concession* that moral guidelines concerning abortions should be offered to our students. But I for one would object if the schools were to usurp this responsibility from the family or church. Since the moral implications of abortion will be different for each student, those implications are best taught by each student's own family or church.

The proposed abortion guide is part of a series on health
education. The questions addressed in it are therefore properly
limited to questions of health and medical procedures.

Sincerely,

A. Reader

Concessions are a part of almost all persuasive writing. For example, the common
ground with which Frances Katano began her article on dining out in Chapter 2 was
really a concession: "Dining out is fun." That it is fun is not Frances' main idea. Indeed,
her main point is that one has to be assertive to make it fun. The common ground in
Janet Fuller's training letter in Chapter 7 is also a concession: "Please don't let them [the
company's rules and regulations] scare you off. After a while, you'll find them easy to
apply." This concedes that the rules are, at least at first, a nuisance.

Concessions need not be limited to the beginning paragraphs of writing. Zabrina
Giron makes concessions throughout the following discussion of the food choices at
Shelton College. You may recognize it from Chapter 3.

A NOONTIME PROPOSAL

Today for lunch I had a Pepsi, a package of nuts layered in salt,
and a burrito supreme. I'll have something similar tomorrow. Am
I becoming a junk food addict? Yes, it appears that way, at least
for as long as I attend Shelton College. Certainly, among
Shelton's four dining options I should find something nutritionally   *concession*
wholesome. Let's visit each of the four and see if I can.

First, we have the lunch wagons to tempt us with a variety of
plate lunches, Mexican food, and hamburgers. But it doesn't take
a discerning eye to spot the grease in which these are prepared.
Along with the lunches, the wagons offer us chips, candy, sodas
... everything to whet the appetite of a junk food junky.

Let's try the cafeteria next. It has a wide range of food,   *concession*
you can't beat the price, and, if you're in the mood for a hot
lunch, they've got it. But that hot lunch comes with greasy meat,
two servings of starch, and, at best, a small scoop of canned
vegetables. And what about the sandwiches? White bread, stained
caramel colored, imitates whole wheat, the meats are smothered in
nitrates, and there's only one slice of tomato, with a sliver of
wilted lettuce.

Our third option is the vending machine--hunger's salvation.
Perhaps we'll find what we're looking for in one of the 10

machines on campus? No, it would seem not. Most of the machines
are empty, and the few that still have food offer only soggy
sandwiches, heavy in mayonnaise and nitrates, but light in
nutritional value. For dessert we're offered candy or an ice milk
bar covered with imitation chocolate.

Admittedly, there's one more option: an innovative idea *concession*
called the Gourmet Dining Room. Certainly it is an adventure in
epicurean dining and the food is nutritious. But the Gourmet Room
has three drawbacks: The dining room holds a total of only
sixteen people, the hours of operation are very limited, and,
above all, it's so expensive that most of us can afford it only as
a special splurge.

Of course I can bring my lunch, but there are no refrigerators *concession*
or lockers in which to store it. I could leave it in the car, but
can you imagine how appetizing that lunch is going to be after it
has sat in a closed car in the boiling heat for four hours? So,
I'd have to lug my lunch to all my classes, thus increasing the
chances of losing it or having it squashed.

Driving off campus to eat is another alternative, but in the
interest of conserving energy, not a viable one. Besides, for
those of us who must return for afternoon classes, the only places
where food can be prepared quickly enough are at the "fast food
restaurants." Surely their food is as high in empty calories as
is the food at the lunch wagon.

Let's face it. There's a problem. Well, what can we do about
it? I suggest that the cafeteria offer certain meals of lean,
broiled meat, accompanied by two servings of fresh vegetables.
There should be real whole wheat sandwiches containing meat not
laced with nitrates. The vending machines should have some
nutritional foods such as fruit juices without sugar or artificial
colorings or flavorings, and whole wheat sandwiches containing
liberal quantities of lettuce and tomatoes (we need the roughage).
Also, the health food stores should be encouraged to send a lunch
truck.

Granted, most students are at school for only one meal a day. *concession*
And many of us don't want to eat nutritiously--at least not every
day. But nutritionists stress that every meal counts. So when
good judgment prevails, shouldn't we be able to find wholesome
foods with relative ease? I'm suggesting that S.C. help us by
giving us a choice at lunch time--a real choice.

Perhaps Zabrina's writing could be strengthened by more factual dietary information. But the concessions she makes are good. By showing that she has considered her reader's point of view, the concessions make her writing more persuasive than it would otherwise be.

Developing the Habit

How can you develop the habit of making concessions in your own writing? A good beginning is to become aware of concessions in the material you read. Be on the lookout for words that may signal the beginning of a concession, words such as: *admittedly, granted, I agree, I concede, of course,* and *naturally*. Notice also the words that usually indicate a concession has ended and the writing is about to continue with the author's own ideas: *however, nevertheless, on the other hand,* and *but*.

Another way to develop your ability to make concessions is to practice looking for comments you can agree with in what others say, especially when their ideas are basically in conflict with your own. In conversation, force yourself to begin, "I agree that . . ." before going on with your own ideas. In class, when the professor or another student is presenting an idea that differs from your own beliefs or interpretation, listen for what you can agree with rather than what you disagree with. To hear what we disagree with is easy; to pick out points of agreement takes conscious effort and practice. In the small group discussions that are a part of many classes, you can suggest that the group members mention at least one previously stated idea that they agree with before making any new, especially contradictory, suggestions or statements of their own. By the way, this technique can be useful in business or club meetings when you're in a position to establish the meeting guidelines.

Finally, when you are doodling, especially for writing that will be persuasive, stop and put yourself in your readers' shoes. How would your readers feel? What would they think? Which of those feelings or thoughts do you have to admit make some sense? They are your concessions. Should you find that you have more concessions than points of your own to make, you may want to reexamine your own position. Perhaps your own ideas need to be modified.

By now, you may be saying to yourself: "Suppose the other guy is simply dead wrong? Suppose there isn't a single thing in his position I can agree with? What then?" Then you should consider waiting a while before you write. Few ideas in life are so simple that they have no exceptions or extenuating circumstances. Few people are 100 percent right or wrong. And, even if you are 100 percent right, how can you hope to persuade a reader as long as you feel that reader is 100 percent wrong?

(For practice activities, see the end of the chapter.)

ANTICIPATE AND ANSWER YOUR READERS' OBJECTIONS

As you consider various ideas that might run counter to your own position, you'll find some points that you simply cannot concede. What do you do? You can still include those points, introducing them as questions or objections that might occur to the reader.[1] Once you've introduced them, you can respond to them.

This is what Dr. Reiffel did in "Why Birds Fly in V Formation" (Chapter 13). In that article Dr. Reiffel anticipated the incorrect explanations that his readers might have been taught regarding the V formation. Rather than ignore them, he introduced these erroneous ideas, tactfully calling them "common sense" and explained why they were wrong.

It's tempting to ignore ideas that run counter to our own. But ignoring them ultimately weakens our own argument since our readers then assume that we're either too blind to see the other side or too rude to admit it exists. Either way, we lose them. Thus even when we can't concede that the reader is right on a given point, it's usually best to do as Reiffel did: include the points you can't concede and then explain why you can't agree with them.

Now we'll see how this technique can work in combination with concessions. Let's suppose you are writing a report on handgun control and it looks as though your thesis is going to be something like: "Privately owned handguns should be outlawed." Let's further say your audience will be people who disagree with you. Before you begin writing, you might make a list of all the arguments you can think of for the *other* side. If you tried hard, your list would probably be fairly long, but it might include the following three points:

We have a constitutional right to protect our life and property.

Guns don't kill; people kill.

The real criminals would still get guns illegally.

Let's further say that on looking over your list, you decide that the last point above is true. You might then decide to concede that point in a passage that might read like this:

```
Of course it's true that criminals will still obtain handguns--and    concession
will still kill people with them.  However, not all murders are
committed by experienced criminals.  Every year people are shot to
death by relatives or acquaintances who have been overcome by
anger or frustration.  Outlawing privately owned handguns could
help prevent these murders....
```

Now, what of the other two points on your list. Suppose you do not agree with your intended readers that people have a constitutional right to handguns, and you think that the "guns don't kill; people kill" slogan oversimplifies a complex issue? In this case you obviously wouldn't concede those points—but you wouldn't ignore them either. You

---

[1]These objections to your own position are sometimes called *counterarguments*.

would include them and then explain why you disagreed. The passages you eventually write might read like this:

Many people are concerned over the constitutionality of a bill to outlaw handguns. They believe that any attempts to limit the rights we enjoy under the Bill of Rights is dangerous in itself and can set a dangerous precedent. *neutral statement*

However, the full text of the second amendment indicates that our forefathers' concern was with the need for a military force: "A well-regulated militia, being necessary to the security of a free State, the right of the people to keep and bear arms, shall not be infringed." Thus it would seem clear that.... *response*

Many people also argue that "guns don't kill; people do." This argument makes the important point that people, not guns, are the problem. The idea is often explained by means of a comparison between automobiles and guns. Automobiles, the argument goes, kill innocent pedestrians. Should we therefore outlaw cars as well as guns? The questions raised deserve a thoughtful answer. *neutral statement*

Let's begin by examining the significant differences between guns and automobiles.... *response*

Notice that the position of those who favor privately owned handguns is stated in neutral, not negative, tones. Also, note that the writer's response to their position is, in fact, a response to their ideas, not to them as people. As soon as disagreements disintegrate into personal name calling, all hope of persuading and of reaching an agreement is lost. Perhaps the first rule of tact, especially when you are disagreeing with someone else's ideas, is to keep it impersonal: focus on the ideas, not the person. (Note: If you personally oppose handgun controls, try turning the above example around. Make a list of all the points you've heard in favor of making privately owned handguns illegal, then decide which of those points you can concede and which you must answer. Try writing the appropriate paragraphs, as in the example above.)

Developing the Habit

As with concessions, one way to develop your own ability in the technique of neutrally stating points of view you can't agree with and then answering them is to look for examples of the technique as you read. Another way is to practice using the technique in conversations and meetings. When someone says something you disagree with, try restating it, neutrally, before you answer.

Three things may happen. First, you may find that the opposing idea makes more sense than you first thought. Second, you may be told that you've misunderstood what the other person was saying. Third, when you do restate the opposing idea accurately and neutrally, you may find that your listeners are more likely to listen carefully to your own ideas. All three of these outcomes are valuable. The first two help you clarify your own thinking; the third helps you communicate effectively. The same benefits apply when you take the time to think of opposing ideas when you write, conceding some and tactfully answering others.

One other way to practice this technique is to join with two or three others who are willing to experiment. Select some topic that you do not agree on. It might be a social issue, such as abortion or gun control, but it may be best, at least at first, to select something less emotional, such as whether or not a particular book, movie, or ball game was "good." After a topic has been selected, everyone should take a minute or two to jot down points in favor of his or her own position. The group can then begin discussing the issue, but with two ground rules. Each speaker (except the first) must neutrally restate what the previous speaker has said, making a concession if possible, before stating his or her own ideas on the subject. If the restatement isn't neutral or accurate, or if the speaker begins to name-call, the group may ask the speaker to "try again." After the discussion has gone around the circle, the first speaker should neutrally restate the position of the last speaker, making a concession if possible. The group should then see how much *agreement* can be reached on the issue under discussion. To practice anticipating points contrary to your own, make two lists at the beginning: one of the arguments supporting your own position, the other of arguments for the opposing view. Check both lists after the discussion is over. How well did you do in anticipating the opposing views? How much have you moderated your own position?

(For practice activities, see the end of the chapter.)

AVOID NEGATIVELY LOADED LANGUAGE

Which would you rather be described as: confident or conceited? Flexible or wishy-washy? As was indicated in the last chapter, many words have feelings or connotations attached to them. These connotations can be positive, as with the word *confident,* or negative, as with the word *conceited.* Yet either word could be used to describe someone with a high self-regard. The *denotation*—that is, the dictionary or factual meaning—is the same for both words. Thus writers who would write tactfully must be aware of the connotations of the words they use. (This is one reason it's so important to use a thesaurus only to jog one's memory, never to locate a brand-new word.) Consider, for example, the following pairs of words:

HOW TO TELL A MALE FROM A FEMALE IN THE BUSINESS WORLD(FROM AN UNKNOWN SOURCE)

A male is aggressive	A female is pushy
He's a go-getter	She's compulsive
He follows through	She's still compulsive
He's confident	She's conceited
He stands firm	She's stubborn
He has the courage of his convictions	She's pigheaded
He's sophisticated	She's "been around"
He's human	She's emotional
He exercises authority	She's power mad
He's discreet	She's secretive
He can make quick decisions	She's impulsive
He's a leader	She's a loud mouth

The connotations of the words on the right are negative, and the connotations of the words on the left are positive. Yet both sets of words could be used to describe the same behavior or person. You can see that in many cases the connotations actually reveal more about the person using the words than about the person or behavior described.

In some ways, connotations are contagious. If we hear a word used often enough in an ugly tone of voice or in a negative context, we may come to feel negative whenever we hear the word used, or even when we use it ourselves.[2] It's as though we catch the emotion from the word.

Since connotations, especially negative ones, can be contagious, it's possible to use negatively loaded words without consciously meaning to. For this reason, it's important for writers who wish to think clearly and write tactfully to become aware of the emotions associated with the words they use. You may want to try an experiment. Listen to yourself and your friends or relatives when you talk. What emotionally loaded words do you habitually use, at least in a particular situation? Ask friends to point out your "loaded language" to you. Once you're aware of the connotations in your own language, ask yourself which negative ones you should change. Try replacing those words with neutral, or, if appropriate, positive words. The results may be interesting: connotations can effect the way you think as well as how tactfully you communicate with others. Maybe your neighbors really are thrifty rather than cheap? Maybe your friend is forgetful rather than dumb?

(For practice activities, see the end of the chapter.)

---

[2]The effect of sound on connotation can be seen in the negative slur words used to identify many ethnic groups. While the full word for the groups' heritage may be long and melodious, as "Italian" or "Japanese," the slur word is typically short and harsh. Such words can be almost spit out of the mouth, contributing to the negative effect.

BE TACTFUL IN LITTLE WAYS

The following brief techniques may help you write tactfully in specific situations.

Don't Complain

Even if you're writing a letter of complaint, avoid the word "complaint." (After all, are you writing to complain or to have a situation corrected?) Put yourself in your reader's shoes: would you want to read that someone has a "complaint"?

Instead of: I'm writing to complain about the awful noise your dog makes barking all day while you're at work.

Try: A watchdog is a great comfort these days. However, I'm concerned about the constant noise your dog makes while you're at work.

Or: A watchdog is a great comfort these days. Unfortunately, Fang's constant barking while you're at work is creating problems in our home.

Or: A watchdog is a great comfort these days. You are probably unaware, however, that Fang barks nearly constantly while you are at work. This is creating problems in our home.

When you have occasion to respond to a complaint, avoid using the word "complaint," even if the person with the complaint used it:

Instead of: We've received your letter of complaint about our dog. . . .

Try: We've received your letter describing the problems our dog is creating for you. . . .

Or, if appropriate: Thank you for your recent note. We had no idea that Fang barks all day. . . .

When Not To Use "You"

When readers read good news, helpful information, or complimentary notes, they enjoy being directly addressed as "you." However, when they read bad news, complaints, or unwelcome advice, they would just as soon not be directly addressed. It's too much like having a finger pointed at them. Who, for example, would want to read:

You made a mistake on our bill.

or

You shouldn't smoke so much while you're pregnant.

A good rule of thumb might be: Avoid using "you" if your reader's reaction is likely to be, "Who me?" The two sentences above could be revised to read:

> There seems to be a mistake on our bill.

> Women who are pregnant should avoid excessive smoking.

In these revisions a reader can agree with the statement without having to admit that she was the one who made the mistake or that she was already smoking excessively. By the way, notice that the revision of the first sentence contains more words than does the original sentence. Remember that wordiness isn't determined by the number of words alone. In this case, the extra words contribute to the sentence's tactfulness.

Sometimes, of course, eliminating the "you" isn't enough. Consider the following example:

> If you want to be less ignorant about international politics, you can. . . .

In this case, simply eliminating the word "you" doesn't help too much. "People who want to be less ignorant about international politics can . . ." still is not as tactful as it could be. The difficulty is the negative tone of the sentence; the solution is to change that tone:

> People who wish to be better informed about international politics can. . . .

> or even

> If you wish to be well informed about international politics, you can. . . .

"As You Know . . ."

When we write, we often must include background information that our readers should already know but probably don't. Or sometimes we must include information that some of our readers already know while others don't. The challenge is to include such information without insulting our audience's intelligence or memory. One way is to introduce the information with a phrase such as, "As you know, . . ." or "As you may have read, . . ." or "As you will recall. . . ." Writers using these phrases must be careful; in some situations they can sound sarcastic or condescending. Often, however, these phrases permit writers to introduce background information in such a way that the intended readers aren't forced to admit, even to themselves, that they didn't already know it.

"What Are the Alternatives?"

Let's say you've written to your favorite aunt and uncle, asking if you can visit them the first week in July. They write back: "We'd love to have you stay with us, but unfortunately we can't because Betty's old college friend will be staying with us then." How would you feel? Probably not as welcome as if they had written: "We'd love to have you stay with us, but unfortunately that week in July is impossible because Betty's old college friend will be staying with us then. But how about coming later in July, or possibly for the last week in June?" The alternative dates would make you feel welcome, even if you couldn't travel at the proposed times.

Offering alternatives when you have to say no is a good habit to develop. For instance, if the phone company wants you to pay your back phone bill by the end of the month and you simply don't have the money, you might be tempted to write: "No, I'm broke and I'm not going to pay it." But that could antagonize your reader, whereas offering an alternative would let your reader know that your goal is to come to an agreement, not a confrontation. You might, for instance, write:

While I recognize my debt for $72.00, I fear I can't pay the full amount by the end of this month. I simply do not have the funds. I can, however, pay $25.00 by the end of this month, and the remaining $47.00 by the end of next month. These payments would, of course, be in addition to my regular monthly phone bill.

Another form of offering alternatives is to make it easy for your reader to do something. For instance, if a family is having trouble with the barking dog next door, they might be tempted to write the following note:

Dear Tom and Sandra,

We've had it with Fang's barking all day. Either get rid of him or make him stop barking.

The Millers

Although the note offers two alternatives, neither of them is practical. It's unlikely that Tom and Sandra would react to this hostile note by getting rid of Fang. And it's equally unlikely that they would make him stop barking—partly because they might not know how to. With a little research, however, the Millers could write a letter that would provide Tom and Sandra with a practical alternative:

Dear Tom and Sandra,

Watchdogs are a great comfort these days, and Fang is certainly a good watchdog. However, you may not be aware that he barks constantly while you are at work. This creates problems for us.

I wonder if we might be able to work something out that would satisfy both your needs and ours. For instance, we've noticed that Fang frequently barks when anyone walks by your house and then continues barking long after they've passed. The Humane Society says that watchdogs can be trained to bark only when someone enters their property. The procedure is simply to throw a cup or two of water at the dog's nose when he barks at the "wrong" times. Usually it takes only a few days before the dog learns that he's not to bark at people on the street. Friends have used this training technique with their dog Rex, and it has worked like a charm. Rex now barks only when people enter our friends' yard or touch the fence surrounding it. Actually, this provides our friends with better protection than before. Now when Rex barks, the neighbors know something is wrong and look out their windows to see if they should call the police.

Please call us if we can help you with the "water training" method or with any other solution for Fang's barking. I'm sure that between us we can work something out.

Sincerely,

The Millers

The Millers

(For practice activities, see the end of the chapter.)

END APPROPRIATELY

The ending of tactful writing can be as important as the beginning. Let's say that you have to turn down someone who has tried out for something, perhaps a position with your musical group or sports team. You might end with a tactful paragraph like this:

We very much appreciate your interest in the Village Alleycats and want to thank you for the time you spent with us during auditions. We wish you every success in the future.

When you want to persuade your readers to do something, consider ending your article or letter with an invitation to action. This doesn't have much to do with tact, but it does increase the effectiveness of tactfully persuasive writing. For instance, if you were writing an article describing the importance of knowing first aid and were trying to persuade your readers to take a first aid class, you might end like this:

If you've ever wondered what you would do if you were alone with someone who suffered a heart attack . . . or choked on a piece of meat . . . or was injured in an automobile accident, stop wondering. Call your local public school or Red Cross chapter today to find out where and when the next emergency first aid class starts. Don't wait until it's too late.

SUMMARY OF CHAPTER

Writing persuasively is partly a matter of putting yourself in your reader's shoes. Making concessions and introducing your reader's arguments, even when those arguments disagree with your own, will help you clarify your thoughts as well as present them more persuasively. Other techniques, such as being aware of the connotations of your words, being careful when you use the word "you," and thinking of alternative solutions to a problem, can also help you write in a way that shows respect for your reader's feelings and ideas.

Persuasive writing is not written to show that the reader is wrong. It's written to bring about agreement. This means that the writer must show that he or she has considered the reader's feelings and point of view.

ACTIVITIES: WRITING TACTFULLY

Many practice activities are suggested within the text of this chapter. Try those suggestions in addition to the activities listed below.

I. A. Often it's easier to see the need for tact in someone else's writing than in our own. As you read material that's written to you (or to people who are similar to you), note places where you feel the writer has totally ignored your point of view. What concessions do you feel the writer could have reasonably made? Which of the writer's words have unpleasant connotations for you? What other aspects of the writing could be changed without the writer's basic idea being altered significantly?

B. Now reread material you've already written yourself. Which of it could be more tactful? How could you improve it?

II. The following three exercises deal with the proposed thesis that the F grade should be eliminated. Read the following passage, assuming that it was written by a student and that the intended audience is teachers who think the F grade should be retained.

ELIMINATING THE F GRADE

The main reason the F grade should be eliminated is that teachers have no business judging students as "Failures." It's high-handed and presumptuous. Just think: the difference between a grade of 59 and 60 means the difference between an F and a D. Yet the F spells disaster for the student, while the D spells hope. How can any teacher be so sure of his or her opinion of a student as to ruin the student's life over a mere 1 or 2 points out of 100?

A second reason for eliminating the F is that it discriminates against students who aren't good in certain subjects. For instance, it's unfair of math teachers to fail liberal arts students just because those students can't do math. Maybe they do English, history, and philosophy very well. Teachers who give F grades are more concerned with showing how smart and tough they are than with helping the student. This is especially true in required courses that students can't drop.

The entire grading system is presumptuous, with the teachers acting like Gods, but the F is especially heartless and discriminatory.

A. If you basically agree with the student's view that the F should be eliminated, revise the draft, making it more tactful. Remember to walk in the teachers' shoes before you begin the revision.

B. If you basically disagree with the student's view, draft a response to the student himself, tactfully persuading him that the F should be retained. Remember to put yourself in his position so you can better understand how he feels.

C. If some people in class do activity A above and some do activity B, read your work out loud to each other, looking for areas you can agree with in the papers that take a position opposite your own.

III. A. Many times we feel that some group we belong to is misunderstood by the public. For instance, cheerleaders, athletes, models, and musicians sometimes find that others think their work involves nothing but glamour and fun. Housewives and members of the military often find that others have erroneous ideas about what they do—or don't do—all day. If you belong to a group that you feel is misunderstood in some way, write a report or article to set the story straight. Take as your audience people who need to be persuaded of the truth as you see it, and remember to write as tactfully as you can. (You may want to review "comparisons," Chapter 12.)

B. To find a different subject to write on, review the lists you made in the "I'm Not Going to Take It Any More" Catalogue (Chapter 4). Select one topic, decide on an audience who could improve that situation for you, and then write to that audience as tactfully, respectfully, and persuasively as you can.

chapter 15

To Write Persuasively, Offer Your Readers Logic and Evidence

There are times when our greatest need as writers is to develop a responsible, closely reasoned argument. This is the type of writing required for most college courses. It's the type of writing required in many other situations, such as persuading college administrators to provide more extensive support services for night students, or persuading readers of an article to adopt a particular political or other viewpoint. It's also the type of writing you would do as a businessperson trying to persuade your company to establish a new line of products or to adopt a new hiring policy. In short, whenever writers want their ideas or suggestions to be taken seriously, they have to present those ideas in a logical, carefully reasoned way.

It's been said that the most persuasive argument is one that sounds like an explanation. This is true, and it explains how to go about writing persuasion. You need to include whatever examples, facts, figures, and details your reader needs in order to understand your point of view. Many of the techniques in Chapter 12 are therefore useful for developing persuasive as well as informative writing. In addition, you need to consider your reader's point of view in order to know what questions and objections he or she needs to have answered. Thus the techniques in Chapter 14 go hand in hand with the techniques in this chapter.

Like other types of writing, logical persuasion presents more than just ideas: it presents an image of the reader and writer as well. In this case, the implied reader is presented as an intelligent person who expects to be given enough facts, logical explanation, and documentation to be able to make up his or her own mind on the issue at hand. In similar fashion, the writing implies that the writer is a mature, responsible person who respects the reader's intelligence. In many ways, this writing implies a pact between the reader and writer: it's as though they agree to certain unspoken ground rules or conventions of rational persuasion.

What are the ground rules readers expect responsible writers to follow? In general, college professors and other readers of serious reports and proposals expect you to:

1. Assume that your readers are intelligent and initially disagree with your position. (They also expect you to give thought to the information they already have and to avoid "telling them what they already know.")

2. Write in a logical, responsible manner, presenting valid evidence to support your position. (They also expect you to evaluate the validity of the sources you may use.)

3. Use good judgment in deciding what—and how much—to quote.

4. Explain how your quotations and other evidence prove your point.

5. Maintain a nonemotional tone and avoid excessive informality.

6. Document the source of your information so that your readers can evaluate your sources themselves.

These are the six main points covered in this chapter. As the following letter to a college newspaper demonstrates, readers can become irritated when they feel these ground rules have been broken:

Dear Editor:

As a member of the student body, I am writing to object to the article in the March 12 issue of the college newspaper concerning nuclear storage at West End. While I am in full agreement that West End should not be selected as the storage area for nuclear weapons, I feel that the article detracted from the validity of that viewpoint. An authority was presented minus credentials, the appeal was emotional, and there were no facts upon which the reader could base a judgment; therefore, the importance of the issue was diminished.

The reporter stated early in the article that much of the information contained was supplied by Mr. Earl Butler. While Mr. Butler was identified as coordinator of "Religious Action of Hawaii," the reporter failed to present Mr. Butler's scientific credentials. Is Mr. Butler an expert in some aspect of the nuclear field in his own right? Is his information based on the recognized credentials of others? As intelligent readers we have the obligation to assess his information based on his credentials.

Another source identified by the article was "The Stockholm International Research Institute." With the help of a school librarian, I attempted to locate information on this group. I was unable to discover any data on an organization with that name. However, I discovered there *is* a "Stockholm International Peace Research Institute," which regularly publishes information on disarmament. If this is the same group to which the article referred, deleting the word "Peace" from its title is an inexcusable omission, for it disallows the reader the opportunity to recognize the possibility of bias.

The nuclear arms issue is a very emotional subject. Any situation which threatens our very existence should be "felt," certainly. However, when presenting the issue to others for consideration, we must not allow emotion to becloud reason. Repeatedly, the article speculates on various hypothetical tragedies—a commercial airliner crashing into the storage facility, a helicopter crash detonating a nuclear weapon. We are informed that the odds are "very high" and the risk is "enormous." What precisely are we discussing? Are we discussing statistical odds or emotional reactions? If we are discussing statistical odds, why are none given in the article? A reader is entitled to objective analysis, not subjective adjectives.

Because this is an admittedly emotional subject, it must be handled in a reasonable and responsible manner. Particularly in an academic community, there should be extra importance attached to data validation and rational argument. To depend on emotionalism and innuendo detracts from the validity of the idea presented, insults the reader, and is unworthy of a college publication.

I appreciate the opportunity to present my views, and I sincerely hope that a more carefully reasoned and documented article will soon appear.

Sincerely,

Nancy L. Summers

With Nancy's letter in mind, let's now look at each of the ground rules mentioned earlier.

ASSUME AN INTELLIGENT READER WHO DISAGREES WITH YOU

The assumption that your reader at least initially disagrees with you is essential to all persuasive writing. Of course, when it's your reader's disagreement that has prompted your writing, it's easy to remember. For instance, if the City Council were about to put a garbage dump next to your favorite park, you'd have little trouble remembering the City Council's view as you wrote a letter or proposal suggesting they move the dump across town. While writing her letter to the college paper, Nancy probably had little difficulty remembering that the paper would, at least initially, disagree with her point of view.

However, when writing is not prompted by a reaction against someone else's ideas or actions, it's harder to remember that our intended readers might disagree with our views. For instance, students writing a proposal for a child care center on campus might find their own arguments so compelling that they could easily overlook the pressures the school administration might feel to spend the money on other services or overlook the possibly complex legal issues involved. Yet a proposal that didn't tactfully anticipate and logically address those issues would not be as effective as one that did.

When writing papers for college classes, it's especially important to assume (or make believe, if necessary) that the teacher initially disagrees with your thesis or main idea.[1] Why? Partly as a test of the thesis. When most college professors assign essays or research reports, they are looking for more than facts or summaries of what other people said. If they merely wanted to know whether you had read some material, they could save themselves considerable time by giving a short-answer or objective test. Therefore the very fact that your history teacher, for instance, assigns a paper is usually an indication that he or she wants your own conclusions regarding a problem, or your own interpretation or analysis of a book, concept, or event. If you can't imagine your professor's disagreeing with your conclusion or interpretation, it might be that you don't have a thesis of your own—that you are really summarizing what other people have said. Unless your professor has asked only for a summary, that's not enough.

Another reason to assume or make believe that your professor will disagree with your thesis is that this assumption will force you to offer enough evidence to be persuasive.

---

[1] If you need to find something to write about for a history, biology, art, or other school course, see the Wish List and the Idea File in Chapter 4. If you've been asked to write about a particular book, see Appendix E.

Even a brilliant idea, or one the professor happens to agree with, doesn't demonstrate that you really understand the subject unless you develop and prove the idea with evidence and logical arguments. Thus the grade a paper receives is usually a reflection of the *evidence* presented.

The following two papers were written for the same teacher. Both received good grades and both, you will notice, assume that the reader, in this case the teacher, probably disagreed with the thesis. As you read these two papers, notice that both writers assume the instructor has already read the book discussed in the writing. There is therefore no need for the students to summarize the plot or tell "what happens" in the book. In fact, if they were to summarize, it would be regarded as "padding." Both writers include evidence from the book, but they include it to prove their own points about the book, not to give information for its own sake.

The assignment given for the following papers was merely to "discuss" some aspect of the book's content or style. The students knew that the instructor had already read the book itself and did not want a summary. The first student, Larry Kimball, decided that he liked the book's approach. The second student, who is Sharon Kimball, Larry's wife, didn't care for the style at all. As you read their papers, see how many of the conventions of rational persuasion you can pick out.

THE TOTAL PICTURE

In *The Year of the Whale,* Victor Scheffer takes many opportunities to depart from his main narration and describe different aspects and lifestyles related to the sea as a whole. In doing this, he often changes the entire style of his writing, usually taking on a more serious scientific approach. For the reader, these sidelights offer a refreshing and informative change of pace, but at the same time they serve an even greater purpose by developing the reader's understanding and appreciation not only of the whale, but of its surrounding environment as well. To accomplish this, Scheffer uses two basic techniques.

First, he describes animals and events that are directly related to the life of the whale. Good examples are found when the whales mingle with schools of dolphin and porpoise. On many such occasions, Scheffer takes the opportunity to explain various aspects of dolphin behavior and research. In one instance, he even offers the interesting story of a porpoise that rescues a drowning woman (p. 35).[1] When the whales encounter a navy ship tracking them with sonar, Scheffer takes time out to explain whale sonar and communication. Later, following a sequence when the whales are feeding on squid, Scheffer traces the mythological story of the Kraken monster. In each case, he departs from the daily routine of the whale to describe a similar or related aspect of the ocean world.

A second method Scheffer uses to broaden our outlook is to describe events that are related solely to man's experiences with the sea. In doing this, he often uses specific examples, usually dealing with oceanic research. Instances of these "mini-stories" are found in his reference to deep diving (p. 61) and in his story of the biologist named "Sea Otter" Hansen (p. 172). Scheffer does not always stick to research-related material, however. Often he seems to enjoy adding a touch of human emotion, such as the fear experienced by Hansen as he encounters a whale underwater. Scheffer also includes a bit of romance by adding frequent references to Herman Melville's *Moby Dick* throughout the book. By skillfully using the element of human experience, Scheffer draws us even closer in our appreciation of the marine development.

Granted, departures from the main character or subject of a story are often distracting and in many cases only serve to confuse the reader. Scheffer, however, smoothly patterns his side trips to complement the story, and his transitions for the most part follow a logical sequence. This not only helps to explain the lifestyle of the whale, but provides us with further bits of information as well.

Overall, by combining relevant facts with human experience, Scheffer greatly enhances our "total picture" of the sea and thereby increases our knowledge and appreciation of its resources.

Larry Kimball

---

[1]Victor B. Scheffer, *The Year of the Whale* (New York: Charles Scribner's Sons, 1969). All page references are to this edition.

FACT OR FICTION?

In *The Year of the Whale,* Victor Scheffer's style of writing is often a confusing combination of descriptive imagery and scientific reality. Scheffer seems to assume the reader requires poetic stimulus to fully appreciate scientific fact. I concede that this style is effective in giving the material human interest. However, while adding human interest, Scheffer often confuses the reader by combining fact with fiction or by using overly descriptive words or phrases.

The whale who dies an "unrecorded death" (p. 61)[1] when it mistakes the Ecuadorian cable for a "squid" (p. 60) is an example of Scheffer's combination of fact with fiction. Fact is the Ecuadorian cable, which truly exists; fiction is the whale's death, which is unrecorded. Scheffer offers no proof that a whale actually died, just as he presents no evidence that the whale mistook the cable for a squid. The events leading to the whale's death are presented in a believable manner; however, the word "unrecorded" raises questions. Did a whale really die? Or does the author feel underwater telephone cables may be responsible for whale deaths? By combining fact with fiction without providing supporting evidence, Scheffer leaves it up to the reader to draw his own conclusions.

In another example, Scheffer weaves a story around a nursing whale and a ship which is cleaning its tank by pumping oil into the sea. Here the nursing whale discovers the milk has an "unpleasant taste" (p. 73), which the author indicates is a result of the oil pollutant. However due to the lack of any real evidence, the reader is left to wonder how Scheffer knows what things taste like to a whale—or, once again, if this particular whale and ship ever existed.

A squid that has met its death from an encounter with a bull whale is described by Scheffer as ". . . a moving gray-pink ghost—a vast membrane streaming through a void, a soft blue of naked whips" (p. 60). Granted, this style of writing is quite lyrical. But it also makes reading rather difficult. These phrases often have to be read numerous times to be fully understood. When describing the ocean setting, Scheffer often uses needlessly descriptive phrases. For example, he describes the ocean as ". . . a haze of crystal sparks"

(p. 170), ". . . struck by a shower of needles" (p. 151). These subjective descriptions contribute to the reader's difficulty in telling the "real" from the imaginary.

Admittedly, Victor Scheffer states in the preface that his story of the whale is "fiction based on fact" (p. vii). However, he too often leaves it up to the reader to determine the truth from the fiction in what he has written. *The Year of the Whale* contains valuable scientific information about the whale and other ocean creatures, but it should have been written in a manner that more clearly separated fact from fiction.

Sharon Kimball

---

[1]Victor B. Scheffer, *The Year of the Whale* (New York: Charles Schribner's Sons, 1969). All page references are to this edition.

Be Careful of "Mere Summary"

Contrast the above papers with the paper below:

THE YEAR OF THE WHALE

The Year of the Whale is about one year in the life of a baby whale.

The reader learns that even during the early years when a baby whale is still nursing, its life is dangerous. From the moment the calf is born, it must travel hundreds of miles with the group or pack. Its mother thus must be able to nurse it through storms, predators, and the dangers of man. The mothers feed their young through nipples on their underside. If a calf loses her mother, the calf will die because no other mother is going to feed that calf.

The book follows the sperm whales' annual migration from the waters of Mexico to the waters near the Arctic Sea. This migration is based on the whales' feeding habits and the areas where food is abundant. The sperm whales travel through storms and currents, through whaling areas and water polluted with oil, even through packs of killer whales to get to their destination. The migration, as presented in the book, is fraught with danger.

The reader follows the baby whale through it all, learning how difficult life can be for the largest of all sea creatures.

The above paper might be appropriately written for people who have not yet read the book and merely want to know what it is about. However, because it is primarily a summary of the book, it is not appropriately written for a college professor who has read the book and wants to know the student's own interpretation, conclusion, reaction, or analysis.

How can you tell when you are summarizing instead of presenting your own thesis? One way is to check the order of the information or evidence you include. If the information is in the same order in which it occurs in the book or magazine article, you may be summarizing. Another indication is whether you include information that the reader doesn't need to know. For instance, in the paper above, the writer includes the sentence, "The mothers feed their young through nipples on their underside." Although this is interesting, it doesn't prove or explain anything else in the paragraph or the paper as a whole. In short, it's a bit of summary the writer has included for its own sake rather than as explanation or proof of the writer's ideas *about* the book.

Another useful technique is to ask a friend to read your draft. (If you are writing about a book, try to find a friend who has read the same book.) Does your friend think you are including evidence in your paper or that you are merely summarizing? Can your friend see what your thesis is? Does your friend think your intended reader could reasonably disagree with your thesis—at least before reading your evidence? If the answer to the last question is no, perhaps you should rethink your thesis.

One last word about assuming your reader disagrees with your thesis. It's probably the best way to be sure that you will include appropriate concessions and will introduce and answer the questions and objections that might be in your reader's mind. (If you haven't yet read Chapter 14, you may want to do so now. The techniques discussed there under *Offer Concessions* and *Anticipate and Answer Your Reader's Questions* are essential to rational persuasion.)

WRITE RESPONSIBLY AND PRESENT VALID EVIDENCE

The second convention of rationally persuasive writing implies that the reader can trust both your honesty and your logic. In such writing, having a "correct" thesis or conclusion isn't enough; the evidence and arguments leading to that conclusion must be reliable. This convention is perhaps at the heart of Nancy Summers' letter to the college paper which appears earlier in this chapter.

When you want to write responsibly, you have to worry about more than your own writing. You're just as responsible for the validity of ideas and information you obtain from others. (That was the main point behind Nancy Summers' letter to the college paper.) The mere fact that something is in print doesn't mean it's reliable. You must decide for yourself if the information is reliable enough to use in your own writing. When you choose to present something as valid evidence, you're giving it your stamp of approval. Fortunately, it's possible to evaluate material you read, even when you're not yet very expert in the field you're reading about. One way is to check the credentials of the author. Look the author up in the appropriate *Who's Who* or check the author listing in *Books in Print,* or in the appropriate guide to periodical literature, to see what else that author has written.[2] Ask yourself if there's any reason to think the author may have a bias or may be less than expert in the subject. You can also evaluate the magazine or publishing company itself. Is it well known? Respected? Perhaps connected with a university? Is there any reason to think it might present a bias of its own? Finally, the date

---

[2]If you don't yet know how to do library research, see Appendix B for help.

is important. Is the book or article recent? This is especially important in scientific and technical subjects.

These methods of evaluating an author and publishing company can only serve as guides, however. After all, even a recognized expert may write occasional foolishness, and an unknown beginner—even one who normally has a bias—may write a responsible, carefully reasoned article. Therefore, evaluating the author or publishing house isn't enough. You must evaluate the material itself, weighing its reliability as you read it.

The following eight questions will help you determine the extent to which you can trust the material you're reading. Of course these questions work two ways: just as you can use them to test material you read, you can be sure that your own readers will use them to test *your* rationally persuasive writing.

1. Is the Source One-sided?

Ask yourself if the writer makes any concessions to opposing ideas or introduces possible questions and objections (see Chapter 14). If not, be suspicious of the writing; it may be slanted or one-sided.

2. Does the Source Contain Overgeneralizations?

Has the writer qualified important statements with words such as *some, may,* or *perhaps?* If not, the writer may be overgeneralizing. If you suspect that important statements are overgeneralizations, try thinking of other information you would need in order fully to weigh the ideas presented.

POSSIBLE OVERGENERALIZATIONS	READERS' QUESTIONS
Today's children can't read.	None of them? What do you mean by read?
If you get a degree in accounting, you'll be able to find a good-paying job.	For how long? Where? What if everyone takes this advice?
The three stores I surveyed as part of this experiment all overcharged for hand-crafted items. This indicates that shoppers should avoid purchasing handmade items from retail outlets.	Were the three stores you surveyed typical of all retail stores? What type of hand-crafted items did you price?

3. Does the Source Include Sufficient Data and Evidence?

Do not accept new or controversial ideas without data and evidence to support them. For instance, if someone wrote, "Chain stores make excessive profits," you could reasonably ask, "All of them?" You should even look for evidence or proof of more limited statements such as "Supermarkets make excessive profits."

4. Does the Source Include False Choices?

Sometimes writers oversimplify issues by presenting the reader with only one or two choices when there are actually other alternatives. Whether the limited choices are offered intentionally (as in much advertising) or unintentionally, they indicate that the author is not a completely reliable source of information. Note the following examples of false choice:

FALSE CHOICE	OTHER OPTIONS
If you want this state to be beautiful, vote for Jim Gonzales for governor.	Perhaps Gonzales' opponent will also beautify the state. Or perhaps the legislature will defeat Gonzales' beautification bills even if he is elected.
The city has two choices: it can widen the highways or it can move to a rapid transit system.	Perhaps traffic congestion could be relieved by staggering school and work hours.

5. Does the Source Contain False Causation?

Much rationally persuasive writing includes an explanation of causes—of *why* something happened or will happen. Yet a responsible explanation of causes is very tricky. For instance, writers sometimes oversimplify by offering just one cause for an event or situation that really had several causes.

FALSE CAUSATION	OTHER POSSIBLE CAUSES
Johnny can't read because he watches too much television.	Johnny's parents don't set an example by reading themselves; Johnny's teacher is asked to promote Johnny whether he can read or not.

In addition to checking whether or not the author has presented all of the important causes, you must also check to be sure the causes presented are, in fact, causes. For instance, if I spray my brand-new ninth-floor apartment with anti-elephant spray the day I move in, I might find after a year that I haven't been bothered by a single elephant. What does that prove about the spray? Or I might hammer a horseshoe over the door of my new apartment and, after a year, realize that I've had marvelous luck during the entire year. What does that prove about the horseshoe? As much as we might enjoy thinking we can ward off bad luck or bring good luck, just the fact that A happened before B doesn't mean that A caused B. Here are some examples of "Before = Because" thinking:

OVERSIMPLIFICATIONS	READERS' QUESTIONS
The history of Western Europe shows that an increase in armaments has always preceded an outbreak of war. (Implication: A buildup in armaments causes wars.)	Perhaps something else caused both the arms buildup and the war? Perhaps there would have been a war anyway?
Most heroin addicts used marijuana before turning to heroin. That proves that marijuana leads to heroin.	But perhaps most heroin addicts also drank milk or chewed gum before turning to heroin. Does that prove milk or gum leads to heroin addiction? Possibly some third cause led to both the marijuana and the heroin?

This last example would prompt some readers to ask, "What percent of the marijuana users turned to heroin? Indeed, if that figure were high, it would strongly suggest a link between the two drugs—but it still wouldn't establish a causal link. In truth, it is very difficult to prove that one thing actually causes another; to do so, the causal connection itself must be established. Unless it can be, careful writers qualify their statements to indicate that the causal connections are only "possible."

6. Does the Source Include Sufficient Documentation?

If the author has made it difficult for you to check up on the sources of the information used, be suspicious. First, the author may be misrepresenting what the sources said. Second, the sources might not exist at all. Third, they may exist but be so unreliable that the writer doesn't want you to know who or what they are. In general, the easier the writer makes it for you to evaluate the sources—and get your hands on a copy of the book or magazine article—the better. In reports written for college classes and scholarly periodicals, this documentation usually takes the form of footnotes or other formal documentation, complete with page references. One typical format used looks like this:

[1]Alden Todd, *Finding Facts Fast* (Berkeley: Ten Speed Press, 1979), p. 26.

Footnotes may appear at the bottom of the page containing the quoted or paraphrased materials or they may be all listed together at the end of the report.

In popular magazine articles the documentation is usually included in the writing itself, and, for simplicity's sake, the page references and publishing information are frequently omitted. Because informal documentation is appropriate for the intended readers of popular magazines, this method doesn't necessarily indicate irresponsible writing. However, it can be frustrating for researchers who want to check the original source themselves. Informal documentation may look like this:

"On election day 1980, in the pages of the *Wall Street Journal,* John Cooper spoke of the need for all political parties to cooperate in an effort to reduce the national debt."

Business reports and proposals may include documentation of either type mentioned above, but, in addition, copies of the important tables and other reference materials referred to in the writing are often attached to the end of the report itself. These attachments (sometimes called an "appendix") are a courteous way to save the readers from having to hunt down copies of the material. (Because of their convenience for the reader, attachments are also used in much scientific writing.)

When writers document their evidence, you can evaluate their sources in the same way that you evaluate sources for your own use. Has the writer used experts in the field? Are the references up to date? Has the writer relied on just one or two sources? Might the writer be overgeneralizing on the basis of very limited sources?

7. Are Statistics Carefully Used?

Statistics are important in persuasive writing. Careful readers don't want to be told that there's a "good chance" that a plane could crash into a nuclear weapon storage site; they want to know what the statistical chance is. They don't want to be told that an accidental detonation is a "likely possibility"; they want to know, statistically, what the possibility is. But to evaluate statistics, you need more than the bare numbers.

In order to evaluate statistics, it's helpful to know who compiled the statistics. (Were they compiled by a group with a vested interest in the subject? Are they government statistics? Do they come from a recognized and respected private research outfit?) In addition, it's often helpful to know how the statistics were compiled. Statistics of "unreported thefts," for instance, must be evaluated on the basis of how those unreported thefts were estimated. Polls must be evaluated on the basis of how the participants were selected. To take an extreme example, a poll showing that "100 percent of the families polled had telephones in their homes" would be meaningless if the families had been polled by phone or were selected from the phone book.

A point of comparison can also be helpful in assessing statistics. For instance, if you were to read that there were an estimated 138,200,000 TV sets in the United States in 1979, you would have no way of interpreting that figure unless you also knew how many households there were, or that there were 444,000,000 radios and 155,173,000 telephones.[3]

Finally, readers must be cautious of the way statistics are interpreted. In at least one state, 55 percent of the heavy drinkers are married and 61 percent of the heavy drinkers are employed.[4] What conclusion can reasonably be drawn from those figures? What other information would a careful reader need to interpret them—or the conclusions

---

[3]*Information Please Almanac,* 1979 (New York: Information Please Publishing, Inc., 1978), p. 5.

[4]"Hawaii State Survey of Substance Abuse, 1979," an unpublished survey conducted for the Alcohol and Drug Abuse Branch, Hawaii State Department of Health, p. 12, table 4.

drawn from them? (Among other things, a reader might want to know what percent of the population is married and/or employed as well as what percent of the married and employed people were heavy drinkers.)

8. Does the Source Include Emotionally Loaded Language?

Does the writer say someone "admitted" or "announced" that a new gene-splicing procedure is being used in laboratories? The difference in emotional impact—and what the difference says about the writer's bias—is great. A friend saying you "admitted" coming home at 2:00 A.M. would be implying one thing. The friend saying you "announced" that you came home at 2:00 A.M. would be implying something different. If your friend merely said you "said" or "reported" that you got in at 2:00 A.M., the implication would be still different—in this case, quite neutral. (See Chapter 13 for more on emotionally loaded language.)

As a test for emotionally loaded language, try substituting words with connotations different from those in the material you're reading. Such substitutions will help you detect and evaluate an author's bias. Several examples follow:

EMOTIONALLY LOADED WORDS	POSSIBLE REPLACEMENTS
The store sells *crumbs* of cheese for high prices.	. . . sells *individually sliced bits* of cheese . . . .
The *cheaply made* homes	. . . the *inexpensive* homes . . . .
Executives who *psychologically manipulate* their employees	Executives who *reward* their employees . . . .

The previous eight questions can help you decide which of your sources are probably reliable and which you should avoid. In addition, they can help you check your own writing to see if it is as responsibly written as it could be.

See activity I at the end of this chapter for practice in evaluating sources.

QUOTE JUST THE RIGHT AMOUNT AND PARAPHRASE WHEN POSSIBLE

There are two ways to include information in your reports. You can either quote information exactly or you can put it into your own words. When you put information into your own words, you can usually shorten it and thus save your reader's time. You can also blend evidence from widely different sources into one consistent style—your own—thus making your writing smoother and easier for your reader to follow.

One difficulty with putting evidence into your own words is that, if you're not careful, it can lead you into pointless summarizing. The trick is to keep your purpose clear: is your purpose to include evidence in as brief a form possible, or is it to summarize for your reader? In persuasive writing your purpose will usually be to include evidence.

(Of course, a brief summary that helps you prove your point isn't "mere summary"—it's evidence. It's a question of purpose, and of how much your reader already knows.)

Paraphrasing

Putting information into your own words is called *paraphrasing* and is an important writing skill. If you reread the Kimballs' writing earlier in this chapter, you'll find that they have paraphrased most of the evidence—that is, they've put it into their own words. By and large, readers prefer paraphrases to long or frequent quotations.

Whenever you paraphrase, the style should sound like you, not like the original author. The ideas, however, should be faithful to the original source; be careful not to distort them. When you paraphrase evidence for persuasive writing, keep your purpose in mind and be careful not to lapse into summary for its own sake. Also, be careful to give credit where it is due. Since the words in a paraphrase are your own, do not put quotation marks around them. However, since the ideas are *not* yours, you *do* have to use a footnote or other method of giving credit to the original author (see Appendix C).

Below is a quotation, a reasonable paraphrase of it, and another paraphrase that borrows too many phrases from the original author:

Quotation

Nowhere in all the sea does life exist in such bewildering abundance as in the surface waters. From the deck of a vessel you may look down, hour after hour, on the shimmering discs of jellyfish, their gently pulsating bells dotting the surface as far as you can see. Or one day you may notice early in the morning that you are passing through a sea that has taken on a brick-red color from billions upon billions of microscopic creatures, each of which contains an orange pigment granule. At noon you are still moving through red seas, and when darkness falls the waters shine with an eerie glow from the phosphorescent fires of yet more billions and trillions of these same creatures.[5]

Appropriate Paraphrase

As Rachel Carson indicates in *The Sea Around Us,* the ocean's surface is teaming with life such as jellyfish and even microscopic creatures that can turn the entire surface red.

Poor Paraphrase

As Rachel Carson indicates in *The Sea Around Us,* nowhere in all the sea is there as much life as on the surface waters. You can see the jellyfish, their bells gently floating on the surface. Or you may suddenly notice that the sea you are passing through is brick red from billions upon billions of microscopic creatures. Each one has an orange pigment granule. At night these same creatures give off a phosphorescent glow.

The second paraphrase has three problems: First, it borrows too many of Rachel Carson's own phrases and therefore plagiarizes. Even though Carson has been given

---

[5]Rachel Carson, *The Sea Around Us* (New York: Oxford University Press, 1950), p. 31.

credit for the ideas, she hasn't been given credit for the style that is really hers. Another problem is that since the style is Carson's and not the paraphraser's, that portion of the writing will stand out from the rest of the writer's paper rather than blend in with it. Finally, it seems to be without purpose. One can imagine the first paraphrase being used to prove a point about the amount of life on the ocean's surface, but it's hard to see what purpose all the detail in the second paraphrase might serve.

If you are concerned that your own paraphrases are too close to the original author's style, try reading some of your paraphrases out loud. Do they really sound like your own writing? If they do, you probably don't have to worry. But if they don't, you may be unconsciously plagiarizing the original author's words. Since plagiarism is both an academic and legal offense, appropriate paraphrasing is worth a bit of practice. See activity II at the end of this chapter.

Quoting

Of course you can't paraphrase everything. There are times when you have to quote. That should be your rule of thumb: Quote only when there's a good reason to. In general, it's a good idea to quote your source exactly in the following situations:

1. When you are going to disagree with what someone is saying. (If you don't quote the person involved, how can your reader be sure you aren't simply misrepresenting that person's view to start with?)
2. When the information itself is very difficult to believe. (In this case, quoting the author's exact words gives the information greater credibility.)
3. When you are discussing someone's style of writing. (There is no way to give evidence of an author's style without quoting some of it.)
4. When you're afraid that by paraphrasing you'll change the meaning. (But be careful: In most cases, if you can't put ideas into your own words, it may be a sign that you don't really understand those ideas yet, at least not well enough to write about them.)
5. When a particular statement is so witty or so perfectly phrased that you want to share it with your reader. (Yet, once again, be careful not to use this as an excuse for padding.)

With these guides in mind, reread the first two papers on *The Year of the Whale*. Would either paper benefit from aditional quotations? From fewer quotations? Why? You may notice that the quotations used in those papers are typically less than one sentence long. That's in keeping with the general principle of quoting only what's necessary. If a phrase proves your point, quote the phrase, not the complete sentence. If a sentence makes the point nicely, quote the sentence, not the entire paragraph. It's part of your responsibility as the writer to select only those portions that are necessary to prove your point. Don't ask your reader to do the selection for you. (If you are not accustomed to quoting less than complete sentences, see Appendix D for help.)

Suppose you end up with no quotations at all. That's possible, but it should be a warning sign that you may have paraphrased in a few cases where a quotation was called for. If they do nothing else, one or two quotations can help reassure your reader that you've read the sources carefully.

EXPLAIN YOUR EVIDENCE

In addition to assuming that your reader will initially disagree with your thesis, you should write with the assumption that, whenever possible, your reader will interpret the evidence you offer differently from the way you interpret it. If you offer statistics that indicate to you that the population in your city is growing too fast, your reader may interpret those statistics to mean the population is growing just fast enough to keep the economy healthy. If you offer evidence that proves, in your mind, that there is a need for handgun control, your reader may interpret that same evidence as proof that handguns should not be controlled. In short, it isn't enough to state the evidence—you have to make clear how or why the evidence proves your point.

In addition, you must make the connection between each paragraph and your main idea clear. This technique is explained in the last section of Chapter 7: Check Each Paragraph's Link to Your Main Idea. You may wish to review that section now.

Sharon Kimball's paper on *The Year of the Whale* illustrates both of these techniques:

FACT OR FICTION?

In <u>The Year of the Whale</u>, Victor Scheffer's style of writing is often a confusing combination of descriptive imagery and scientific reality. Scheffer seems to assume the reader requires poetic stimulus to fully appreciate scientific fact. I concede this style is effective in giving the material human interest. However, while adding human interest, Scheffer often confuses the reader by combining fact with fiction or by using overly descriptive words or phrases. *[thesis]*

The whale who dies an "unrecorded death" (p. 61)[1] when it mistakes the Ecuadorian cable for a "squid" (p. 60) is an example of Scheffer's combination of fact with fiction. Fact is the Ecuadorian cable, which truly exists; fiction is the whale's death, which is unrecorded. Scheffer offers no proof that a whale actually died, just as he presents no evidence that the whale mistook the cable for a squid. The events leading to the whale's death are presented in a believable manner; however, the word "unrecorded" raises questions. *[evidence / explanation of above evidence]*

[thesis]

[links back to thesis]

Did a whale really die? Or does the author feel
underwater telephone cables may be responsible for whale
deaths? By combining fact with fiction without
providing supporting evidence, Scheffer leaves it up to
the reader to draw his own conclusions.

links back to thesis

In another example, Scheffer weaves a story around
a nursing whale and a ship which is cleaning its tank by
pumping oil into the sea. Here the nursing whale
discovers that milk has an "unpleasant taste" (p. 73),
which the author indicates is a result of the oil
pollutant. However, due to the lack of any real
evidence, the reader is left to wonder how Scheffer
knows what things taste like to a whale--or, once again,
if this particular whale and ship ever existed.

evidence

explanation of above evidence

A squid that has met its death from an encounter
with a bull whale is described by Scheffer as "...a
moving gray-pink ghost--a vast membrane streaming
through a void, a soft blue of naked whips" (p. 60).
Granted, this style of writing is quite lyrical. But it
also makes reading rather difficult. These phrases
often have to be read numerous times to be fully
understood. When describing the ocean setting, Scheffer
often uses needlessly descriptive phrases. For example,
he describes the ocean as "...a haze of crystal sparks"
(p. 170), "...struck by a shower of needles" (p. 151).
These subjective descriptions contribute to the reader's
difficulty in telling the "real" from the imaginary.

evidence

explanation of above evidence

links back to thesis

Admittedly, Victor Scheffer states in the preface
that his story of the whale is "fiction based on fact"
(p. vii). However, he too often leaves it up to the
reader to determine the truth from the fiction in what
he has written. The Year of the Whale contains
valuable scientific information about the whale and
other ocean creatures, but it should have been written
in a manner that more clearly separated fact from
fiction.

links back to thesis

Sharon Kimball

---

[1]Victor B. Scheffer, *The Year of the Whale* (New York: Charles Scribner's Sons, 1969). All page
references are to this edition.

MAINTAIN A NONEMOTIONAL TONE AND AVOID EXCESSIVE INFORMALITY

Don't be misled by the personal behavior of the people for whom you're writing. Often a teacher or boss seems very informal—perhaps curses or jokes around—yet that same person may be upset if you write a very informal report.

The conventions of rationally persuasive or responsible writing include an appropriate tone. In general, you should avoid language that's so emotional as to call your judgment into question. Also avoid slang. That doesn't mean going to the other extreme. There's no need to turn yourself into a machine that writes with all the warmth and grace of a computer.

The best style to strive for is one that is clean, easy to read, and straightforward. It should sound businesslike but natural. Perhaps the best test, as always, is to read it aloud or have someone read it to you.

DOCUMENT YOUR SOURCES

Just as you should check the sources of the writers you read, your own readers will want to be able to evaluate the sources you use. Appendix C provides guides for two different types of formal documentation. As you use those guides, however, don't become so obsessed with where to put commas and periods that you lose sight of the overall purpose of documentation.

That purpose is to make it as easy as possible for your readers to evaluate the sources you have used, and, if they want, to locate copies of those sources. When you document your sources, you should therefore ask yourself two main questions:

1. What information would help my readers evaluate this source?
2. What information would help my readers find a copy of this information?

The details of format—where commas and parentheses go, for instance—are means to an end, not ends in themselves. A standardized format simply makes it easier for readers to find what they want within a footnote or bibliographic entry.

In general, if readers are going to be able to evaluate your sources and locate copies when they want to, they will need the following information

Books:

Author (both to evaluate the author's reliability and to help locate the book in the library or bookstore).

Title (to help locate the book).

Date (to evaluate whether the information is up to date and to know which edition the page references refer to).

Publishing house (to help evaluate the reliability of the book and to make the page references useful for books that are published by two or more companies).

City of publication (traditionally included; helpful in locating books published by new or little-known publishing houses).

Page references (helpful in evaluating whether or not all the references are from the same few pages; essential if the reader wants to read the original materials).

Magazines

Author (to evaluate the author's reliability).

Title of article (to help locate the article).

Name of the magazine (to evaluate the article's reliability and to help locate it).

Page reference (to help locate the original material).

Inclusive pages (used in the bibliography; helpful in assessing the length of the article and in locating it).

In addition to helping your readers evaluate and locate copies of your sources, documentation serves another purpose. It enables you to strengthen your own position by showing that you did use reliable sources.

SUMMARY OF CHAPTER

The type of writing discussed in this chapter depends upon an unspoken pact between the reader and writer. The reader agrees to consider what the writer has to say, and to be persuaded by it if the evidence presented is sufficiently logical and compelling. In exchange, the reader expects the writer to carefully weigh evidence and to write in a reasonable, responsible manner. The writer agrees to do just that.

Writing responsibly means not only weighing evidence carefully, but also anticipating and answering the reader's questions and objections. It means avoiding oversimplifications and half-truths. It means presenting evidence in such a way that the reader can easily evaluate both the evidence itself and the source of the evidence. In short, it means respecting the reader's intelligence and appealing to his or her sense of logic. It's writing with integrity.

Here's a copy of a student research paper on the nursing shortage in the student's home state. The paper was written by Mark Andruss. As you read it, notice how it observes the six conventions of responsible writing discussed in this chapter.

WHERE ARE ALL THE NURSES?

Recently a friend of mine was in the hospital. One day while I
visiting him, he rang the call bell for assistance. We waited for fifteen
minutes but had no response. We thought perhaps the bell was faulty. So I
walked down to the nurse's station to inquire if they had received my
friend's call. They had. Politely, I asked why the call had not been
answered. The nurse replied, "If you knew the staffing shortage we have you
would understand our problems."

Curious, I did a little research and found that nationally, hospitals
and nursing organizations are deeply concerned about an acute shortage of
nurses, and Hawaii is no exception.

According to the U.S. Department of Labor, employment opportunities in
the health field are expected to grow much faster than the average for all
occupations through the mid-1980s.[1] Why the shortage of help in a growing
field? Admittedly, it is difficult to earn a degree in nursing, but this
cannot be the reason for the shortage of Registered Nurses (RN's)
nationally. From the Great Lakes to the Gulf of Mexico, and from coast to
coast, health care facilities confront a crisis situation in obtaining
sufficient numbers of skilled nurses.[2] Why?

It seems that there are a significant number of reasons why there is a
shortage of nurses. According to Kathy Titchen, Honolulu Star Bulletin
staff writer, at Queens Medical Center, with a permanent staff of 200 RN's,
119 nurses resigned in the 15-month period from January 1977 to March 1978.[3]

---

[1] U.S. Department of Labor, Bureau of Labor Statistics, Occupational
Outlook Handbook, 1978-79 Edition (Washington, D.C.: Government Printing
Office, 1978), p. 448.

[2] Letitia Cunningham, "Nursing Shortage," American Journal of Nursing, 79
(March 1979), 471.

[3] Kathy Titchen, "Concern Is Mounting Over Nurse Shortage," Honolulu Star
Bulletin, March 30, 1979, Section A, p. 14.

The reasons nurses gave for resigning were job dissatisfaction and   2

understaffing. Some nurses complain that they are not involved in decision

making on such things as remodeling units or making changes in procedures to

facilitate patient care. Others say that understaffing in some units is so

critical that patients' lives are at stake. Nurses charge that they are not

performing their jobs. They are often given nonnursing functions such as

paper work or scheduling laboratory and X-ray appointments.

In addition to the previously mentioned factors of job dissatisfaction

and understaffing, another problem that has led to the lack of nurses is

poor financial compensation. Admittedly, financial compensation for the

nursing field has improved in the last couple of years, but it has been

found that nurses make less than trainee traffic-signal repairmen. An even

greater disparity exists with doctors whose median income is now more than

$65,000 a year.[4] Nurses are not compensated as well as some professions

where a comparable amount of education is required. A beginning nurse in

Hawaii earns from $10,000 to $12,000 a year, and nurses can't expect to earn

more than $16,000 a year even after several years' service. Working all

those hours, under stress, for that kind of pay is extremely discouraging.

Another controversial issue is the sporadic working hours. In Hawaii

nurses work on a rotating schedule. It is not uncommon for them to work

double shifts and on their days off to cover understaffed units. Since most

nurses are women and have families, many find the shifting hours incompatible

with child rearing and other family responsibilities. Traditionally,

nursing has been a woman's occupation. Data developed from the 1970 census

revealed that there were 2,819 female RN's and 100 male RN's employed in

Hawaii at that time.[5] It is important to realize that because of new job

opportunities there are not enough women to fill the demand for nursing

---

[4]"Rebellion Among the Angels," Time, August 27, 1979, p. 62.

[5]U.S. Department of Commerce, Bureau of Census, 1970 Census of
Population: Detailed Characteristics (Hawaii), Final Report PC (1)-D 13
Hawaii (Washington, D.C : Government Printing Office, 1972), p. 295.

personnel. Also nursing has expanded to encompass a wide variety of job possibilities. Nurses can now find employment in industry, clinics, schools, and public and private agencies, where they have more autonomy, regular hours, and less stress.

As a result of the problems stated above, some nurses have resorted to part-time nursing jobs. There are now four agencies in Hawaii that provide relief nurses. These agencies become the employers who recruit nurses on an "on-call" basis, paying their wages, workmen's compensation, etc. These agencies are modeled after the firms that have supplied temporary office help all over the country. The four national agencies include: Western Medical Services, a division of Western Temporary Services, Inc., first to establish here in 1975; Upjohn Health Services, a subsidiary of Upjohn Pharmaceutical Co., opened in 1976; Medical Personnel Pool of America, a subsidiary of H & R Block; and Kokua Nursing, opened in 1979. Hospital administrators are reluctant to use these agencies, but because of the lack of nurses there is no choice. Administrators also grumble that these agencies are exploitative, charging the hospitals exorbitant prices. According to _Time_ magazine, pay at Hollywood Presbyterian Hospital, for example, is $93 a day (after agency fees) for a temporary vs. $64 for a hospital paid staff member.[6] There have also been complaints that these agencies send inadequately trained nurses. Additionally, orientating these nurses tends to slow responses from staff nurses.

The causes of the current nursing shortage are complex, yet working conditions and wages seem to be at the heart of them. Perhaps it's necessary for the hospitals to take time out and examine the root causes before the present reliance on temporary help becomes all too permanent.

---

[6]"Rebellion Among the Angels," p. 62.

BIBLIOGRAPHY

Cunningham, Letitia. "Nursing Shortage." _American Journal of Nursing_, 79 (March 1979), 469-480.

"Rebellion Among the Angels." _Time Magazine_, August 27, 1979, pp. 62-63.

Titchen, Kathy. "Concern Is Mounting Over Nurse Shortage." _Honolulu Star Bulletin_, March 30, 1979, Section A, p. 14.

U.S. Department of Commerce, Bureau of Census, _1970 Census of Population: Detailed Characteristics (Hawaii)_, Final Report PC (1)-D 13 Hawaii (Washington, D.C.: Government Printing Office, 1972).

U.S. Department of Labor, Bureau of Labor Statistics, _Occupational Handbook_, 1978-79 Edition (Washington, D.C.: Government Printing Office 1978).

I. Evaluating Sources

    A. Let's say that you were planning to write a report on the shortage of nurses in hospitals and you came across the following article. Keep in mind that the author's thesis is not in question—it's the reliability of the arguments and evidence she presents. Here's a quick summary of the eight basic questions to ask yourself:

        1. Is the writing one-sided?

        2. Does the writing contain overgeneralizations?

        3. Does the writing include sufficient data and evidence?

        4. Does the writing include false choices?

        5. Does the writing contain false causation?

        6. Does the writing include sufficient documentation?

        7. Are statistics carefully used?

        8. Does the writing include emotionally loaded language?

HOW TO SOLVE THE NURSING SHORTAGE

Nursing has been considered a profession since 1903, when North Carolina began to require a written examination and a license for nurses to practice. Other states followed this precedent—but nursing is still a profession in name only.

Although there are male nurses, nursing is still a predominantly female profession. This is a big part of the problem. Male chauvinist doctors have traditionally expected nurses to serve as handmaidens, doing everything from cleaning bedpans to assisting in surgery. Doctors expect nurses to be "quiet, docile, and respectful." They feel that nurses are "rather like household help" brought in to do the dirty work only. Now, however, nurses are refusing to play this old male–female game and are rebelling. The most telling sign of this rebellion is the current nursing shortage which is seen throughout the country. If doctors won't treat nurses as fellow professionals, nurses will simply leave the "profession."

Another difficulty with the nursing profession is salary. In 1979 the average salary for nurses was around $13,000 a year—that's less than cashiers make at the large grocery store chains! But studies show that 48 percent of the doctors think that nurses are paid just about right, and 10 percent actually feel that nurses are overpaid. What other "profession" rewards it workers with $13,000 a year? If the salary paid to nurses were raised to $20,000 a year or more, nursing would become the "profession" it is supposed to be and the nursing shortage would disappear.

In conclusion, our nursing shortage is caused by unprofessional working conditions. Doctors visit patients in the hospital for an average of five minutes per patient. It's the nurses who treat patients and help them get well. Yet the May 1979 issue of *Good Housekeeping* reveals that a questionnaire conducted among 2,000 doctors and 2,000 nurses showed that 85 percent of the nurses respected the doctors but only 13 percent of the doctors respected the nurses. The low regard and low pay must end. When they do, the nursing shortage will end too.

B. Compare Mark Andruss' report on nursing with this one. What strengths does Mark's have that this one lacks? What makes Mark's more responsibly written? Be as specific as possible in your answers.

C. As you read magazines and books, evaluate the writing not only for clarity and interest, but also for the extent to which it seems responsibly written. When you notice writing that is less responsible than you feel it should be, share that writing with others. Do they agree with you? Why or why not?

II. Paraphrasing

A. Select one page from a book or magazine. Decide what the author's main point is on that page, then paraphrase that idea as though you were going to use it as an example or evidence in a paper. Try to shorten it by at least half, probably more. (If you select something in which the writer or characters use *I* to refer to themselves, you'll have to change the *I* to *he* or *she*.

B. After you've written your paraphrase, read it out loud. Does it sound like your own writing? As a more mechanical check, circle all the words you've used that are the same words the author used. (Circle words even if you changed the word order or the endings, but don't circle words like *the* or *to*.) If you find that you've circled several words in a row, or that one-fourth or more of your words are circled, you may be borrowing too much of the original writer's style. Looking away from your paper and saying the ideas out loud, in your own words, will help you write a paraphrase.

III. Writing

A. Review the persuasive writing you've already written, whether it's in draft or final form. Should some of it be rewritten using the techniques in this chapter? If so, try rewriting it, even if just for the practice.

B. Review writing you've done for other college courses other than English. Did you summarize when the teacher really wanted your own thesis or ideas? Did you offer enough evidence? Did you explain how the evidence proved the points you were trying to make? If you feel dissatisfied with a paper you've written for a course other than English, review the assignment to be sure you understand what the professor was asking for. If you think he or she wanted the type of writing described in this chapter, and if you are still taking that course, see if the professor might let you redo the paper using the techniques presented in this chapter.

IV. Review the "I'm Not Going to Take It Anymore" Catalogue, and the Wish List in Chapter 4. Use those techniques to locate a subject or idea that calls for rationally persuasive writing. (You may, of course, already have a subject in mind.) If you already know how to do library research, research the idea then write on it. If you're not sure how to do library research, read Appendix B, then start. Either way, write the more rationally persuasive report you can.

appendix A

A Brief Grammar Guide

This appendix is not designed to teach you grammatical terminology, nor is it designed to teach you all about grammar. Rather, it's designed to give you practical guidance in rewriting your own sentences to avoid very common grammatical problems. Each problem is briefly explained with examples. After the explanation, there's a brief exercise so you can test whether you understand the examples. Since the answers to the exercises are at the end of this appendix, you can test your understanding immediately. If you get the exercises right, you can then revise your own sentences. If you don't, you should ask your teacher or someone else for help before working on your own sentences.

The following topics are covered in this appendix:

Sentence fragments

Run-on sentences

Subject-verb agreement

Pronoun agreement and non-sexist language

Parallelism

Spelling, contractions, and possessives

Punctuation

If you don't find what you are looking for in the list above, please use the alphabetical index at the back of the book. It will help you find grammar tips located in earlier chapters. It will also help you find what you need even if you are using words different from those used in this book. (For instance, some people say *comma splice* while others say *run-on sentence*. Both words are listed in the index.)

SENTENCE FRAGMENTS

As you read the following sentences, notice that each has a subject (underlined once) and a verb (underlined twice). These sentences are grammatically "complete" because they contain a subject and a verb in a way that "sounds" as though the whole sentence is there:

1. <u>Cars</u> <u>move</u>.
2. <u>Cars</u> <u>move</u> swiftly along the freeway.
3. <u>Moving</u> swiftly along the freeway <u>is</u> dangerous.
4. Moving swiftly along the freeway, <u>cars</u> <u>are</u> dangerous.

Notice that in sentences 3 and 4, *moving* is not the verb. In sentence 3, *moving* is the subject. (What *is dangerous? Moving* is dangerous.) In sentence 4, *moving* is an adjective that describes the car. *Cars* is now the subject. (What *are dangerous? Cars* are dangerous.)

When a verb has *-ing* on the end, it no longer counts as a verb unless a "helping verb" such as *is, am,* or *has been* accompanies it. The following sentences contain helping verbs:

1. <u>He</u> <u>is moving</u> swiftly down the freeway.
2. <u>He'</u> <u>s moving</u> swiftly down the freeway.
3. <u>He</u> <u>was going</u> very fast.

Sentence Fragments: -ing

A sentence fragment is a group of words that isn't quite a sentence; an essential element, such as the subject or verb, is missing. The following are sentence fragments:

Going to the library and doing research.
Walking slowly away with his hand in his pocket.

One way to test a sentence fragment is to see if it would sound complete with the words "I believe that . . ." in front of it.
　　I believe that going to the library and doing research . . . .
　　I believe that walking slowly away with his hand in his pocket . . . .

Neither of these statements sounds complete. To correct sentence fragments, it's necessary to rewrite them so they contain both a subject and a verb and sound complete. This can be done in several ways:

Fragment

Going to the library and doing research.
REWRITE 1: <u>Going</u> to the library and <u>doing</u> research <u>bores</u> me. (Verb added.)
REWRITE 2: <u>I</u> <u>went</u> to the library and <u>did</u> research. (*Going* and *doing* have been changed to the verbs *went* and *did*. Notice that one subject can have two verbs.)

Fragment

Walking slowly away with his hand in his pocket.
REWRITE 1: <u>He</u> <u>is walking</u> slowly away with his hand in his pocket. (The subject *he* and the helping verb *is* have been added.)

REWRITE 2: I <u>saw</u> him walking slowly away with his hand in his pocket. ("<u>I saw</u> him" has been added.)

The four rewrites above all pass the "I believe that . . ." test. Check them to see.

Exercise I:

Rewrite whichever of the following are sentence fragments. (Use the "I believe that . . ." test.) The first one is done for you. Answers are at the end of this appendix.

1. Reading about New Mexico and realizing that she could move there, Mrs. Howell becoming interested in the subject.

   By reading about New Mexico and realizing that she could move there, <u>Mrs. Howell</u> <u>became interested</u> in the subject.

   or

   <u>Mrs. Howell</u> <u>became</u> interested in New Mexico when she <u>read</u> about it and <u>realized</u> that she could move there.

2. The dark gray ship floating at the pier. The cargo was unloaded quickly.

3. Wagging his tail, the dog barked ferociously. He knew there was no real danger.

4. Reading silently in the library, John and his three buddies working on research papers.

Sentence Fragments: Dependent Clauses (*Because, which,* etc.)

Sometimes a statement can contain both a subject and a verb without being a complete sentence. Consider the following fragments:

Fragments:

> *Because* he laughs too much.
> The green grass *which* she had just finished mowing.

The "I believe that . . ." test can reveal this type of fragment also.

> *I believe that* because he laughs too much . . . .
> *I believe that* the green grass which she had just finished mowing . . . .

Each of these statements leaves the reader feeling that something is missing. The reason is that words such as *because* or *which* make one clause (a group of words with a subject and verb) dependent on another clause to complete the sentence. There are usually two ways to make dependent clauses into grammatical sentences:

DEPENDENT CLAUSE: Because he laughs too much.

> REWRITE 1: He <u>laughs</u> too much.

> REWRITE 2: Because he laughs too much, <u>he</u> <u>is</u> not taken seriously.

In rewrite 1 the word *because* has been dropped. In rewrite 2 "he is not taken seriously" has been added to the dependent clause. Both of the rewrites pass the "I believe that . . ." test. Try it.

Here's another:

FRAGMENT: The green grass which <u>she</u> <u>had</u> just <u>finished</u> mowing.

REWRITE 1: <u>She</u> <u>had</u> just <u>finished</u> mowing the green grass.

REWRITE 2: The green <u>grass</u>, which she had just finished mowing, <u>was</u> now covered with snow.

Following are some of the other words that create dependent clauses:

after	unless
although	until
before	what
how	when
if	where
since	who

You'll notice that many of these words are used to begin questions. A question is *not* considered a fragment.

Exercise II:

Rewrite whichever of the statements below are sentence fragments. Use the "I believe that . . ." test. The first one is done for you. Answers are at the end of this appendix.

1. He thought the American Civil War was ancient history. Because it took place over 100 years ago.

   He thought the American Civil War was ancient history because it took place over 100 years ago.

   or

   Because it took place over 100 years ago, he thought the American Civil War was ancient history.

   (Other grammatical rewrites are also possible.)

2. The librarian showed her how to use the card catalogue. Which she used a great deal during the next two weeks.

3. Although he seemed to enjoy the party. We noticed he left early with Sue.

4. Next week you can help out in the Hardware Department. While they take inventory in Ladies' Jewelry.

5. Because the store is almost out of canned tomatoes, we must limit each customer to five cans only. Next week, however, we should receive an additional shipment.

Exceptions: In informal writing situations, sentence fragments are more accepted than they are in very formal situations. Even in formal situations, fragments may be considered acceptable after questions:

> How many items are they permitted to buy? Five each.

Sentence fragments that are used for special effect may also be acceptable in many formal writing situations:

> From the first paragraph it's clear that she is an old woman. A frail, but lovable, old woman.

Run-on Sentences

Whereas sentence fragments are incomplete pieces of sentences, run-on sentences are two sentences that have been run together as though they were one. The following are examples of sentences that have been run together:

> <u>Computers</u> <u>can</u> "crunch numbers" quickly <u>they</u> <u>are</u> useful office machines.
> <u>Computers</u> <u>can</u> "crunch numbers" quickly, <u>they</u> <u>are</u> useful in businesses.
> <u>Computers</u> <u>can</u> "crunch numbers" quickly when the work is repetitious <u>they</u> <u>use</u> a small <u>computer</u> in their office.

In the first two examples, readers obviously can tell where one sentence should stop and the next begin: after the word *quickly*. In the third example readers can't be sure whether the dependent clause "when the work is repetitious" explains when computers can crunch numbers fast or whether it explains when they use a computer in their office.

One way to detect run-on sentences is to read your writing aloud. When you detect sentences you have run together in your writing, you can rewrite them in several ways, depending on what you want to say. Here's how each technique works:

1. Use a period. This makes a strong division between the two ideas.

> RUN-ON: Computers can "crunch numbers" quickly they are useful office machines.
>
> REWRITTEN: <u>Computers</u> <u>can</u> "crunch numbers" quickly. <u>They</u> <u>are</u> useful office machines.

2. Use a semicolon. This implies to your reader that there is a close, but unstated, connection between the two ideas.

> RUN-ON: Computers can "crunch numbers" quickly they are useful office machines.
>
> REWRITTEN: <u>Computers</u> <u>can</u> "crunch numbers" quickly; <u>they</u> <u>are</u> useful office machines.

Note: When you use a semicolon, be certain that you have a subject and verb both before and after the semicolon.

3. Use a semicolon plus a word like *however* or *therefore*. This tells your reader what the connection is between the two ideas. Because it can sound rather stiff or formal, make sure the writing situation is appropriate.

> RUN-ON: Computers can "crunch numbers" quickly they are expensive machines.
>
> REWRITTEN: <u>Computers</u> <u>can</u> "crunch numbers" quickly; however, <u>they</u> <u>are</u> expensive machines.

Note: When *however, therefore,* or *consequently* is used in this way—with a subject and verb both before and after—the normal punctuation is a semicolon before the word and a comma after. In other types of sentences, however, the semicolon is not necessary: "I cannot, however, agree with you."

4. Use a word such as *and, but, yet, for,* or *or.* This shows the reader that there's a close connection between two equally important ideas. Further, it states what the connection is.

> RUN-ON: Computers can "crunch numbers" quickly they are expensive machines.
>
> REWRITTEN: <u>Computers</u> <u>can</u> "crunch numbers" quickly, but <u>they</u> <u>are</u> expensive machines.

Note: When you have a subject and verb on *both* sides of words like *and* or *but,* you usually put a comma before the joining word.

5. Use a "dependent" word such as *because* or *although.* This lets the reader see that one idea is less important than the other. It also lets the reader see exactly how the two ideas are related.

> RUN-ON: Computers can "crunch numbers" quickly they are expensive machines.
>
> REWRITTEN: Although <u>computers</u> <u>can</u> "crunch numbers" quickly, <u>they</u> <u>are</u> expensive machines.

Note: When you use a dependent word at the *beginning* of a sentence, you'll usually also need a comma, as in the example above.

Exercise III:

A. Which of these are run-on sentences? Answers are at the end of this appendix.

1. We must assume more responsibility for the elderly in our society, it's to our own benefit as well as theirs.

2. The restaurant on the corner will soon be out of business.

3. The restaurant on the corner will soon be out of business because it has poor management.

4. Television presents mindless situation comedies it also presents *Nova* and political debates.

B. What's wrong with the following sentence?

    1. Your job is; however, well paid.

C. Rewrite the following sentences to show the relationship indicated. Answers are at the end of this appendix.

    1. *Rewrite to show a complete division of ideas:*
    Let's go to the concert tomorrow, the music should be good.

    2. *Rewrite to show the exact relationship between the ideas:*
    John now sings with the Hot Flash group the money is better.

    3. *Rewrite to show the connection between the ideas, using a technique that is fairly formal:*
    Your proposal to increase the security of the parking areas is well thought out, we don't have the funds available.

    4. Rewrite the run-on sentences in exercise A.

SUBJECT–VERB AGREEMENT

In the following sentences the verbs and subject agree because they are both singular or both plural:

SET 1:   The <u>book is</u> on reserve.
           The <u>books are</u> on reserve.
           The <u>book and magazine article are</u> on reserve.

SET 2:   The <u>book</u> that he wants to check out <u>is</u> on reserve.
           The <u>books</u> that he wants to check out <u>are</u> on reserve.

SET 3:   The art <u>book</u> on the library shelf in the next room <u>is</u> on reserve.
           The art <u>books</u> on the library shelf in the next room <u>are</u> on reserve.
           <u>One</u> of the books <u>is</u> on reserve.

SET 4:   There <u>is</u> one <u>book</u> on reserve.
           There <u>are</u> five <u>books</u> on reserve.

Set 1: The first set of sentences if fairly straightforward. The subjects and verbs are close together: *the book is, the books are,* and *the book and magazine article are.* In this last example the verb is plural because there are two subjects: the book and the magazine article.

Set 2: This set has *who, which,* and *that* complications. The sentences in the second and third sets present more difficult situations for a writer. In both sets the subject and verb are separated by other words. When writing or revising such sentences, writers must decide which subjects and verbs go together. In the second set the verb *wants* goes with *he*, not with *book*. (A quick test would be "Who or what wants to check out the book? *He* does.) The verb *is* goes with *book*, even though they are widely separated in the sentence. (Quick test: Who or what is on reserve? *The book* is.) Thus *book* and *is* must agree.

    Set 3: The difficulty in the third set of sentences is that the verb is separated from the subject by prepositional phrases. (A prepositional phrase is a short group of words beginning with *up, down, in, out, of,* and similar words.) Prepositional phrases are important to the meaning of sentences, but from a strictly grammatical point of view they are "invisible" or don't count. Thus writers must mentally eliminate them to find the true subject. Below are the sentences from set 3 with the prepositional phrases placed in parentheses.

    The art <u>book</u> (on the library shelf) (in the next room) <u>is</u> on reserve.

    The art <u>books</u> (on the library shelf) (in the next room) <u>are</u> on reserve.

    <u>One</u> (of the books) <u>is</u> on reserve.

Mentally eliminating prepositional phrases can help you find the true subject of a verb.

    Set 4: When the sentence begins with the word *there*, the true subject often comes after the verb. This is tricky to remember because in speech we often use the singular "there is," or "there's" while we are trying to decide what to say next. In writing, however, we can double check the sentence to make the subject and verb agree.

Exercise IV:

In the following sentences, underline the subject once and the verb twice. If necessary, use arrows to indicate which subjects go with which verbs. Some of the subjects and verbs already agree. If they don't, correct them by changing *the verb.* Answers are at the end of this appendix.

1. The women is ready to go now.
2. Chemistry and math are her favorite subjects.
3. The people doesn't understand all the difficulties involved.
4. One of the subjects they will study are business management.
5. The student who received two scholarships is very lucky.
6. There is two rules that we insist on at this store.
7. The microscopes in the cabinet on the right is available for use at any time.

PRONOUN AGREEMENT AND NONSEXIST LANGUAGE

Singular and Plural Pronouns

    Just as verbs should agree with their subjects, pronouns should agree with the words to which they refer. In the following sentences, the pronoun agreement is correct:

Parents often read to *their* children.
Mary reads to *her* daughter.
One of the men on that shift lost *his* job.
Everyone on the women's swim team should bring *her* own towel. (Words like *everyone* and *someone* are singular.)

Pronouns and Sexism

One difficulty with making pronouns agree with the words to which they refer is that there is no English pronoun that, in the singular, refers to men and women both. This creates problems with sentences such as the following:

Everyone should vote according to_____conscience.

A parent should read to_____children as often as possible.

A lawyer should not accept a case_____doesn't agree with.

All three of the above sentences require a singular pronoun, but in none of the sentences is there any reason to think the noun refers exclusively to males or females. In the past, people regularly used *he* or *his* in such situations, with the understanding that *he* and *his* included women as well as men. Many people now find this use of *he* and *his* to be sexist and therefore unacceptable. There are several ways to rewrite sentences so that they do not appear sexist.

1. Use the plural rather than the singular:

   ORIGINAL: A lawyer should not accept a case he doesn't agree with.

   REWRITE: *Lawyers* should not accept cases *they* don't agree with.

   Note: Be sure you make *all* the appropriate words plural, not just some of them.

2. Use *we* or *you* instead of *everyone* or *everybody*.

   ORIGINAL: Everyone should vote according to his conscience.

   REWRITTEN: *We* should vote according to *our* consciences.

   ORIGINAL: Each member of the tennis team should bring his own towel to practice.

   REWRITTEN: *You* should bring *your* own towel to practice.

3. Use the phrase *his or her:*

   ORIGINAL: Each applicant supplied a transcript from his current school.

> REWRITTEN: *Each* applicant supplied a transcript from *his or her* current school.

Each of these methods has a drawback. Too many plurals can make writing less crisp and clear. *We* and *us* aren't always appropriate. *His or her* is awkward. For this reason, writers are still experimenting with ways to write clearly and smoothly without giving the appearance of being sexist.

PARALLELISM

Parallelism is discussed in more detail in Chapter 15, Polish Your Sentence Style. In brief, it's a way of presenting related ideas in similar grammatical form:

> He enjoys swimming, golfing, and playing pool.
> My mother has three admirable qualities: a sense of humor, respect for other people, and a willingness to work hard.

Exercise V:

The following sentences lack parallel form where they could easily have it. Note the suggested revisions of the first one, then try the others for yourself. Sample answers are at the end of this appendix.

1. He enjoyed photography, playing the guitar, and to relax with friends.
   He enjoyed photography, playing the guitar, and relaxing with friends.
   or
   He liked to take photographs, play the guitar, and relax with friends.
2. It's important to have fun as well as working hard.
3. The form asked us to list our educational backgrounds as well as if we had any experience.
4. The major sections of this report are: (1) making a budget, (2) how to find bargains, and (3) consumer protection groups.

SPELLING, CONTRACTIONS, AND POSSESSIVES

Spelling "rules" have so many exceptions that they are often no help. Therefore one of the best ways of learning to spell is by making a list of words you frequently misspell. Then you can concentrate on just those.

Speech/Writing Problems

As you check your list, you may find that one problem is that you are spelling words the way they are pronounced in casual conversations. The following words present such problems:

WRONG	RIGHT
1. He could *of* finished it.	He could *have* finished it.
2. He was *discourage an* sad.	He was *discouraged and* sad.
3. He *walk* to the next room.	He *walked* to the next room.

The list on the left represents the way we pronounce words, especially when we are speaking casually. For instance, we often run "could have" together into "could've," which we then pronounce "could of." That leads us into the incorrect spelling. The same is true of "discouraged and sad." In casual conversation, it's easy to slur the words so that they sound like "discourage-an-sad." That leads to misspellings.

Frequently Confused Words

Words such as *two* and *to* often confuse people. They sound the same but are spelled differently. Below are the most important sets of words you are likely to misspell.

ACCEPT/EXCEPT *Accept* means to receive or agree to something. *Except* means "excluding."
TIP: "I will *accept* them all *except* that one."

AFFECT/EFFECT *Affect* is the verb. *Effect* is the result.
TIP: "It will *affect* you in one way. The *effect* will be good."
Note: In some businesses and legal situations, *effect* can also be a verb with a slightly different meaning.

ALL READY/ALREADY When it is spelled as one word, you need the whole word. When it is spelled as two words, you can omit the *all*.
TIP: "We are all ready." (You could say "We are ready.")
"It's already too late." (You can't say "It's ready too late.")

IT'S/ITS *It's* always means "it is." *Its* is possessive.
TIP: "*It's* too early for the store to advertise *its* sale."

THAN/THEN *Than* compares two things. *Then* tells "when."
TIP: "I'd rather get an A *than* a B." "She went to the library, *then* home."

THEIR/THERE/THEY'RE *Their* is possessive. *There* tells "where."
They're means "they are."
TIP: "*Their* house is *there* at the corner and *they're* home now."

TO/TOO/TWO *To* is a preposition or part of an infinitive.
Too implies "too much." *Two* is the number.
TIP: "The *two* students were *too* smart *to* be tricked by the test."

WEATHER/WHETHER *Weather* refers to "wet" or "sunny" conditions.
Whether means "if."

Tɪᴘ: "Who knows *whether* or not we'll go in this wet *weather*."

WHO'S/WHOSE   *Who's* means "who is" or "who has." *Whose* is a possessive.
Tɪᴘ: "*Who's* been playing this record?" "*Whose* record is it anyway?"

YOU'RE/YOUR   *You're* means "you are." *Your* is possessive.
Tɪᴘ: "*You're* going to get *your* reward."

Contractions

Words like *it's, we'll* and *you're* are called contractions because two words have been shortened, or contracted, into one word. An apostrophe is used to show where a letter or two has been dropped. The most common spelling mistake with contractions is putting the apostrophe in the wrong place or leaving it our entirely. Remember that the apostrophe goes wherever the letters have been dropped.

ORIGINAL WORDS	CORRECT CONTRACTIONS	MISSPELLING
they are	they're	theyr'e
do not	don't	do'nt
cannot	can't	ca'nt
is not	isn't	is'nt
there is	there's	theres
I will	I'll	I'l
let us	let's	lets
who is	who's	whos
they are	they're	theyr'e
they have	they've	theyv'e
will not	won't (Notice that this contraction is different.)	

As the last section indicates, contractions are often confused with other words that they sound like.

Possessives

Possessives are convenient. Instead of writing "the book of the woman," we can write "the woman's book." It's quicker and smoother to do so. The only trick is remembering to use the apostrophe. One way to tell where to put the apostrophe is to ask "Who or what owns X?" If the answer is a word that ends in *s* (whether it's singular or plural), the apostrophe goes after the *s*. If the answer does not end in *s*, then an *s* must be added.

records of Mike = Mike's records ('*s* added since the word *Mike* does not end in *s*.)

home of the Smiths = The Smiths' home (apostrophe added to the *s* that's already there)

boat of the boys = The boys' boat (apostrophe added to the *s* that's already there)

boat of the women = women's boat ('*s* added since the word *women* doesn't end in *s*)

The important exceptions to this rule are possessive pronouns. The following words are already possessive: they do *not* use apostrophes.

its	his
ours	hers
their	yours
theirs	mine

Exercise VI:

Decide which of the following words are misspelled and correct them. Remember that apostrophes should be used only when there is a reason for their use. Answers are at the end of this appendix.

1. Its his last two papers we're concerned with. Accept for the spelling, their excellent. I doubt whether anyone would disagree.

2. The mans first job was very interesting. He all ready had a good backgroun, but he soon learn more about the work.

3. The countries history is not easy too summarize. Their have been to many different political parties for that. Still, we can't really say that anarchy prevailed.

4. Their not at home tonight because of the symphony. We could of gone with them, but the paper's for Johns new business must be filed by tomorrow.

PUNCTUATION

Much punctuation is covered elsewhere in this book. For the use of punctuation for stylistic effects, see Polish Your Sentence Style in Chapter 13. For the punctuation of quotations, see Appendix D. For the use of semicolons, see "Run-on Sentences" in this appendix.

Here, then, is a quick summary of the most troublesome punctuation problems not covered elsehwere:

1. Comma used to set off long introductory passage:

    Despite his lifelong commitment to public service, John Ramsy retired at age 50.

2. Commas used to set off "interrupters":

    I will, of course, be happy to vote for him.
    I will not be pleased, however, if he is elected. (*Note: However* functions as an interrupter in this sentence. Compare it with the use of *however* to join two sets of subjects and verbs: "I will vote for him; however, I do not care if he wins.")

3. Comma used before a *BUT, AND,* or *OR* that joins two sets of subjects and verbs:

    I will vote for the man gladly, but I do not expect him to win.

4. Comma used after a dependent clause that begins a sentence:

    Because he is the best candidate running, I will vote for him. (*Note:* A comma is not used when a dependent clause comes at the *end* of the sentence: "I will vote for him because he is the best candidate running.")

5. Commas used to set off a *who* or *which* clause that does not restrict the meaning of the sentence:

    Elaine Nakamura, who is an excellent secretary, makes our department run very smoothly.
    The Jones' house, which was designed by Frank Lloyd Wright, is scheduled for demolition.

These last two examples call for a bit more explanation. The reason we say that the *who* and *which* clauses do not "restrict" the meaning is that they do not tell us *which* "Elaine Nakamura" or *which* "Jones' house." Presumably we already know.
    Compare those sentences with the following:

    The woman who has short dark hair makes our department run very smoothly.
    The house which was designed by Frank Lloyd Wright is scheduled for demolition.

In these two sentences, the *who* and the *which* clauses are necessary to let the reader know *which* woman and *which* house. Therefore they cannot be set off with commas. A quick test to see if a *which* clause should be punctuated is to substitute *that* for *which*. If the word *that* sounds right in the sentence, the chances are that no commas should be used:

    The house that was designed by Frank Lloyd Wright is scheduled for demolition.

Exercise VII:

Punctuate the following sentences. Answers are at the end of this appendix.

1. I will however accept your recommendation.
2. Mark Webb who is a student here has written two books.
3. The photograph which you took of the banyan tree may be the best of the group.
4. I appreciate your offer of help but if we work hard we can do it ourselves.
5. I appreciate your offer of help and gladly accept it.

ANSWERS TO EXERCISES

Exercise I: (Other revisions could also be correct.)

2. The dark gray <u>ship</u> <u>was floating</u> at the pier. The <u>cargo</u> <u>was unloaded</u> quickly.

or

The <u>cargo</u> <u>was</u> quickly <u>unloaded</u> from the dark gray ship floating at the pier.

3. The sentence is correct.
4. Reading silently in the library, <u>John</u> and his three <u>buddies</u> <u>were working</u> on research papers.

or

<u>John</u> and his three <u>buddies</u> <u>were reading</u> silently in the library. <u>They</u> <u>were working</u> on research papers.

Exercise II: (Other revisions could also be correct.)

2. The librarian showed her how to use the card *catalogue. She used it* a great deal during the next two weeks.

or

The librarian showed her how to use the card *catalogue, which she used* a great deal during the next two weeks.

3. Although he seemed to enjoy the *party, we noticed* he left early with Sue.

or

He seemed to enjoy the party, but we noticed that he left early with Sue.

4. Next week you can help out in the Hardware Department while they take inventory in Ladies' Jewelry.
5. The sentences are correct.

Exercise III: (Other revisions could also be correct.)

A. 1. Run-on. 2. Correct. 3. Correct. 4. Run-on.
B. When a semicolon is used with *however*, there should be a subject and verb on *both* sides: "Your <u>job</u> <u>is</u> well paid; however, other <u>jobs</u> <u>pay</u> even better." This original sentence could be correctly written: "Your job is, however, well paid."

C. 1. Let's go to the concert tomorrow. The music should be good.

   2. John now sings with the Hot Flash group because the money is better.

   3. Your proposal to increase the security of the parking area is well thought out; however, we don't have the funds available.

   4. We must assume more responsibility for the elderly in our society; it's to our own benefit as well as theirs.
Although television presents mindless situation comedies, it also presents *Nova* and political debates.

Exercise IV:

1. The <u>women</u> <u>are</u> ready to go now.

2. Correct. (Chemistry and math are . . . .)

3. The <u>people</u> <u>don't</u> (or <u>do not</u>) understand all the difficulties involved.

4. <u>One</u> of the subjects they will study <u>is</u> business management.

5. Correct (The student . . . is very lucky.)

6. There <u>are</u> <u>two rules</u> that we insist on at this store.

7. The <u>microscopes</u> in the cabinet on the right <u>are</u> available for use at any time.

Exercise V: (Other revisions could also be correct.)

2. It's important to have fun as well as work hard.

3. The form asked us to list our educational backgrounds as well as any experience we had.

4. The major sections of this report are: (1) making budgets, (2) finding bargains, and (3) using consumer protection groups.

or

The major sections of this report are: (1) budgets, (2) bargains, and (3) consumer protection groups.

Exercise VI:

(Changes are in italics.)

1. *It's* his last two papers we're concerned with. *Except* for the spelling, *they're* excellent. I doubt whether anyone would disagree.

2. The *man's* first job was very interesting. He *already* had a good *background*, but he soon *learned* more about the work.

3. The *country's* history is not easy *to* summarize. *There* have been *too* many different political parties for that. Still, we can't really say that anarchy prevailed.

4. *They're* not at home tonight because of the symphony. We could *have* gone with them, but the *papers* for *John's* new business must be filed by tomorrow.

Exercise VII:

1. I will, however, accept your recommendation. (Commas added.)

2. Mark Webb, who is a student here, has written two books. (Commas added.)

3. No additional punctuation necessary. The *which* phrase is necessary to let us know *which* photograph. You could use *that* in place of *which*.

4. I appreciate your offer of help, but if we work hard we can do it ourselves. (Comma added.)

5. No additional punctuation necessary. (The *and* merely joins two verbs: *offer* and *accept*.)

appendix B

A Brief Research Guide

This appendix is designed to serve as a starting point and preliminary guide to writers undertaking a research project. It does list some of the most basic and popular research and reference works and contains useful tips on writing college research papers, but it is not a complete treatment of the subject. Your teacher or reference librarian can refer you to complete books on the subject. For information on how to write the paper (as opposed to how to conduct the research) see Chapter 15 of this book, and also Appendices C and D.

THE COLLEGE RESEARCH PAPER

During your college career you will probably be required to prepare a number of research papers for humanities and science courses. Writing these papers can be either a very memorable learning experience (many people who have been out of school for twenty years or more can still describe in great detail one or more of their college research projects) or a frustrating waste of time.

You can be fairly sure that what you get out of writing a research paper will be related to the effort you put into it, provided you don't just work hard but also "work smart." The sections that follow should help you to avoid many of the time-wasting pitfalls that beginning researchers fall into. It should help you produce a paper that will represent a good return on the time you invest.

START WITH A QUESTION

The very word "research" implies that there is going to be an effort to discover something that is not already known, that there is a question that needs an answer. You do not ordinarily start a research effort with your final conclusion firmly in mind. True, a scientific reseacher may suspect that he knows the answer to a question, but he suspends judgment and calls the possible answer a "hypothesis" until he completes the experiments and verifies that the hypothesis is indeed correct.

Whether your instructor assigns you a subject to research or gives you complete freedom in choosing your own topic, you will have the opportunity to structure the project as a search for the answer to a question or questions. If you can make the question one that you are *personally* curious about, you will bring more enthusiasm to the project and increase your chances of producing an interesting paper.

In English class many of the ideas from your Wish List and "I'm Not Going to Take It Anymore" Catalogue (Chapter 4) would make good subjects for research. In other classes, such as History or Psychology, your instructor may assign a subject. However, if the instructor doesn't, you might find one for yourself by brainstorming on the following ideas, keeping the course subject matter in mind:

I wish I could understand why . . .

I wonder if . . .

I wish I could decide if . . .

I'd like to know whether or not . . .

I wonder what caused (or causes) . . .

I wonder how . . .

Here are some questions that can be asked about many different subjects:

What is . . . ?

What caused (or causes) . . . ?

What was the result of . . . ?

What happened when . . . ?

How does_____differ from_____?

How does one go about . . . ?

Who was responsible for . . . ?

Why did . . . ?

Where did . . . ?

When did_____first . . . ?

Narrow the Focus

Once you have a basic question or two in mind, you may have to narrow the scope of the question so that you can cover it with reasonable completeness in the time and space you have available. A question that can be treated adequately by a Ph.D. student in a 400-page dissertation produced over a year's time will be quite different from one you can expect to cover in a 10-page paper due in three weeks. For example, the question "What were the results of World War II?" would be far too broad for even a doctoral dissertation. A narrower focus on specific results of the war, such as economic results, political results, or social results might be manageable in a book-length manuscript or a lengthy article. For a typical college research paper, however, an even narrower focus would be needed. Someone with an interest in economics or business, for instance, might narrow the question to the effects of the war on the housing industry in the five years immediately after the war. A writer interested in sociology might work on the effects the war had on immigration to the United States from Germany in the postwar years.

Often you will see ways to narrow your focus *after* you begin your research. Therefore it's important to regard your original subject and question as just a starting place.

LOCATE INFORMATION

Your instructor will probably expect you to do your research in the college library working with books, magazine articles, and newspaper articles written by others who are investigating your subject; these sources are commonly referred to as *secondary sources*, since the information in them is secondhand. In some cases, you may work with firsthand information or *primary sources* such as original historical documents, old letters, sets of statistics, responses to questionnaires you yourself have distributed, and so forth.

Locating Information in the Library

The starting point for finding the answers to your questions is the Reference Department or Reference Room of the library. Begin with an overview of your subject in the major encyclopedias available, such as:

> *The New Encyclopaedia Brittanica*
>
> *Encyclopedia Americana*
>
> *World Book Encyclopedia*

This overview may help you narrow your focus. Now is the time to begin making notes (each on a separate 3- by 5-inch card) of other articles or books referred to in the encyclopedia articles. Be sure to write down author's name, full title, and publishing information for future use.

Next locate the *Readers' Guide to Periodical Literature*, a collection of green volumes which indexes articles from more than 150 general magazines. Look up the subject of your research in the most recent volume and work your way backward chronologically for additional articles. (The index goes back to 1900.) For articles before 1900, refer to *Poole's Index to Periodical Literature 1802–1907*. On a note card, jot down the title, author, and relevant publishing information of sources that may help you.

If newspaper articles might be a source of information on your subject, refer to the *New York Times Index,* which covers articles from 1913 to the present that have appeared in the *New York Times,* probably the most comprehensive newspaper in the United States. Articles more than a few years old will be available on microfilm; microfilm readers are available in most libraries. For subjects of recent interest (1972 to the present) refer to

Newspaper Index, which covers articles that have appeared in eight major U.S. newspapers from coast to coast.

The library's main card catalog is another important stop. The card catalog has three cards for each book in the library's collection, all filed alphabetically: one by author's last name, one by title of the book, and one by subject. You can start by looking up your subject; then see if there are any books by authors of the magazine and newspaper articles you found in the periodical and newspaper indexes. Once again, fill out a note card for each title that may be of interest to you. These note cards need contain only the author's name, the title, and the library call number.

By this point you will probably have a substantial collection of note cards listing books and articles of possible interest to you. If you have been able to locate only one or two books and a few articles related to your subject, you will want to consult the reference librarian for help in locating additional sources. If your subject is very technical or of limited interest to general readers, the reference librarian may be able to refer you to specialized indexes such as the *Social Sciences Index,* the *General Sciences Index,* or the *Humanities Index,* each of which indexes over 100 scholarly journals, or the *Public Affairs Information Service Bulletin,* which indexes over 1,000 periodicals containing articles on politics, government, and public affairs generally. Finally, the librarian may be able to show you a specialized bibliography or list of books and periodicals that will help you.

The reference librarian will be most helpful to you if you can provide information as to both your general subject *and* the particular limited question you are researching. The more clues you provide, the more sources he or she may think of. Many large libraries now also provide computer searches of articles and even speeches on academic subjects. These computer searches typically cost $20 and more, but can be very helpful provided you have first narrowed your question.

The Tentative Bibliography

Once you have a substantial stack of note cards containing references to books and articles, you can begin deliberately weeding out items that appear not to be directly related to your subject. In some cases you will discard items without even scanning the book or article because its title clearly indicates that it is of less interest to you than other items you have. Next you will do some involuntary weeding out: when you try to obtain a book or article you may find:

That it is out on loan to someone else.

That it has mysteriously disappeared.

That the library's file of a periodical doesn't go back as far as the volume you need.

That a periodical you need is "at the bindery" being bound into a complete volume.

You should indicate these problems on a note card and save them for future reference.

What you have left after your voluntary and involuntary weeding out is your Tentative Bibliography, a list of references you will consult. As you proceed in your research, you will find still more sources of information by reading the footnotes and bibliographies of the works you consult.

TAKE NOTES

You have now reached the point where you are actively seeking answers to the questions you have posed for yourself. You will want to start by skimming a given book or article. Before taking a single note on a reference source, ask yourself: "Does this book/article contain information I need to find out?" In the case of books, look at the chapter titles in the Table of Contents. Turn directly to chapters that may have information you need. Skim the chapter or skim the article. If the information is irrelevant to your project, make a note to that effect, as shown here. Don't waste your time on irrelevant material, but do keep track of which sources you skim and dismiss. Otherwise, you'll find yourself looking at an item a second time, having forgotten that you've already skimmed it once.

Note Card with Irrelevant Material

Gunning, *Rape Crises.*
KF4799
C2L43

No help

If a reference does contain usable material, then immediately write a *bibliography note card* containing all the information you'll need to write footnotes and bibliographies. (See Appendix C for footnotes.) In brief, this bibliography card includes author, title, publishing information, including date, and, for magazine articles, the first and last pages. In addition, it should have the library call number. You won't use this number in the finished paper, but it will save you time if you need to recheck a book or article that you don't have at home.

> KF 8745
> D6A3
>
>   William O. Douglas
>   Go East Young Man : The Early Years
>   N.Y. Random House 1974
>   493 pages

You are now ready to begin taking your actual notes. Once again, use index cards, putting just one idea on each card. When you are through with your research, your note cards will be similar to a brainstorm list. You can arrange your cards into logical groups, just as you arrange items in a brainstorm into logical groups. If you have more than one idea on a note card, it becomes much more difficult to organize the cards into appropriate groups. To help yourself with this organization, you should label each card with a quick word or two telling the *specific* subject of that card.

In addition to the idea itself and a word or two identifying the subject, each idea card should also contain a quick reference to the appropriate bibliography card, some indication of whether you've quoted or paraphrased, and the specific pages you've used.

Idea Card

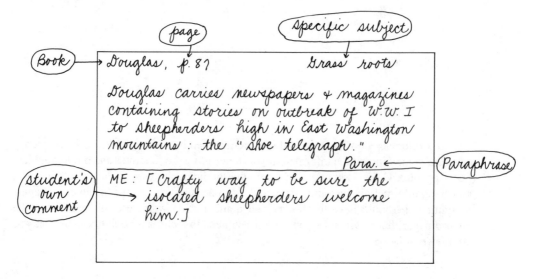

Generally speaking, your notes should summarize in your own words whatever ideas you wish to use. (In those cases where your source states a thought so well or so clearly that it would be hard to summarize well, quote the words exactly and use quotation marks.) Remember that in your writing you must give credit to your source for ideas that you borrow, even when you put the ideas into your own words.

If you find that you are unable to summarize source material without looking at it, you probably haven't completely understood it. And if you are not understanding the materials, you are not going to be able to synthesize these materials in your own mind into a coherent answer to your research question. Instead you will end up with a disjointed series of other people's thoughts pasted together. (See Chapter 15, "Quote Just the Right Amount and Paraphrase when Possible", for more information on paraphrasing and quoting.)

In addition to summarizing the material you read, you must also be judging the quality of the material as you go. The fact that something is printed in black and white does not make it true. You may well come across unreliable or biased sources as well as out-of-date "factual" material. Experience (and Chapter 15 of this book) will soon enable you to evaluate how reliable your source is. Any information you take from such sources should be clearly marked on your note cards as being of questionable value. *You are responsible for the validity of the information you choose to include in your writing.*

You may want to write your own comments and reactions at the bottom of a note card. If you do, put your ideas in brackets so that your own ideas don't become confused with those of your source. You may also want to write some cards that will contain just your own ideas. These should be clearly labeled "me" or "my own," so you won't later spend time trying to track down the source.

CONDUCT INTERVIEWS

Don't limit your research to the library. Other methods of obtaining information may be equally important. For instance, you may wish to interview someone who is an expert in the subject. Such an expert can give you valuable information and suggest other sources to you. Other times you may wish to interview people who can provide firsthand insights into a problem you are investigating. For instance, if you were researching the community facilities available to elderly people, you might want to interview elderly people as well as "the experts."

When you interview, keep the following tips in mind:

1. Establish in advance how long the interview will be and do not run overtime. Arrive on time.

2. Do not use a tape recorder without first asking permission.

3. Decide in advance what questions you will ask. (Make believe that you are paying the person you're interviewing $25 per hour. That should help you keep the interview to the point and courteously short.)

4. Ask permission to use the person's name in footnotes. Do not use the name without permission.

5. If you are not using a tape recorder, take careful notes of important information, and be sure you have names and dates correct. (Make believe the person you're interviewing is leaving on a long trip the day after the interview. That will help you "get it right the first time.")

6. Be patient with long pauses while the person you're interviewing is deciding what to say next. Don't try to rush things and don't fill in the pauses with your own conversation. Remember: The person you are interviewing should do most of the talking, not you.

7. Send a thank you note to the person you've interviewed. If you've quoted the person extensively you might also send a copy of the finished report.

appendix C

A Brief Documentation Guide

There are two formal methods of citing sources. One is used primarily for research papers in English, history, art, philosophy, and other humanities. The other is used primarily for science, business, and social science papers. The first is often called "Footnotes and Bibliography"; the second is often called "References Cited." If you aren't sure which format you should use, ask your teacher before writing your paper.

FOOTNOTES AND BIBLIOGRAPHY METHOD

As you write footnotes, keep the purpose in mind. It's to let your reader know exactly what source you used and to make it as easy as possible for your reader to evaluate your source and/or obtain a copy of the same material. In general, that means your reader needs the following information:

Book: The author, title, edition, publishing company, date of publication, and page.

Article in a book: The author of the article, the title of the article, the editor of the book, the title of the book, the publishing company, date, and page.

Magazine or newspaper article: The author of the article (if known), the title of the article, the name of the magazine or newspaper, the date, and the page. In addition, the section and column numbers of newspapers are helpful to readers, as are the volume numbers of magazines that have them. In addition, the first and last pages of a magazine article are helpful, although they are included only in the bibliography, not in the footnote itself.

If you have difficulty locating the necessary publishing information from the copyright and title page of a book or government periodical you are using, check the library index card pasted in the front of the book. It often has all the information you need.

A second major purpose of footnotes is to give another writer credit for any ideas or words that you are borrowing. You should give credit in a footnote for ideas you have borrowed from other writers, even when you put the ideas into your own words. When you use another writer's exact words, then you should use quotation marks as well as footnotes.

Failure to give proper credit to another writer is *plagiarism,* a form of theft that is taken very seriously by most instructors and in some cases is grounds for expulsion or a failing grade in a course.

All of the conventions regarding how to write footnotes and bibliographies—where to put the commas, what order the information goes in, and so forth—are designed to help readers find the information they need as quickly as possible. When writers all use the same format, it's easier for readers to find what they need. Thus as you write your footnotes and bibliography, keep your reader and the *purpose* of footnoting in mind.

Footnote Location

Footnotes may be placed all together at the end of a paper or on the bottom of the appropriate pages. The advantages of putting them all at the end are that they are easier to type and the pages of the writing itself are not cluttered with footnotes. The advantage of putting them at the bottom of the appropriate page is that readers can check a reference without having to flip pages back and forth. Where you put the footnotes should thus be determined by the likelihood that your reader will want to check them while reading your paper. However, you must use one system consistently throughout the paper.

Within your writing, the footnote number should usually be put at the end of the appropriate sentence. It should be slightly raised and placed outside any quotation marks. See the sample below.

Footnote Appearance

The first line of a footnote is indented, with the footnote number slightly raised as it is in the text. When footnotes are placed at the bottom of the pages, there should be a line an inch or two long separating the footnotes from the writing itself. When footnotes are located at the end of the paper, they are placed on a separate sheet of paper, *not* on whatever room is left at the bottom of the last page. In either case, footnotes are *single-spaced,* with double spaces between notes.

Notice in the following example that the footnotes are numbered consecutively. Do *not* begin renumbering footnotes with each page, and do *not* use the same number more than once.

```
An even greater disparity exists with doctors whose
median income is now more than $65,000.00 a year.⁴
Nurses are not compensated as well as some professions
where a comparable amount of education is required.  A
beginning nurse in Hawaii earns from $10,000.00 to
$12,000.00 a year, and nurses can't expect to earn more
```

footnote # is raised slightly and placed after the period

than $16,000.00 a year even after several years service.
Working all those hours, under stress, for that kind of
pay is extremely discouraging.

Another controversial issue is the sporadic working
hours. In Hawaii nurses work on a rotating schedule.
It is not uncommon for them to work double shifts and on
their days off to cover understaffed units. Since most
nurses are women and have families, many find the shifting hours incompatable with rearing children and other
family responsibilities. Traditionally, nursing has
been a woman's occupation. Data developed from the 1970
census revealed that there were 2,819 female RN's and
100 male RN's employed in Hawaii at that time.[5] It is
important to realize that due to new job opportunities
there are not enough women ....

---

[4]"Rebellion Among the Angels," Time Magazine, August
27, 1979, p. 62.

[5]U.S., Department of Commerce, Bureau of Census,
1970 Census of Population: Detailed Characteristics
(Hawaii), Final Report PC (1)-D 13 Hawaii (Washington,
D.C.: Government Printing Office, 1972), p. 295.

short line above notes
indent first line
double space between footnotes
footnotes used to give credit information
single space

For the appearance of a complete research paper, see pages 221–223.

Footnote Format

The following footnotes are models that you can refer to when you write your own
footnotes. Note that the author's first name comes first and that the general order is
author–title–publishing information–page used. Notice also that titles of articles are placed
in quotation marks, while titles of books and names of magazines are underlined.

Magazine Article

[1]Harold Goldstein, "Improving Policing: A Problem-Oriented Approach," Crime
and Delinquency, 25 (April 1979), 238.

Note: 25 is the magazine *volume number* and 238 is the *page number*. The footnote would
look like this if there were no volume number:

[2]Harold Goldstein, "Improving Policing: A Problem-Oriented Approach," Crime
and Delinquency, April 1979, p. 238.

Because the first footnote includes a volume number, the parenthesis separates the date from the page number. Because the second footnote does not use a volume number, the "p." separates the date from the page. (Thus a given footnote would have *either* a volume number *or* the abbreviation "p." but not both.)

Newspaper Article

[3]"Legal Help Union Ends Long Strike," <u>New York Times</u>, 30 Jan. 1980, Sec. 2, p. 3, col. 5.

Note: If the author's name were given, it would be placed before the title. If this were an editorial, the word "editorial" would be placed after the title.

Article in a Book of Collected Essays

[4]Kenneth Cloke, "The Economic Basis of Law and State," in <u>Law Against the People</u>, ed. Robert Lefcourt, (New York: Vintage Books, 1971), p. 69.

Note: Some people are tempted, when they find a book that has several different essays by different authors, to write the footnotes as though they had read the essays in whatever magazines or newspapers they originally appeared. This is a form of plagiarism, however, since an editor, not the student, did the hard work of tracking down the various essays. In addition, the pages in the book will not be the same as the pages in the original source.

Book

[5]William O. Douglas, <u>Go East, Young Man: The Early Years</u> (New York: Random House, 1974), pp. 49–50.

Note: If this were a second or later edition, the edition would come right after the title: "3rd ed." If there were more than one author, the two authors would both be listed: "William O. Douglas and Hugo Black."

The abbreviation *pp.* means *pages*.

Government Publication

[6]U.S. Department of Labor, Bureau of Labor Statistics, <u>Occupational Outlook Handbook</u>, 1978–79 Ed. (Washington, D.C.: Government Printing Office, 1978), p. 367.

Note: Government Printing Office may be abbreviated "G.P.O."

Interview

[7]Sgt. Sandra Reilly, personal interview on crime detection, San Francisco, 20 Jan. 1982.

Note: When you conduct personal interviews, include whatever information would interest your reader. Typically, that's the name and position of the person interviewed, the subject, the place, and the date.

It's no longer necessary to use Latin phrases such as "ibid." or "op. cit." in repeated references to the same work. The newer style is simply to give the author's last name and the page referred to. If you have already cited two different sources by the same author, give a short version of the title in addition to the author's last name. *It does not matter if other footnotes come in between the two.*

First footnote:

⁸William O. Douglas, <u>Go East, Young Man: The Early Years</u> (New York: Random House, 1974), pp. 49–50.

Later footnote to same book:

⁹Douglas, p. 89.

Bibliography Format

The purpose of the bibliography is different from the purpose of the footnotes. The bibliography is designed to let your reader see in one place, at a glance, what materials you've used. In addition, the bibliography shows the length of magazine articles by including the first and last pages. (With popular magazines this can be misleading, since articles beginning at the front may be continued in the back; in such cases it may be best to list the actual pages the article was printed on, such as: *pp. 9, 32, and 60.*

The bibliography format is different from the footnote format in several ways:

1. The author's *last name* comes first.
2. The bibliography is arranged in *alphabetical* order. When the author's name is not known, the entry is alphabetized by the first word of the title, excluding *a, an,* or *the.*
3. When two or more sources are by the same author, the author's name is listed just for the first one. Ten hyphens are used in place of the author's name for the second source.
4. The punctuation is different. In bibliographies, a period, not a comma, is used to separate the author's name from the title of the book or article and also to separate the title of the book or article from the publishing information.

Following is a bibliography made up of the sources in the preceding footnotes.

BIBLIOGRAPHY

CLOKE, KENNETH. "The Economic Basis of Law and State." In <u>Law Against the People</u>. Ed. Robert Lefcourt. New York: Vintage Books, 1971, pp. 65–80.

DOUGLAS, WILLIAM O. Go East, Young Man. New York: Random House, 1974.

GOLDSTEIN, HAROLD. "Improving Policing: A Problem-Oriented Approach." Crime and Delinquency, 25 (April 1979), 236–58.

"Legal Help Union Ends Long Strike." New York Times, 30 Jan. 1980, Sec. 2, p. 3, col. 5.

REILLY, SGT. SANDRA. Personal interview. San Francisco, 20 Jan. 1982.

U.S. Department of Labor, Bureau of Labor Statistics. Occupational Outlook Handbook, 1978–79 Ed. Washington D.C.: Government Printing Office, 1978.

AUTHOR/YEAR METHOD

Up to this point we have been outlining the "footnotes and bibliography" method for documenting sources consulted in writing research papers. This method, frequently referred to as the MLA (Modern Language Association) method, is the preferred method for most arts and humanities papers.

There is another method of documentation known as the "name and year/references cited" method. This method is the preferred method of documentation for science, social science, business, and other technical types of papers. This "references cited" format has at least two advantages over the "footnote and bibliography" style. First, it's more convenient for readers, since the documentation is included right in the text rather than in separate footnotes. Second, it is more convenient for the writer for reasons that will be apparent below.

The precise format for the "references cited" method varies slightly from one academic field to another. The examples below follow the widely used format of the American Psychological Association, commonly known as *A.P.A.*

In Place of Footnotes:

The references cited method replaces footnotes with brief parenthetical references right in the body of the paper. These refer to publications which are fully described in a list of references cited at the end of the paper:

> "A boyhood hero who was to play an important role in
> my life many years later was William E. Borah of Idaho.
> Borah was elected to the Senate in 1906 and served until
> his death in 1940" (Douglas, 1974, p. 66). Statements
> such as this show Douglas' respect for mentors.

instead of footnote

period goes outside parentheses

When the author's name is included in your own writing, you should put just the year and page in parentheses:

> Cloke (1971, p. 66) suggests that lawyers, by filing lawsuits, may be deluding immature clients into believing they have legally enforceable claims, when, in fact, no court would find in their favor.

In Place of a Bibliography:

References Cited replaces the bibliography used in the MLA method. The References Cited is quite similar to a bibliography: It is an alphabetical list of works used and it appears at the end of the paper. There are a number of minor differences in format, however:

1. Initials are used instead of the author's first name.
2. Titles of articles are ordinarily not capitalized, except for the first word.
3. Titles of articles are not enclosed in quotation marks.
4. Names of technical periodicals are frequently abbreviated.
5. If you refer to more than one work by a given author, repeat the author's name. Do not use dashes as in a bibliography.

You may wish to compare the format in the following list with the M.L.A. bibliography given earlier.

REFERENCES CITED

CLOKE, K. The economic basis of law and state. In: Law against the people. Ed. Robert Lefcourt. New York: Vintage Books, 1971, 65–80.

DOUGLAS, W. O. Go east, young man. New York: Random House, 1974.

GOLDSTEIN, H. Improving policing: a problem-oriented approach. Crime and delinquency, 1979, 25, 236–258.

Legal help union ends long strike. New York Times, 30 Jan. 1980, Sec. 2, p. 3, col. 5.

REILLY, SGT. S. Personal interview. San Francisco, 20 Jan. 1982.

U.S. Dept. of Labor, Bureau of Labor Statistics. Occupational Outlook Handbook, 1978–79 Ed. Washington D.C.: GPO, 1978.

Keep in mind that slightly different documentation formats may be used in different scientific and technical disciplines, or at particular schools. It is always wise to find out if your instructor prefers a particular format.

appendix D:

A Brief Format Guide

This appendix is designed to help you give your writing the physical appearance that knowledgeable readers expect. In addition to a sample letter, memo, press release, and academic paper, it includes a guide to the proper punctuation of quotations.

PAPER AND OTHER SUPPLIES

Informal, friendly letters and notes may be handwritten or typed in almost any manner on almost any type of paper. However, reports for school as well as letters written from or to businesses, committees, public officials, or other similar sources should look businesslike. The paper should be bond, the typewriter ribbon should be fresh, and mistakes should be corrected with one of the correction fluids now available at most drug stores. Flimsy and erasable paper should be avoided, as it easily smudges and can be difficult to read.

If your typing is good, you should make a carbon copy of your letters and reports. A copy is useful if the original is lost or if you need a copy for future reference. If you make many corrections as you type, it's more efficient to make a photocopy when you're finished.

LETTERS

The following is an example of a letter with a businesslike format.

Another letter format can be seen on page 260. It uses no paragraph indentations and thus gives a more efficient, businesslike impression. It also shows how to address a letter when you don't have a specific person's name to use. One method is to write "Dear Sir or Madam," but that's a bit awkward. "To Whom It May Concern" is gaining in popularity.

344 Trinity St.
Providence, Rhode Island 02901
March 19, 1982

Mr. Jake Myers
Jake's Records
18 South Street
Boston, Mass. 02106

Dear Mr. Myers:

I've always been pleased with your mail order records in the past. The bill for my last order, however, presents problems.

On February 11, 1982, I ordered the following three records from you:

Album Title	Your Order #	Your Price
1 - Best of Chopin	CL-201	$4.99
1 - Blues on Jazz	J-419	$5.99
1 - French Music for Harp	CL-304	$4.99

Early this month, I received the Chopin record and the Blues on Jazz. However, when I played these records for the first time, I discovered the Chopin record is badly warped.

In addition, I have not yet received the French Music for Harp, although I did, last week, receive the enclosed bill for all three records.

You can see my difficulty. Enclosed is a check for the Blues on Jazz. I would still like to receive the French Music for Harp but naturally do not wish to be billed for it until I've received it.

As to the Chopin, I'm not paying for the defective record. However, despite the inconvenience to me, I'm willing to return the record to you, at your expense, if you wish me to. In your reply, please let me know if you have good copies of the Chopin in stock, should I wish to reorder the record.

Sincerely,

Trudy Dela Cruz

Trudy Dela Cruz

single-space

double-space between paragraphs

signature

typed name

344 Trinity St.
Providence, Rhode Island 02901
March 19, 1982

Jake's Records
18 South Street
Boston, Massachusetts 02106

To Whom It May Concern:

I've always been pleased with your mail order records in the past. The bill for my last order, however, presents problems.

On February 11, 1982, I ordered the following three records from you:

Album Title	Your Order #	Your Price
1 - Best of Chopin	CL-201	$4.99
1 - Blues on Jazz	J-419	$5.99
1 - French Music for Harp	CL-304	$4.99

Early this month, I received the Chopin record and the Blues on Jazz. However, when I played these records for the first time, I discovered that the Chopin record is badly warped.

In addition, I have not yet received the French Music for Harp, although I did, last week, receive the enclosed bill for all three records.

You can see my difficulty. Enclosed is a check for the Blues on Jazz. I would still like to receive the French Music for Harp but naturally do not wish to be billed for it until I've received it.

As to the Chopin, I'm not paying for the defective record. However, despite the inconvenience to me, I'm willing to return the record to you, at your expense, if you wish me to. In your reply, please let me know if you have good copies of the Chopin in stock, should I wish to reorder the record.

Sincerely,

Trudy Dela Cruz

BUSINESS MEMOS

Most businesses have memorandum forms printed as in the following example. All that's necessary is to fill in the appropriate spaces.

```
TO:  Joy Smith                    ⌐initials⌐        DATE:  Sept. 4, 1983
                                   └of writer┘
FROM:  Mark Lerner   M. L.

SUBJECT:  Training new receptionists

     We've long talked of the need for a manual to help train our new
receptionists.  At Sue's suggestion, I've written the attached draft.  I'd
appreciate your reviewing it and suggesting any changes that would make it
clearer or more helpful.  Since Sue wants the manual out by November, could
I have your reactions by the end of next week?  If that's too soon, let me
know.
```

If you want to write a memo but do not have a printed form, you can simply type the words *TO, FROM, SUBJECT,* and *DATE* yourself. Memos are normally used to communicate *within* a given company.

NEWS RELEASES

When you want a newspaper or radio station to announce an activity, promotion, or anything else, you send them a "news release" that should look similar to the one that follows. If possible, call the paper or radio station to find out the exact person or department your release should be mailed to. Also, if possible, each one you send should be freshly typed, not photocopied.

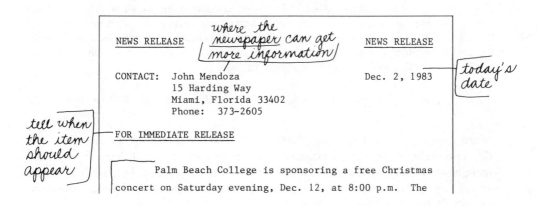

```
                    where the
NEWS RELEASE        newspaper can get        NEWS RELEASE
                    more information

CONTACT:  John Mendoza                       Dec. 2, 1983   ⌐today's
          15 Harding Way                                     date
          Miami, Florida  33402
          Phone:   373-2605

tell when ┌ FOR IMMEDIATE RELEASE
the item  │
should    │     Palm Beach College is sponsoring a free Christmas
appear    └ concert on Saturday evening, Dec. 12, at 8:00 p.m.   The
```

```
                  concert will be held in the Memorial Auditorium.  As

                  seating is limited, all wishing to attend should pick up

                  their free tickets in advance at the Memorial Auditorium

                  box office.  Tickets will be available between 9:00 a.m.

                  and 1:00 p.m. weekdays until the concert.

                       This free concert will feature Palm Beach music

                  students performing rock, jazz, and seasonal music.
```

this is the information that will be printed or read

`#####`

Shows "the end." use in press releases only

PUNCTUATING QUOTATIONS

As Chapter 17 pointed out, you should generally quote no more than is necessary to illustrate or prove your point.

Long Quotations

On those occasions when the material you quote would be more than three lines in your own paper, you should set off the quotation in the following manner:

> The way Taylor makes scientific ideas both clear and interesting to a nonscientific audience is especially interesting. For instance, he begins one chapter with an anecdote:
>
>> The crowd stands at the graveside: a funeral is taking place. Suddenly one of the onlookers, a boy, bursts into uncontrollable laughter. The mourners are shocked at first, then realize something strange has happened. He is led away. It turns out that a blood-vessel in his brain has burst, flooding the third ventricle—the open space in the centre of the brain. An event known to doctors as a subarachnoid haemorrhage.
>
> This anecdote prepares the reader for the scientific discussion that follows.

When you set off, or indent, a long quotation, you do *not* also use quotation marks. You do, however, single-space the material. This has two advantages: It lets the reader see more easily exactly what material is quoted and what isn't. Also, because it is single-spaced, the quotation takes up less space than it would otherwise. Indented quotations are usually introduced with *colons*.

262

Short Quotations

Short quotations are identified by quotation marks. If a comma or a period comes at the same point as the closing quotation mark, it is *always* put *inside* the quotation mark, even when the comma or period is not part of the quotation. This isn't always logical. The only reason for doing it this way is that it makes typing easier.

> Taylor writes, "The mourners are shocked at first, then realize something strange has happened."

Notice that this quotation is introduced with a *comma*. This is often the case when complete sentences are quoted and are introduced by phrases like "he wrote" or "she said." Other times, for variety, you may wish to use a colon to introduce a quotation that is a complete sentence:

> Taylor plays on the reader's curiosity: "The mourners are shocked at first, then realize something strange has happened."

Since they are complete sentences, both of the quotations above begin with a capital letter.

Unlike periods and commas, question marks and exclamation marks do not always go inside the closing quotation marks. They are placed outside the quotation marks when the question or exclamation is the writer's and not the part of the material being quoted:

> Did Taylor write, "The mourners are shocked at first, then realize something strange has happened"?

Since the question isn't Taylor's question, the question mark is appropriately placed outside the quotation mark. Note also that the period after "happened" has been dropped.

Still Shorter Quotations

When you can illustrate or prove your point by quoting less than a complete sentence, do so. Just be careful not to change the writer's meaning in any way. In addition, follow these three conventions:

1. Some quotations do not have to be introduced by either colons or commas, and the first word is often not capitalized:

   > When we read "a funeral is taking place," we wonder whose it is.

2. Ellipses (three periods) *must* be used to indicate that you've omitted material in the middle of a quotation:

   > The explanation is clear: "It turns out that a blood-vessel in his brain has burst, flooding . . . the open space in . . . the brain."

Ellipses can also be used to indicate that *important* material has been omitted from the beginning or end of a quotation. In most situations, however, the readers can tell that something came before or after the words you are quoting, and ellipses are therefore not necessary there. Indeed, they can be distracting to the reader. Should you need to use one at the end of a quotation, and should that occur at the end of your own sentence, use four dots instead of the usual three: one for the period and three for the ellipses:

Our curiosity is satisfied when we read that "a blood-vessel in his brain has burst, flooding the third ventricle. . . ."

3. Use brackets when it is necessary to add your own words to quotations. Sometimes a date or name must be added to a quotation if the reader is to understand it. Other times a simple word or an *s* must be added to make the brief quotation fit into the rest of your sentence. If you add anything at all to a quotation, you must alert your reader that you've done so by using square brackets, not parentheses:

Taylor writes that "a blood-vessel in his [the boy's] brain has burst."

You either can write the brackets in with pen or can use your typewriter's slash mark "/" and then complete the bracket by hand. This method results in a slanted bracket, but you're less likely to forget it than if you count on adding the entire bracket later.

Page References and Quotation Marks

When you use a page reference in parentheses at the end of a quotation, place the period after the parentheses:

He wrote that the mourners "are shocked at first" (p. 1).

That way your reader clearly knows which of your sentences the page number refers to.

When you have a parenthetical page reference at the end of a long quotation, place the parenthesis on a separate line, putting the period at the end of the last sentence quoted.

The crowd stands at the graveside: a funeral is taking place. Suddenly one of the onlookers, a boy, bursts into uncontrollable laughter. The mourners are shocked at first, then realize something strange has happened. He is led away.

(p. 1)

Footnote numbers are placed outside quotation marks.

ACADEMIC PAPERS AND REPORTS

A sample format of a short academic paper follows. (For help with the documentation of full research papers, see Appendix C. The footnote format is appropriate for papers in which you refer to only *one* book.)

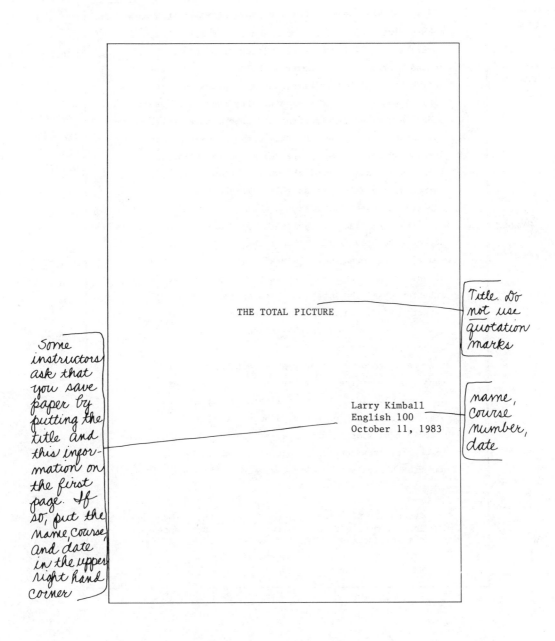

THE TOTAL PICTURE

Title. Do not use quotation marks

Larry Kimball
English 100
October 11, 1983

name, course number, date

Some instructors ask that you save paper by putting the title and this information on the first page. If so, put the name, course, and date in the upper right hand corner

1

Title
on
title
page
only

*double-
spaced*

*margins
roughly
1 inch
wide*

*Para-
graphs
are
indented*

In <u>The Year of the Whale</u>, Victor Scheffer takes many
opportunities to depart from his main narration and
describe different aspects and lifestyles related to the
sea as a whole. In doing this, he often changes the
entire style of his writing, usually taking on a more
serious and scientific approach. For the reader, these
sidelights offer a refreshing and informative change of
pace, but at the same time they serve an even greater
purpose by developing the reader's understanding and
appreciation not only of the whale, but of its
surrounding environment as well. To accomplish this,
Scheffer uses two basic techniques.

First, he describes animals and events that are
directly related to the life of the whale. Good
examples are found when the whales mingle with schools
of dolphin and porpoise. On many such occasions,
Scheffer takes the opportunity to explain various
aspects of dolphin behavior and research. In one-
instance, he even offers the interesting story of a
porpoise that rescues a drowning woman (p. 35).[1] When
the whales encounter a navy ship tracking them with
sonar, Scheffer takes time out to explain whale sonar
and communication. Later, following a sequence when the
whales are feeding on squid, Scheffer traces the
mythological story of the Kraken monster. In each case,
he departs from the daily routine of the whale to
describe a similar or related aspect of the ocean world.

*appropriate
footnote*

---

[1]Victor B. Scheffer, <u>The Year of the Whale</u> (New York:
Charles Scribner's Sons, 1969). All page references are
to this edition.

A second method Scheffer uses to broaden our outlook is to describe events that are related solely to man's experiences with the sea. In doing this, he often uses specific examples, usually dealing with oceanic research. Instance of these "mini-stories" are found in his reference to deep diving (p. 61) and in his story of the biologist named "Sea Otter" Hansen (p. 172). Scheffer does not always stick to research-related material, however. Often he seems to enjoy adding a touch of human emotion, such as the fear experienced by Hansen as he encounters a whale underwater. Scheffer also includes a bit of romance by adding frequent references to Herman Melville's <u>Moby Dick</u> throughout the book. By skillfully using the element of human experience, Scheffer draws us even closer in our appreciation of the marine development.

Granted, departures from the main character or sub-ject of a story are often distracting and in many cases only serve to confuse the reader. Scheffer, however, smoothly patterns his side trips to complement the story, and his transitions for the most part follow a logical sequence. This not only helps to explain the lifestyle of the whale, but provides us with further bits of information as well.

Overall, by combining these related facts with human experience, Scheffer greatly enhances our "total picture" of the sea and thereby increases our knowledge and appreciation of its resources.

word divided at syllable. Words cannot be divided except at syllables

end of paper. Do not write "the end."

appendix E

Tips for College Writing

ESSAY EXAMS

When you write an essay exam, write as if your instructor will grade your paper at midnight, half asleep, after reading 30 other papers that are similar to yours. In addition, write as though your teacher were going to disagree with everything you say. These assumptions will help you feel the need to write clearly enough so that someone half asleep can follow your ideas, and to offer enough evidence and proof so that even if you are wrong in what you say, you'll still get credit for making a good case for your ideas.

Clarity and sufficient examples or evidence are the heart of good essay exam writing. Most instructors are unwilling to give credit unless they can understand exactly what you say. Otherwise they worry that they may be reading their own ideas into what you've written and giving themselves, rather than you, a grade. They are also unwilling to give credit unless you offer enough examples to demonstrate clearly that you understand what you're writing about or to "prove" the point you are making. Without evidence and proof, you might just be repeating a clever idea without really understanding it. When you study for an essay exam, remember that your instructor will be looking for a display of more than rote memory. It's much faster to grade objective exams, so if your instructor is taking the time for an essay exam, it must be because he or she wants to test your understanding, not just your memory.

Specific Tips

1. To prepare for an essay exam, try to imagine the questions your teacher might ask, then see if you can answer them. In particular, try to make up questions that begin in these ways:

   Why. . . .
   Compare. . . .

What changes. . . .
What caused. . . .
What results did. . . .
Do you agree that. . . .
Evaluate. . . .

2. If the exam will be an open-book exam, do *not* count on using the book more than two or three times. If you have to use it more than that, you may waste precious time. To save time on open-book exams, be sure you've marked very important passages with a colored marker and put paper clips on the four or five pages you're most likely to use. In addition, you might ask your instructor if it is permissible to make a list of dates, names, or important words on the inside cover.

3. If you are very nervous during the exam, do one of the following: take deep *slow* breaths, shake out your hands, or put your hands in an open, relaxed position.

4. Read the questions carefully. If one question looks much easier than the others, be careful before selecting it as the one you'll answer. It might be that you are over-simplifying the question, in which case you won't get full credit. Or it might be that the question really *is* easier than the others, in which case you may be limiting yourself to a grade no higher than B or C just because you chose the easy question.

5. When you select a question to answer, reread the question carefully to be sure you understand what is being asked of you. For instance, the following questions involve *hidden comparisons:*

Explain when noise becomes noise pollution.
Discuss the changes that occur when a society becomes industrialized.

The following questions ask you to *take a stand,* even though they don't use the words "argue" or "position," or "your own opinion":

Explain why it is (or is not) in the nation's best interest to provide free medical care for all.
Discuss whether evolution is a fact or a theory.

Be especially careful when questions contain the following words:

significant
main
to what extent

The first two words indicate that the instructor sees the possibility of many true but trivial answers. This is a clue for you to weed the unimportant answers out before you begin the writing. The last phrase is a clue that the instructor feels the answer isn't "black or white," but some shade of gray. For instance, if the question were

"To what extent can computers help small businesses?" the teacher probably would expect you to say that they can help in some ways but not in others.

6. Take at least five minutes to *brainstorm* at the beginning of the exam. Only by quickly jotting down the ideas that come to mind can you weed the unimportant from the important and organize your response before you begin writing. In addition, brainstorming can help you quickly recall the details and ideas you studied.

7. In an essay exam, put your thesis or main idea in your first sentence. (You'll know what it is if you brainstorm first.) There is, unfortunately, no time to see what you really want to say by freewriting or writing a messy draft. Since clarity is so important in essay exams, and since your teacher may be very tired by the time he or she reaches your exam, a good plan is to include in your first sentence the number of points you'll be making. For instance:

Five major changes can occur when a society becomes industrialized.

If, at the end of the exam, you find you've included only four changes, you can change the *five* to *four* in your first sentence. An alternate plan is to leave the number blank in the first sentence, filling it in when you have finished writing. (But then you must be certain you remember to do so.)

It's usually not necessary to spend time copying the entire question before you begin answering. However the way you write your first sentence should let your teacher clearly know *which* question you are answering. For instance, an instructor might become confused if your first sentence read: "Five major changes can occur when this happens." The instructor might wonder: "When what happens? What question are you answering?" Use the key words of the question to form your thesis sentence. A good rule of thumb is that your first sentence, as well as your entire essay, should make sense to someone who has not seen the question.

8. Essay exams are, by nature, make-believe situations. In an essay exam you are explaining things to someone who already knows them. In real life that doesn't (or shouldn't) happen too often. This make-believe aspect can be confusing unless you recognize it and accept it from the very beginning.

One way around this problem is to pretend that you are writing not to your real flesh-and-blood instructor, but rather to someone who happens to be just like your instructor. In this way you can feel comfortable explaining things that you know your instructor already knows.

Remember: Write *as if* your teacher disagrees with your thesis when you are taking a stand.

9. Do try to allow time at the end to write at least a quick summary or conclusion and to reread what you've written. Check for words you might have omitted while writing fast and also for obvious grammar mistakes.

10. Remember that in-class exams are a specialized species of writing. You don't have time for a full, rich writing process. You don't have time to discover and play with

new ideas. It's therefore best to accept the limitations of in-class essays and focus on presenting clear, well-organized ideas.

You might organize a very clear essay exam in this way:

1ST paragraph — State your thesis, briefly listing the <u>main points</u> you'll make.
2ND paragraph — 1. Explain your <u>first point</u>.   2. Offer evidence.   3. Explain <u>how</u> your evidence proves or explains the first point.
3RD paragraph — 1. Explain your <u>second point</u>.   2. Offer evidence.   3. Explain <u>how</u> your evidence proves or explains the second point.
Other paragraphs — Continue above pattern.
Last paragraph — Conclude quickly, briefly restating the points you've made.

Of course this is just a bare skeleton. As you explain your main points, you will also need to make concessions as appropriate, as well as anticipate and answer your reader's objections. Still, if you have trouble expressing your ideas clearly in exams, a plan similar to the above could help you. If you brainstorm and organize *before* you start writing, you can know what your main points will be.

COLLEGE PAPERS

Chapter 15 presents many tips for writing the types of papers often required in history, psychology, science, and other college classes. In general, college papers should present your own viewpoint, your ideas or conclusions about a given subject. They should be written as if your instructor were an expert in the subject but disagreed with your specific viewpoint or conclusions. In short, your task is to persuade the instructor while writing as logically and carefully as possible. As with essay exams, the evidence and proof you offer may be more important than your actual thesis. See Chapter 15 for more help with persuasive college papers.

Of course not all papers written for college classes are persuasive. Sometimes professors assign papers as a test of how well their students can summarize or paraphrase information that's already been presented in class or in a book that both the professor and student have read. This situation is similar to an essay exam in that you have to make believe the instructor knows less than he or she really knows. One way around this difficulty is to write the paper as a popularization—as though you were writing for people who did *not* already know or understand the ideas you are explaining. Sometimes it helps to make believe that you are writing a textbook or article of your own, explaining the ideas to other college students. When you are writing this type of paper, the tips and techniques in Chapter 12 may help you, as well as the information on paraphrasing given in Chapter 15.

Usually you'll know from the assignment itself what type of paper is expected. If you're not sure, ask your instructor. For instance, if you have been asked to write a paper about a particular book, ask whether you are to assume that your instructor has or has not read the book. Ask if the instructor wants you to summarize what the book says or wants you to avoid summarizing. It's much better to ask in advance than to find out later that you guessed wrong.

FINDING INTERESTING SUBJECTS BASED ON YOUR READING

The lists below are designed to help you discover ideas about what you've read. Remember, unless you've been asked to, or unless you are writing for people who didn't read the book you did, do not just summarize.

Method 1: Be Bold

1. Disagree:

   If you disagree with the author's ideas, say so and explain why.

   If you disagree with what most *other* people think about the book, say so and explain why. (But be prepared to explain how you know what other people think.)

   If you agree with the author's ideas but disagree with his method or style of writing, say so and explain why.

2. Compare:

   Compare what the book "is" with what you think it "ought" to be.

   Compare what the book "seems" to be with what you think it really "is."

   Compare two people in the book. (Which is more honest? More intelligent? Happier?)

Compare the book you've just read with another (similar) book. Which is better? Which is more interesting?

3. Evaluate:

Is the book "good"? Why or why not?

Is the book important or significant? Why or why not?

Is the book "true"?

Is the book dangerous in any way?

4. Imagine:

Imagine "what if" and change the facts in the book, one by one. This will help you see what's really important in the book and what isn't. It is especially helpful in thinking about novels.

Example: What if you changed the setting? How much difference would it make to the book as a whole? Does this tell you something about the book?

What if you changed the sex of the main character?

What if you changed the personality of a minor character?

What if you eliminated certain people?

What if . . .

Note: This little game can give surprisingly good results if you keep in mind that you are looking for insights that you might otherwise miss.

5. Look for problems:

Do any parts of the book seem to contradict other parts? Are there parts that don't seem to fit together?

6. Look for paradoxes and ironies:

A *paradox* is something that seems contradictory but really makes sense. Irony is incongruity between what might be expected and what actually happens. Identifying and explaining paradoxes and ironies can be a very good way of finding interesting subjects.

Method 2: Ask Questions

1. What:

What is the author really saying? What does he seem most interested in? (*Note:* Only if people who have also read the book could disagree with you would this make a good subject.)

What "kind" of book is this? (*Note:* Only if people could disagree with you would this make a good subject.)

2. Why:

Why did the author write the book or article? Does he seem most interested in educating people, in entertaining them, in expressing himself, or in some combination?

Why do the things that happen in the book happen? Why do the people in the book act and think the way they do? (*Note:* The less obvious the answer is, the better subject it will make.)

3. How:

How did the author write the book? Did he seem to take much time? Do much research? (Remember, only if people could disagree . . .)

How could you apply the ideas in the book to your own life? How could the ideas be applied in your city or state?

How do you like the book? Why?

4. Who:

Who wrote the book? What kind of a person does the author seem to be? What kind of background does he or she have? How much difference would it make if the book had been written by someone with a different personality or background? (This last is the real question to answer.)

Who seems to be the author's intended audience?

Who should read the book? Who shouldn't read it? Why?

5. When:

When was the book written? Does the time in which it was written affect the content? The style? Is the book out of date?

6. Where:

Where is the book set (that is, where do the events take place)?

Is the location of the book important? Why? If the location were changed, what else would change?

Index